Hiking
Arizona's
Cactus Country

Erik Molvar

D1304721

FALCON®

HELENA, MONTANA

Falcon® is continually expanding its list of recreational guidebooks. All books include detailed descriptions, accurate maps, and all the information necessary for enjoyable trips. You can order extra copies of this book and get information and prices for other Falcon guidebooks by writing Falcon, P.O. Box 1718, Helena, MT 59624 or calling toll free 1-800-582-2665. Also, please ask for a free copy of our current catalog and visit our website at www.falconguide.com.

©1995 by Falcon® Publishing, Inc., Helena, Montana.
3 4 5 6 7 8 9 0 MG 03 02 01 00 99 98

Printed in the United States of America.

All black-and-white photos by author.
Cover photo by Eric Wunrow.

Library of Congress Cataloging-in-Publication Data

Molvar, Erik.
    Hiking Arizona's cactus country / by Erik Molvar.
        p.   cm.
    ISBN 1-56044-316-2
    1. Hiking—Arizona—Guidebooks.   2. Hiking—Sonoran Desert—
Guidebooks.   3. Trails—Arizona—Guidebooks.   4. Trails—Sonoran
Desert—Guidebooks.   5. Arizona—Guidebooks.   6. Sonoran
Desert—Guidebooks.
GV199.42.A7M65   1995
796.5'1'09791—dc20   95-25320
                                                        CIP

CAUTION

    Outdoor recreation activities are by their very nature potentially hazardous. All participants in such activities must assume the responsibility for their own actions and safety. The information contained in this guidebook cannot replace sound judgment and good decision-making skills, which help reduce the risk exposure, nor does the scope of this book allow for disclosure of all the potential hazards and risks involved in such activities.

    Learn as much as possible about the outdoor recreation activities you participate in, prepare for the unexpected, and be safe and cautious. The reward will be a safer and more enjoyable experience.

 Text pages printed on recycled paper.

CONTENTS

*This book is dedicated to Private Johann and
Arnie Krammer, who introduced me to the desert.*

ACKNOWLEDGMENTS

Several land managers helped shape the focus of this book, provided information on the hiking areas contained in it, and participated in the review process. Foremost among these is Jim Schmid, who served as a clearinghouse of information from the headquarters of Coronado National Forest. Other key contacts included John Williams of Saguaro National Park, Dominic Cardea of Organ Pipe Cactus National Monument, and Sue Morgan and Steve Knox of the Bureau of Land Management. Thanks to the mechanics of Western Distributor for keeping my truck on the road; may the toes of the camel bring you good fortune. Little Joe Manley deserves thanks just for being himself. Thanks to Ed Zink for making my computer mobile, and to the crew of the tugboat Umatilla for letting me take over their galley while I wrote this book. Edward Abbey provided the inspiration for all of my desert explorations.

OVERVIEW MAP

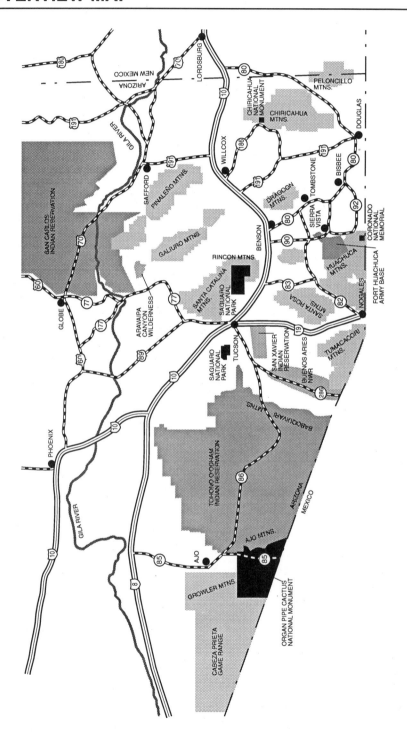

LEGEND

▦ ﹢ ▦ ﹢ ▦ ﹢	WILDERNESS/NATIONAL PARK BOUNDARY
▬▬▬▬▬▬	PAVED ROAD
≡≡≡≡	INTERSTATE HIGHWAY
=========	JEEP ROAD
═══════	IMPROVED GRAVEL ROAD
────────	PERMANENT STEAM
────── ⋯─	INTERMITTENT STREAM
░░░░░░░░░	NATIONAL FOREST BOUNDARY
─── · ───	STATE BOUNDARY
▬▬▬▬	RIVERS
▬ ▬ ▬ ▬ ▬	DESCRIBED TRAIL
─ ─ ─ ─ ─	OTHER TRAIL
▪▪▪▪▪▪▪▪▪▪▪	DESCRIBED ROUTE
· · · · · · · · ·	OTHER ROUTE
⬭	LAKE
x⁷⁵²⁴	MOUNTAIN PEAK
Λ	CAMPSITE
▌	RANGER STATION
♠	VISITOR CENTER
⁾ᵣ	PASS/SADDLE
▪	BUILDING
○	TRAILHEAD
▢178	FOREST ROAD
④	STATE HIGHWAY
②	US HIGHWAY
====↰====	PERMANENTLY LOCKED GATE
====⁋====	SEASONALLY LOCKED GATE
⁋	SPRING
⚒	MINE
⊙	POINT OF INTEREST
⊼	PICNIC AREA
◪	RUIN
⤫	TUNNEL
☗	NATIVE AMERICAN PETROGLYPHS
☗	WINDMILL
⚲	TANK
♄	CORRAL

INTRODUCTION

Welcome to Cactus Country, America's winter hiking wonderland. Arizona offers unlimited opportunities for backcountry exploration, from soaring mountains to secluded canyons, from coniferous forests to stands of giant cacti. Arizona deserts are dotted with reminders of a not-so-distant past when holdups and gunfights were commonplace and the country was inhabited by tough trappers, prospectors, and cowhands. Hikers may discover pre-Columbian rock art, abandoned mining claims, and moldering corrals in the midst of the trackless backcountry. This, too, is the land of heartbreaking sunsets and magical moonrises, of brilliant constellations and the vast, humbling silence of the desert. Here is an entire region where the encroachment of civilization is only a puny and fitful scrawl across an endless sea of basins and ranges.

WHAT IS CACTUS COUNTRY?

Cactus Country is a broad swath of the Sonoran Desert that extends northward across the Mexican border to encompass the southern third of Arizona. For the purposes of this book, the northern boundary of Cactus Country will be established at the Gila River. This slice of territory belonged to Mexico even after the Mexican-American War, and finally was added to the United States under the Gadsden Purchase of 1853. As one would expect, it is a region flavored by its native and Spanish cultures.

The dominant and unifying element in this diverse landscape of cloud-scraping peaks and broad basins is the cactus. Varying species of this spiny, leafless plant are scattered from the lowest desert basin to the highest mountaintops. Cactus country's plant communities range from desert scrub to pine woodlands. Giant saguaros and organ pipe cacti rise in stately ranks above the thorn scrub of many desert basins here, and these are the dominant plants in the classic Sonoran Desert ecosystem.

Because of its low economic value, much of Cactus Country remains in public hands. Most of its higher mountain ranges fall within Coronado National Forest, while the broad desert basins are largely in state and private ownership. There are a dozen designated wilderness areas to explore, and several national parks offering a more developed experience. Hiking and backpacking are allowed on most state and federal lands, although many of these areas do not have developed trail systems. Respect all private property and "No Trespassing" signs, and always inquire about land status before proceeding with an expedition. Finally, tread lightly on the desert, so that it can remain pristine and accessible to future generations of explorers.

SKY ISLANDS AND LOW DESERTS

The modern landscape of southern Arizona began to take form during a period of great mountain building known to geologists as the Laramide Orogeny.

Sun sets beyond a saguaro in the heart of the Cactus Forest.

During this cataclysmic time, between 75 million and 50 million years ago, the continent of North America slid over the floor of the Pacific Ocean. Block faulting and volcanism built up a mountain range of enormous magnitude. These mountains were worn down for 25 million years, after which a new round of block faulting and volcanic activity created the basins and ranges that presently stretch from southern Arizona to eastern Oregon. The basins were filled to a great depth with rocky debris washed down from the mountains. During wetter times, they became the beds of encroaching seas and vast freshwater lakes.

The collection of plant communities that we see in Cactus Country today has roots in the Pleistocene Era. During this time, glaciers covered the northern half of the North American continent, and a boreal forest of spruce and aspen extended all the way into southern Arizona. The end of the ice ages brought a warmer, drier climate, and desert vegetation gradually began to encroach from the south. Coniferous forests and boreal animals were stranded at the tops of mountain ranges that rose from a sea of arid desert. These "sky islands" became ecological arks, bearing isolated populations of plants and animals that could not interbreed with their neighbors because of intervening deserts. As a result of genetic drift, some of these plants and animal populations have evolved into new species specific to small regions or even single mountain ranges.

The modern stratification of plant communities on the sky islands of southern Arizona reflects the retreat of cold-weather plants to higher elevations. Sky island plants thrive where the climate is cooler and wetter, and they have shorter growing seasons. The great biologist C. Hart Merriam studied these patterns in 1889 and developed a system of "life zones," wherein every thousand feet of elevation gain is roughly equivalent to traveling 500 miles north. Thus, the spruce-fir-aspen forest on the highest peaks of southern Arizona is quite similar to the boreal forest of the southern Yukon. Between 7,000 and 8,000 feet, Douglas-firs dominate the forest as they do in British Columbia. The pine forests found between 5,000 and 7,000 feet are the ecological equivalents of lowland forests in Montana. Below, pines mix with evergreen oaks in a woodland that gradually favors hardwoods at lower elevations. The oak woodland breaks into grassy savannahs at its lower edge, and the desert grassland dominating the lowest slopes holds succulents and even a few small cacti. On the skirts of the mountains, soil structure is the dominant factor in determining plant distribution. Water is most available in the loose, coarse-grained soils of the bajadas, or alluvial slopes, at the feet of the mountains. Here, one finds the most diverse communities of desert plants: giant cacti, drought-tolerant deciduous shrubs, and thorn scrub, hallmarks of the Sonoran Desert.

As runoff waters drain into the desert basins, they lose speed and drop coarser particles of sediment. The basins themselves have sandy soils. A barren community of bursage and creosote bushes dominates the basin landscape, along with a few mesquites along the washes. The centers of these desert basins have extremely fine silt soils, which are often alkaline from chemicals leached by runoff waters and deposited through evaporation. Saltbush is one of the few plants that can survive here. Where soil alkalinity is highest, the basins may become barren playas, or alkali flats.

Looking across the upper basin of Aravaipa Creek at the Santa Theresa Range.

THE ORIGINAL ARIZONANS

During the Pleistocene Era, glaciers covered much of the northern hemisphere. At that time, southern Arizona was a land of lakes and mountains, coniferous forests, and grassy savannahs. A diverse fauna featuring mammoths, mastodons, camels, and dire wolves roamed the landscape. The first primitive human cultures shared the steppes with these enormous beasts and left finely worked stone points to mark their passage. These people, known to archaeologists as members of the Clovis culture, ranged this area as much as 11,200 years ago. Their relics have been found in conjunction with mammoth bones, indicating that theirs was a hunter-gatherer culture with some proficiency at hunting even the largest animals.

When the glaciers retreated and the Ice Age mammals disappeared, the region's indigenous people broadened their diet and began relying more heavily on wild plants. These evolving gatherers, known variously as the Cochise or Archaic culture groups, left behind a variety of stone implements used for the grinding seeds into coarse flour. Perfectly round mortar holes were worn into the bedrock and grinding pits, and flat grinding stones called manos and metates were fashioned to crush the seeds. Archaic culture flourished from 7000 B.C. to A.D. 150, and may have represented a fairly nomadic lifestyle.

These desert nomads soon gave rise to three pre-Columbian cultures of great social advancement. The Anasazi inhabited northern Arizona, Utah, and western Colorado; the Mogollon people lived in central Arizona along the Mogollon Rim; and the Hohokam inhabited the desert basins of southern Arizona. The Anasazi and Mogollon people were cliff dwellers who built sturdy adobe villages beneath rock overhangs. They shared with the Hohokam a propensity for intricate petroglyphs, or rock art, that may have had religious or mystical significance. The Hohokam lived in walled villages on the basin floors and engineered complicated systems of irrigation canals to bring water to their crops. These people traded extensively with the mighty civilizations that lay to the south, in present-day Mexico: the Aztecs, Mayans, and Toltecs. It is likely that the modern tribes of Pima, Sobaipuri, and Tohono O'odham Indians are direct descendants of the Hohokam people.

As the first Spanish missionaries and explorers probed northward along the frontier of New Spain, a new group of Native Americans arrived on the scene: the Apaches. The fierce Apache confederation of hunter-gatherers swept down from the northern plains into eastern Arizona. These latecomers spoke an Athabaskan tongue, like the tribes of northwestern Canada. The Apaches were nomadic and warlike, and so dominated the eastern part of Arizona that the Spanish knew this region as Apachería. Spanish missionaries were able to forge a lasting peace with the Pimas, Sobaipuris, and Tohono O'odham peoples, but

The remains of Hohokam dwellings.

The agave, or century plant, may live for over thirty years before expending all of its energy in a single blooming effort before dying.

the Apaches resisted Spanish culture. They waged guerrilla war against the influx of Europeans, and this bitter conflict burned through the Mexican Revolution, the Mexican-American War, and the Gadsden Purchase.

PLANNING YOUR TRIP

It is important to gather as much current information as possible before starting on a wilderness expedition in Arizona, as anywhere. Permits are not required for expeditions into most public lands, although they are required for all National Park Service holdings as well as the Aravaipa Canyon Wilderness. It is always wise to check in at a local ranger station to get the latest report on trail conditions. Ask for the trail supervisor or wilderness manager, who will be best equipped to answer your questions. A list of addresses and phone numbers for these ranger stations is provided in Appendix B of this book. Since there are no designated camping spots in most backcountry areas, campers are asked to practice minimum-impact camping techniques, as outlined later in this section. In the wilderness, humans are visitors and should leave no trace of their activities to mar the wilderness experience of other travelers.

Hikers should pay close attention to trail mileages and levels of difficulty. Travelers who underestimate the distance or time required to complete a trip may find themselves hiking in the dark, a dangerous proposition at best. An experienced hiker traveling at a fast clip without rest stops can generally make 2.5 miles per hour on desert terrain, perhaps more if the distance is all downhill. Novices and hikers in poor physical condition generally have a maximum speed of 1.5 miles per hour. Note that these rates do not include stops for rest and refreshment, which add tremendously to a hiker's enjoyment and appreciation of surroundings. Eight miles a day is a good goal for travelers new to backpacking, while old hands can generally cover 10 miles comfortably. We recommend traveling below top speed, focusing more attention on the region's natural beauty and less on the exercise of hiking itself. In addition, desert heat and aridity make it unwise to push one's limits.

WEATHER

The Sonoran Desert is unique in that it has two distinct wet seasons. In winter (November through February), northwesterly winds bring cooler air and moisture from the Pacific Ocean. At lower elevations, moisture falls as a steady rain, which soaks into the soil. On mountaintops, it falls as snow, which may accumulate to a depth of several feet at higher elevations. During late July and August, afternoon thundershowers produce a second greening of the desert. These storms are born in the unstable air above the Gulf of Mexico, and unleash a sudden deluge that can turn a dry wash into a raging river in minutes. From October through April, high temperatures hover in the 60s and low 70s in the desert basins, while the mountains are substantially cooler. From May through September, temperatures in the desert basins may soar to 105 degrees Fahrenheit in the shade. The lofty mountains are much cooler, and rarely get much hotter than 90 degrees. Bring warm clothes at all times of year, because the desert cools off quickly once the sun goes down.

DESERT HIKING

Hiking in the desert poses special challenges encountered nowhere else. Much of Cactus Country is free of trails, and hikers may have to rely on map-and-compass skills to find their way. Low deserts with their broadly spaced shrubs make the easiest hiking, while the cactus scrub of the alluvial bajada slopes may be somewhat challenging. Some arroyos are lined with thorn scrub that is difficult to negotiate without getting thoroughly perforated. In the foothills, cross-country hikers may encounter a chaparral of manzanita or other shrubs; this is virtually impenetrable, even though these bushes lack thorns. And note: staying on an established trail is no guarantee that these obstacles will not be encountered. Many of the trails in Cactus Country receive little, if any, maintenance.

The pads of prickly pear are not spiny enough to discourage the culinary efforts of hungry javelinas.

Perhaps the most obvious challenge of desert hiking is the climate. Hikers should wear broad-brimmed hats, long-sleeved shirts, and baggy pants to protect themselves from the intense desert sun. Exposed skin should be covered with sunscreen lotion. During the hottest parts of a summer day, the temperature can reach 130 degrees several feet above the desert floor. Take a lesson from local wildlife and hike in the cooler mornings and evenings. Rest in the shade during the heat of the day.

Desert air wicks moisture away from the body at an amazing rate, and active hikers should plan to drink about a gallon of water per day. Desert water sources may run dry for part of the year and, when not dry, often contain exotic microbes that can cause intestinal disorders. Always carry enough water to meet your daily needs, and filter all surface water to remove the harmful microbes.

Many desert-dwelling animals have evolved poisons as protection and may bite or sting when provoked. The rattlesnake is the most notorious of these, although its reputation for aggressiveness is undeserved. These snakes, like most nocturnal predators, will flee when given a chance. They rarely bite unless surprised or cornered. To avoid snakebites, always watch where you are putting your hands and feet and avoid reaching into dark places or overturning boulders. This practice will also save you from scorpions, most of which have painful stings. Scorpions like to hide in dark, moist places; hikers who leave their boots outside overnight may be in for a nasty surprise in the morning. The Gila monster, a slow-moving lizard with a beaded black-and-orange hide, is also poisonous but poses no threat to hikers unless handled.

One of the salient features of desert vegetation is the abundance of spiny plants. Some plants have barbed spines, while others have thorns coated with chemicals that interfere with the healing process. Several species of cholla cactus have evolved a strategy of dispersal using mammals as carriers. The sharp, hooked spines penetrate the skin and hold on while a joint breaks away from the living plant. After this clinging section is removed by the mammal, it puts down roots and grows into a new cactus. Chollas attack desert travelers with such frequency that one species has been named "jumping cholla." Hikers who get impaled by a cholla joint should not try to remove it with their hands. Instead, the joints can be removed with a comb, pliers, or (the author's favorite method) with two dead branches held like chopsticks. Travelers who spend time in the desert backcountry will learn quickly to give thorny plants a wide berth.

Desert hikers must be particularly careful not to upset the ecological bal-

Cactus wrens protect their eggs from predators by building their nests among the spiny branches of the cholla cactus.

ance of desert communities. Many plants and animals are living on the edge of their capabilities, and any added stress may result in death. Give a wide berth to nesting birds, animals with young, and wildlife using a water source. Feel free to observe these wild inhabitants of the desert, but do so at a respectful distance so that your presence does not disturb them. Finally, hikers who are traveling in low desert should watch out for cryptogamic soils and avoid walking on them. These dark and granular soils contain algae and other microbes that come alive after rains. Through photosynthesis, they form an important link in the desert's ecological web. Cryptogamic soils are very fragile and may not recover for years after trampling.

SHARING THE TRAIL

Visitors should expect to encounter a wide variety of different user groups in southern Arizona. This magnificent wilderness is a magnet for hunters, fishermen, and solitude-seekers of all descriptions. In the interest of a safe and pleasant wilderness experience for all, exercise consideration and good manners when meeting other parties on the trail. Respect for others is the cornerstone of the traditional western ethic, a code still in force in the Arizona wilderness. Backpackers must share the trail with stock users and mountain bikers in many parts of the state. A few common-sense guidelines will help backcountry travelers avoid a bad experience when encountering others.

Because pack and saddle stock are less maneuverable than foot travelers, hikers should yield to horse parties when the two meet on a trail. In such a situation, the best thing that a hiker can do is to hike away from the trail for at least twenty feet and allow the stock to pass. It often helps to talk to the animals in reassuring tones as they pass by. This keeps the animals from panicking and tangling up the pack string.

Mountain bikes are not allowed on most trails in national parks and are prohibited in designated wilderness areas. Bikers who use traditional hiking trails should proceed slowly and with caution, especially when approaching blind corners. Always bike at a speed that allows instant braking if an unexpected obstacle or traveler appears in the path. Bike users should yield the right of way to horsemen, hikers and backpackers. Walkers should yield to horses.

HOW TO FOLLOW A FAINT TRAIL

Many of the trails that appear on topographic maps in this part of the world are faint or even nonexistent. Visitors to desert country should have a few elementary route-finding skills in their bag of tricks, in case a trail peters out or a snowfall covers the pathway. A topographic map and compass, and the ability to use them, are essential insurance against disaster when a trail is hard to find or disappears completely. There are also a few tricks that may aid a traveler in such a time of need.

Maintained trails in southern Arizona are marked in a variety of ways. Signs bearing the name and/or number of the trail are present at some trail junctions, although weathering and inconsiderate visitors sometimes remove or obscure these plaques. These signs rarely contain mileage information, and where they do, the information is often inaccurate. Along the trail, several kinds of markers indicate the location of maintained trails. In forested areas, cuts in the bark of living trees, known as "blazes," are made immediately beside the path. In spots where a trail crosses a gravel streambed or rock outcrop, piles of rocks called "cairns" mark the route. These cairns are typically constructed of three or more stones placed one on top of the other, a formation that almost never occurs naturally.

In the case of an extremely overgrown trail, markings of any kind may be impossible to find. On such a trail, the techniques used to build the trail serve as clues to its location. Well-constructed trails have rather wide, flat beds. Let your feet seek the flat spots when traveling through tall brush and you will almost always find yourself on the trail. Look for check dams and other rock-work on the trail that may have been placed to prevent erosion. Old sawed logs from previous trail maintenance can be used to navigate in spots where the trailbed is obscured; if you find a sawed log, then you must be on a trail that was maintained at some point in time. Switchbacks are also a sure sign of an official trail; wild game travels in straight lines, and horsemen traveling off-trail seldom bother to zigzag across hills. Previous travelers have also left clues to the location of old trails: watch for footprints or hoof marks as you go along.

When attempting to find a trail that has disappeared, ask yourself where the most logical place would be to build a trail given its source and destination. Trail builders tend to seek level ground where it is available, often following natural contours of streamcourses and ridgelines. Bear in mind that most trails avoid up-and-down motion in favor of long, sustained grades culminating in major passes or hilltops. Old trailbeds can sometimes be spotted from a distance as they cut across hillsides at a constant angle.

NO-TRACE CAMPING TECHNIQUES FOR THE DESERT

Most of the backcountry areas in southern Arizona do not have established, hardened camping areas. As a result, backpackers have unlimited choice in choosing a spot to bed down. With this freedom comes the responsibility to leave the campsite exactly as it was found. It is easy to see that if even half of the backcountry campers left evidence of their passage, Arizona's wilderness would soon be dotted with damaged campsites. Travelers should inspect their campsites when they leave and camouflage any spots that have been impacted. Pack out what you brought in with you, and pick up any trash that may have been left by less considerate campers.

Campsite selection is a key component to an enjoyable backpacking trip. Choose a level spot that is already free of vegetation so that it doesn't have to be cleared. Flash floods are a real threat to desert campers—even under blue skies, a rainstorm 20 miles away can send a wall of water down an arroyo in minutes—so be sure to pitch your camp on high ground, well away from streams and dry washes. When traveling along a major canyon, do not camp in the mouth of a side canyon or across from it. Finally, seeps and permanent streams are critical features of wildlife habitat. Camp at least 200 yards away from such water sources so that animals will be undisturbed; as a result you will get a good night's sleep.

Campers should move their camp every night so that their impacts are not concentrated at any one spot. Soils of the low deserts are particularly vulnerable to compaction. Compacted soils do not absorb water as well as loose soils, and this leads to an increase in runoff. This results in greater soil erosion, and less water for desert plants, which may die as a result. By moving camp frequently, soil compaction will be less severe and can be repaired by the activities of burrowing animals and insects. In addition, your presence will be less likely to disturb the behavior patterns of local wildlife.

There is something magical about having a campfire in the desert, beneath stars scattered across the infinite heavens like so much sparkling dust. Campfires can affect the desert community, however, and campers who build them should practice minimum-impact techniques so that their fire-building activities do not scar the landscape. To build a no-trace fire, dig a pit 6 inches deep in mineral soil. Do not surround the pit with rocks; they will only get scorched and will not stop a fire from spreading. Gather dead and downed twigs of small diameter—these will burn completely and leave no charred stumps. When your fire is spent, make sure it is cool to the touch, then bury it with the original soil. Scatter twigs sparsely across the site to camouflage it. Campfires are not allowed in some areas, and firewood may be hard to find in others. Come prepared by bringing a lightweight backpacking stove and using it instead of a campfire for all of your cooking needs.

Finally, wilderness sanitation may be one of the next great problems facing land managers in southern Arizona. There are few outhouses to be found in the Arizona backcountry, so hikers must practice no-trace techniques while having a bowel movement. When relieving yourself, select a site that is well away from any stream, spring, or wash that might potentially become contaminated. Dig a "cat hole" 4 to 6 inches deep in mineral soil, relieve yourself, and cover the site over with soil. An even better solution is to carry a "poop tube" to pack out your solid wastes. Such a tube can be constructed of a short length of PVC pipe, with screw-on caps at either end. It is inexpensive and lightweight, and may represent the wave of the future in these desert lands.

DRIVING ON DESERT ROADS

Most roads that access Arizona's wilderness areas are remote, lightly traveled, and unpaved. Each trail description in this book includes a section on finding the trailhead, with a description of roads leading to it. Improved gravel roads are suitable for all types of vehicles and are shown on maps by two parallel, solid lines. Some of these may become slippery or washed out in wet weather; these are listed as "fair-weather" roads. Primitive roads are shown by dashed lines on the map and may be passable to high-clearance vehicles with two-wheel-drive during favorable weather. During wet weather, four-wheel-drive is a must. Finally, four-wheel-drive roads are completely impassable to two-wheel-drive vehicles, and jeep trails are challenging even for four-wheel-drives. These roads are also indicated by dashed lines.

Every year, desert travelers become stranded on remote roads. Help may not come along for days, and unprepared travelers can sustain severe dehydration or even die if they become stranded. All hikers should carry a basic desert survival kit in their vehicles in case they become stuck. Such a kit should include five gallons of water, enough food for at least five days, a first-aid kit, and several blankets. Lack of preparedness can turn an adventure into a disaster.

USING THIS GUIDE

The primary intent of this guide is to provide information that helps hikers choose backpacking trips according to their desires and abilities. This book also provides a detailed description of the trail and interpretation of its natural and historic features. The guide is intended to be used in conjunction with topographic maps, which can be purchased at some ranger stations, local gift and sporting goods stores, or through the U.S. Geological Survey, Denver, CO 80225. The USGS has stopped making the larger 15-minute map series and now publishes only the 7.5-minute maps. Several fine topographic maps of larger areas have been put out by various private organizations; these are available in local stores.

Each trail description begins with an outline of the physical characteristics of the trail, for quick and easy reference. A general description of the trek comes first, complete with overall distances listed in miles. Extended trips cannot be reached by road, while wilderness routes represent abandoned trails and cross-country routes where the only indication of a trail might be an occasional blazed tree. This brief description is followed by notes on the best season for attempting the trail. The "Best Season" may be influenced by summer heat, winter snows, and/or wet season flooding.

Next comes a difficulty rating, which can be interpreted as follows: Easy trails can be completed without difficulty by hikers of all abilities; hikes rated Moderate will challenge novices; Moderately Strenuous hikes will tax even experienced hikers; and Strenuous trails will push the physical limits of the most Herculean hiker. Difficulty ratings may be followed by stars, which indicate difficulty in following the trail. Trails with one star typically had a well-defined tread at one point, but may have become overgrown in places and it might be necessary to follow cairns for short distances. Hikers who pay close attention to the trail should not have much difficulty following such routes. If the difficulty rating is followed by two stars, then the trail may be faint or even nonexistent for long stretches. Be prepared to use a compass and topographic map frequently on such hikes.

Water availability along the trail is described according to its reliability. Even perennial, or year-round, water sources may dry up during drought years, while intermittent sources hold water only during the wet months. Wise hikers will bring their own water rather than relying on natural supplies.

Next, the appropriate 7.5-minute quadrangle maps for each featured hike are listed in plain type. Maps that show the trail incorrectly are indicated

Author at Window Rock in the Santa Catalinas.

by an "(inc.)" beside the map name. Maps published by sources other than the USGS appear in italics. The managing agency responsible for the area is then listed. Look in the back of the book for the addresses and phone numbers of each agency. Brief directions for reaching the trailhead rounds out the opening statistical section.

Following this statistical section is a mile-by-mile description of landmarks, trail junctions, and gradient changes. The official distances given by the land management agency are presented for all trails that had them at press time. Where official distances were unavailable, they were developed using an instrument called a planimeter, which measures two-dimensional distances on a topographic map. These distances were then corrected for altitude gain or loss. The resulting mileages should be looked upon as conservative estimates, because they do not account for small-scale twists and turns or minor ups and downs.

The reference section is followed by a detailed interpretive description of the trail, including geologic and ecological features, historical sites, campsites, and other important information. Photographs have been included to give the reader a visual preview of some prominent geographic features. An elevation profile accompanies each trail description, providing a schematic look at major elevation gains and losses incurred during the course of the trip.

THE CHIRICAHUA MOUNTAINS

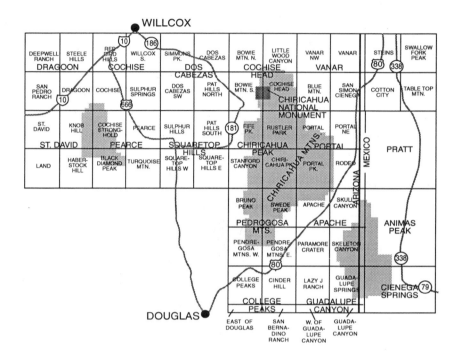

A verdant range of rounded mountains, the Chiricahuas rise from the grassy altiplanos of Arizona's southeastern corner. The range had its genesis in a huge volcanic caldera, or basin. The volcano's violent eruptions filled the Sulphur Springs Valley with ash to a depth of hundreds of feet. Geologists believe that the edge of the caldera can be traced along Witch Ridge, the Chiricahua Crest, then west through Johnson Peak. The floor of the caldera has become the Turkey Creek basin. This volcanic activity also included ash flows, which produced the fantastic pillars of Chiricahua National Monument, known to the Apaches as "Land of the Standing-Up Rocks." The multicolored rhyolite formations of Cave Creek and Rucker Canyon also originated in volcanic eruptions.

Atop this igneous core, the Chiricahuas have a sky-island ecosystem. Pines predominate, but Douglas-firs, Englemann spruces, and quaking aspens can be found above 8,000 feet. The foothills are clothed by oak woodlands, grading into grasslands at the edges of the mountain range. Abundant springs provide ample water for both wildlife and hikers. Coatimundis, Chiricahua fox squirrels, and Coues white-tailed deer are spotted here often, and a diverse and

Punch and Judy Rocks.

exotic assemblage of birds can be found during springtime in the riparian forests. Ridgetops are excellent places to spot raptors.

The heart of the range burned severely in 1994. The fire leveled the forests of Chiricahua Crest and spread onto surrounding ridges. A large number of trails were affected by the blaze, which caused numerous deadfalls and bared slopes to the ravages of erosion. Only the Chiricahua Crest trail received intensive rehabilitation following the blaze; hikers on other trails in the burn may have trouble finding their routes.

Forest fires are a natural part of this ecosystem, but a catastrophic blaze like the 1994 fire is a direct result of a century of fire suppression. In the absence of man, fires burned in small patches, creating a mosaic of timber classes. Older stands had lots of downed wood and burned readily, while younger stands, without enough fuel to carry a blaze, served as natural firebreaks and kept fires small. The Chiricahuas are filled with fire-adapted species. Some, such as the pines, have thick bark that insulates them from fire. Others, such as aspen and raspberry, depend on fires to create openings where they can grow in direct sunlight.

The heart of the Chiricahua Mountains is protected within the Chiricahua Wilderness Area, which is administered by the USDA Forest Service. There is plenty of auto-accessible recreation around the edges of the wilderness, with developed campgrounds at Camp Rucker, Sunny Flat (along Cave Creek), and Rustler Park. There are also primitive campgrounds throughout the range where no fee is charged for camping. Backcountry camping is permitted everywhere within Coronado National Forest, but Chiricahua National Monument only allows day hiking. There is an auto-accessible campground across from monument headquarters.

The nearest services are along U.S. Highways 191 and 80; Dos Cabezas, to the northwest, has an interesting mining museum but no visitor services.

1   THE HEART OF ROCKS LOOP

General description: A day loop through the head of Rhyolite Canyon, 8.4 miles round-trip.
Best season: September-May.
Difficulty: Moderate.
Water availability: None.
Elevation gain: 1,405 feet.
Elevation loss: 1,405 feet.
Maximum elevation: 7,055 feet.
Topo maps: Chiricahua National Monument, Arizona.

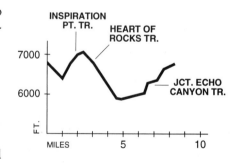

Jurisdiction: Chiricahua National Monument (NPS).
Finding the trailhead: From Willcox, take Arizona Highway 186 southeast to reach the monument. The trail leaves from the Echo Canyon

trailhead, on a spur off the Bonita Canyon Road, 0.3 mile from Massai Point.

0.0   Echo Canyon Trailhead. Follow Ed Riggs trail eastward.
0.2   Junction with Massai Point spur trail. Stay right.
0.9   Junction with Hailstone trail. Turn left onto Mushroom Rock trail.
3.1   Junction with Inspiration Point trail (0.5 mile, easy). Keep going straight on Big Balanced Rock trail.
4.1   Junction with Heart of Rocks spur loop (0.9 mile, moderate). Bear left to complete the larger loop.
5.7   Trail exits Sarah Deming Canyon. Junction with Rhyolite Canyon trail. Turn right to complete the loop.
6.8   Junction with Hailstone trail. Turn left and enter Echo Canyon.
7.0   Echo Park.
8.4   Trail returns to Echo Canyon trailhead.

The trail: This popular route makes a long day loop, visiting the most spectacular rock formations in Chiricahua National Monument. These formations were once a giant bed of superheated ash spewed forth from a caldera in the heart of the Chiricahua Mountains about 25 million years ago. The

1   Heart of Rocks

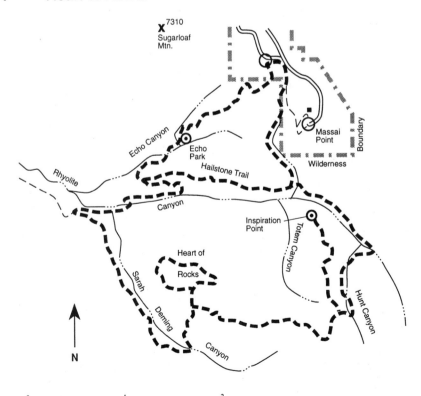

Pillars of welded tuff soar above Echo Canyon.

ash solidified into a rock called "welded tuff" as it cooled, with bands of varying widths marking different eruptions. Later, a dome-shaped uplift raised this layer of tuff unevenly, and stress fractures called "joints" crept down through the rock in a geometric pattern. These joints provided avenues for storm runoff, and over the centuries erosion dissected the formerly solid sheet of stone into the columns, spires, and hoodoos we see today. Some of these formations have suggestive shapes and have been named by passing travelers. The trail also takes in the upper watershed of Rhyolite Canyon, which is closed to backcountry camping.

From the Echo Canyon trailhead, follow a marked footpath east toward Massai Point. This area was named for the Apache warrior Bigfoot Massai, who escaped from an Oklahoma reservation by jumping a train in Kansas; he made his way back to the Chiricahuas undetected. Massai raided a ranch in Bonita Canyon in 1890, stealing a horse and provoking a local manhunt. The posse lost his trail near this area, and Bigfoot Massai escaped again.

The trail drops into a shallow draw and passes a spur track that climbs to the parking area at Massai Point itself. Stay right as the draw deepens. A diverse woodland of oaks, Arizona cypresses, and junipers soon provides splashes of shade. The first scattered pillars rise from the slopes surrounding the draw. The draw ultimately empties into Rhyolite Canyon, where clusters of pinnacles rise rank on rank like a petrified choir.

The trail reaches a marked junction at the mouth of the side draw; turn east into the main arm of Rhyolite Canyon to begin the loop trip. The trail descends to cross the mouth of a boulder-strewn gully with tall pines and cypresses growing up through the rocks. The path then makes its way up the head of Rhyolite Canyon through a pine-oak woodland that obscures much of the surrounding scenery. Keep an eye peeled for Mushroom Rock, which rises among the pinnacles near the canyon rim on the opposite slope.

A wooded gulch enters from the south. The path ascends along its watercourse to reach the top of a rolling plateau. Here, the Inspiration Point trail takes off to the south; it is discussed in detail at the end of this section. The main trail runs west across the plateau, which rises gradually to a small dome. A sparse growth of piñon allows 360-degree views that include Cochise Head to the west and the Dos Cabezas Range to the north, as well as the loftier Chiricahua Mountains to the south. The path then glides down across an inclined table of stone to enter the Heart of Rocks area.

Big Balanced Rock rises to the south of the trail. This 1,000-ton sphere is perched precariously upon a narrow pedestal. Just beyond this unlikely formation lies a junction with a spur loop that takes the traveler deep into the Heart of Rocks. This short but challenging side trail descends into a depression filled with Chihuahua pines and Arizona cypresses, where it splits at a trail register. Following the loop in a clockwise manner leads the hiker up a vigorous ascent to the west. Pinnacle Balanced Rock rises like a graceful obelisk along the way, and Old Maid Rock greets the traveler at the top of the grade. Camel's Head Rock and Thor's Hammer are the next prominent pillars; each takes the form of a substantial cap rock that is perched atop a slender gooseneck of less-resistant stone. Punch and Judy Rock, named for the famous puppets, soon appears through a window in the stone as the trail dips and climbs on an eastward heading. The unusual Duck on a Rock formation, created by diagonal jointing in the stone, perches to the east of the trail ahead. The popular Kissing Pock is the final named feature, composed of a slender, wasp-waisted spire joined to a more stout pillar in a caricature of a human kiss. The path returns to the wooded depression to close the loop.

Back at the main trail, the trek continues with a cliff-hanging descent into Sarah Deming Canyon. The path follows the western slope of this defile through a pine-oak forest, offering occasional views of the spires rising along the eastern rim of the canyon. Near the mouth of Sarah Deming Canyon, the bedrock is shot through with vertical and horizontal joints that give it the appearance of an adobe ruin. It does not form massive pillars because of its structural weakness. This canyon soon merges with the much wider cleft of Rhyolite Canyon, where the loop hike turns east on the Rhyolite Canyon trail.

This trail drops to the valley floor, then follows the streamcourse upward through a riparian forest notable for its abundant Arizona madrones among more common oaks and pines. The trail ultimately switchbacks steadily up the north wall of Rhyolite Canyon to reach a junction with the Echo Canyon and Hailstone trails.

To complete the loop, turn left into Echo Canyon. The trail winds upward to reach a grove of Apache pine and Arizona cypress known as Echo Park. The path then climbs vigorously, winding through some of the most spectacular pinnacles of the entire route. The cunningly crafted footpath hugs pillars and passes fascinating grottos as it ascends through welded tuff to reach a finger ridge. It then follows the ridgetop northeast to return the traveler to the Echo Canyon trailhead.

INSPIRATION POINT TRAIL

This path ascends gradually for 0.5 mile to reach an overlook above the head of Rhyolite Canyon. It traverses the stony crest of a finger ridge cloaked in piñon pine and manzanita. The pinnacles lining the north rim of the canyon stand out particularly well from this vantage point, and the overlook also boasts a superb view of Cochise Head.

HAILSTONE OPTION

This trail runs for 0.8 mile of level traveling between the mouth of Echo Canyon and the Massai Point trail. It allows a 3.3-mile loop of moderate difficulty, which features the spectacular formations of Echo Canyon. The Hailstone trail follows the base of a palisade above Rhyolite Canyon's north side. The vegetation on this south-facing slope is typical of semi-arid uplands. Piñon pine, evergreen oak, and alligator juniper are the prevalent trees, while yucca and manzanita are well-represented in the understory. In contrast, the north-facing slopes across the valley support a montane forest of ponderosa pines, Arizona cypresses, and even Douglas-firs. While hiking this trail, watch for the tiny "hailstones" of volcanic origin that gave the route its name. These tiny spheres of rock are called "spherulites," and were formed in place as a result of crystalline growth.

2   RHYOLITE CANYON

General description: A day hike along Rhyolite Canyon from Chiricahua National Monument Visitor Center to the Echo Canyon trail, 2.6 miles.
Best season: September-May.
Difficulty: Moderate.
Water availability: None.
Elevation gain: 950 feet.
Elevation loss: 50 feet.
Maximum elevation: 6,290 feet.

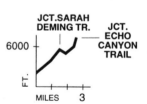

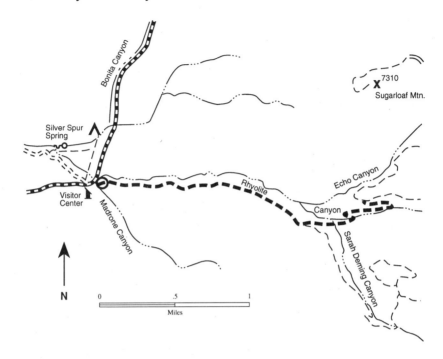

Topo map: Chiricahua National Monument.
Jurisdiction: Chiricahua National Monument (NPS).
Finding the trailhead: This trail leaves from the Chiricahua National Monument Visitor Center parking lot.

0.0	Trail leaves visitor center parking lot.
1.5	Junction with Sarah Deming Canyon trail. Turn left.
1.8	Trail reaches floor of Rhyolite Canyon.
2.6	Junction with Echo Canyon and Hailstone trails.

The trail: This trail links the Chiricahua visitor center with the Heart of Rocks loop. The hike begins by following the bottom of Rhyolite Canyon eastward from the visitor center. A diverse forest of pines, oaks, and cypresses supports an abundance of birds during spring and summer, including the seldom-seen elegant trogon. The canyon floor is buried in alluvial gravel that has been washed down by periodic floods, but the streambed itself is generally dry here, even during the rainy season.

The path climbs steadily along the south wall of the canyon, and the pinnacles of welded tuff for which the canyon is famous rise in parallel ranks above the valley. Look for Arizona madrones along the path as it ascends. These unusual trees are characterized by shiny leaves and terminal branches of polished red.

Views expand as the trail gains elevation and joins the Sarah Deming Canyon trail. Both the Sarah Deming and upper Rhyolite Canyon trails are discussed in detail under Trail 1, The Heart of Rocks Loop.

3   SUGARLOAF LOOKOUT

General description: A short day hike to the top of Sugarloaf Mountain, 0.9 mile.
Best seasons: September-November; March-May.
Difficulty: Moderate.
Water availability: None.
Elevation gain: 495 feet.
Maximum elevation: 7,310 feet.
Topo map: Chiricahua National Monument.
Jurisdiction: Chiricahua National Monument (NPS).
Finding the trailhead: Within Chiricahua National Monument, this trail leaves from the end of a marked spur road that departs Bonita Canyon Road 0.3 mile from Massai Point.

No photographs of the Apache chief Cochise exist to tell us whether his profile is accurately reflected in the stone of Cochise Head.

| 0.0 | Trailhead. |
| 0.9 | Sugarloaf Mountain fire lookout. |

The trail: This trail makes a brief climb to the top of Sugarloaf Mountain, where a fire lookout commands views encompassing Chiricahua National Monument. The path starts out on sidehills across the northern slope of Sugarloaf Mountain, which looks out over the clustered pinnacles of Bonita Canyon. After passing through a man-made tunnel, the grade steepens a bit. The path follows the base of an exposed layer of tuff, a rock made of conglomerated volcanic ash. It is structurally weak, and weathers easily into a fine dust. The layer above it is welded tuff, which has been bonded under great heat and pressure to form stone. This formation becomes particularly apparent as the trail swings onto the eastern slope of the mountain.

As it passes along the southern face of the hill, the trail offers a broad panorama of Rhyolite Canyon, filled with rows of stone pillars. The forested massif of the Chiricahua Mountains rises beyond the canyon. The final stretch of trail climbs through a dense thicket of manzanita on its way to the fire lookout at the summit. The lookout commands sweeping view of the Bonita Canyon watershed, Cochise Head, and the Dos Cabezas Range to the north.

3   Sugarloaf Lookout

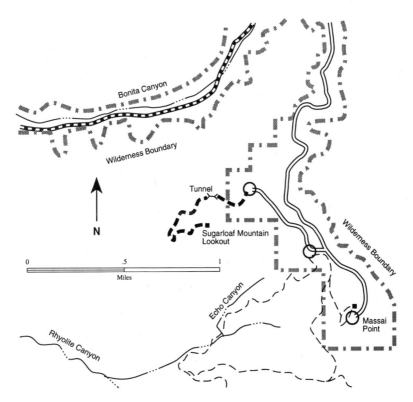

General description: A day hike to an overlook of Natural Bridge, 2.4 miles.
Best season: September-May.
Difficulty: Moderately strenuous.
Water availability: None.
Elevation gain: 645 feet.
Elevation loss: 250 feet.
Maximum elevation: 6,050 feet.
Topo map: Chiricahua National Monument.
Jurisdiction: Chiricahua National Monument (NPS).
Finding the trailhead: The trail departs from a marked trailhead 1.3 miles beyond the Chiricahua National Monument Visitor Center on Bonita Canyon Road.

0.0   Trailhead.
1.7   Picket Park.
2.4   Natural Bridge overlook.

4   Natural Bridge

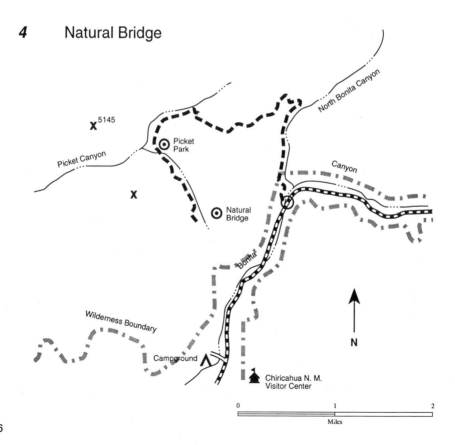

Tuff formations rise above the pines of Preston Park.

The trail: This rewarding trail penetrates a hidden corner of Chiricahua National Monument to reach a small stone bridge formed of bedrock weathered by centuries of erosion. The trail begins by crossing the wash of Bonita Canyon and following a side canyon northward through an oak-pine woodland. A spur ridge soon takes the traveler upward, revealing the clustered spires that line the canyon walls. The path climbs at a steady clip, topping out on a high plateau where piñon pine and alligator juniper rise above a chaparral community of manzanita, bear grass, and yucca. Two buttes faced with cliffs and spires rise ahead as the trail runs westward, and the tawny grasslands of the Sulphur Springs Valley stretch away beyond them.

After a gradual descent across the plateau, the trail drops into a small canyon to the north. It follows the oak-clad bottoms toward the two buttes, then doglegs back to the southeast to enter Picket Park. This enchanting woodland of ponderosa and Chihuahua pines occupies a flat basin surrounded by fascinating rock formations. The basin soon tapers down to become a rocky side canyon, and the tall pines fall away as the trail climbs to an overlook spot that marks its terminus. High on the far wall of the canyon, the natural bridge spans a narrow gulch lined by oak trees. This stout, 30-foot span of welded tuff has been weathered out of the bedrock by the passage of water, which eroded the weaker rock beneath what's left.

5   JOHNSON PEAK LOOP

General description: A day hike around Johnson Peak, 6 miles.
Best seasons: September-November; March-May.
Difficulty: Moderately strenuous.
Water availability: None.
Elevation gain: 2,030 feet.
Elevation loss: 2,443 feet.
Maximum elevation: 8,555 feet.
Topo maps: Chiricahua Peak, Chiricahua Mountains.

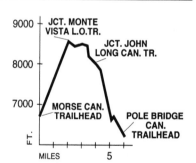

Jurisdiction: Chiricahua Wilderness, Douglas Ranger District, Coronado National Forest.
Finding the trailhead: From Arizona Highway 181 east of Sunizona, take the Turkey Creek Road (Forest Road 41) to its end to reach the Morse Canyon trailhead. The Pole Bridge trailhead is 1.2 miles farther down the canyon.

0.0	Morse Canyon trailhead.
2.0	Head of Morse Canyon. Junction with Monte Vista Lookout trail. Turn right.
2.5	Junction with Turtle Mountain trail. Bear right.
3.4	Junction with spur track to helipad. Turn right.

5   Johnson Peak Loop

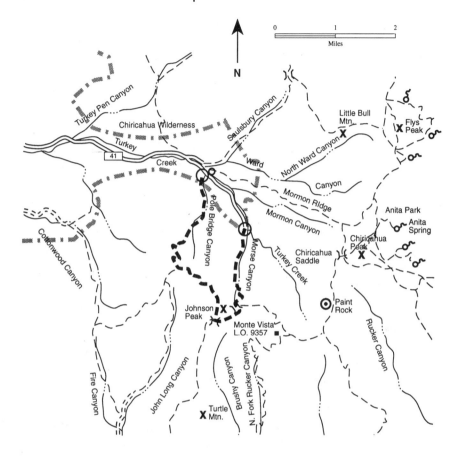

3.9   Junction with John Long Canyon trail. Turn right for descent into
       Pole Bridge Canyon.

6.0   Pole Bridge Canyon trailhead.

The trail: This hike combines the Morse Canyon and Pole Bridge Canyon
trails to form a semi-loop that takes in nice views of the western
Chiricahuas. The loop makes a circuit of Johnson Peak, one of the few
accessible peaks spared by the fire of 1994. Travelers can look forward to
cool pine forests and grassy glades on higher ridges as the trail takes in the
high country along a major divide. Ambitious hikers can add a side trip of
1.6 miles from the top of the loop to reach Monte Vista Lookout. (Ask permission from the lookout before climbing onto the tower.) There is no surface water along the route, so carry plenty of water bottles.

The trek begins with an ascent of Morse Canyon, a steep-sided valley
clothed in a magnificent forest of mature ponderosa pines and Douglas-firs. A
steady, zigzagging ascent leads to a lofty saddle at the foot of Johnson Peak,

where the trail reaches a marked junction. The Monte Vista Lookout trail climbs the ridgeline to the east, while the Johnson Peak route rounds the south side of the mountain. Monte Vista Lookout and Turtle Mountain are visible along the way to a slightly higher saddle, where the path meets the Turtle Mountain trail. Bear right as the Johnson Peak loop rises to meet the westward-running ridgeline. It follows the ridgetop for a time, with views of Cochise Head and Chiricahua Peak to the northeast. The trail then passes to the south of another high point, affording vistas down John Long Canyon toward the jumble of lesser peaks that trail away to the south.

A grassy meadow crowns the next high saddle, after which the trail descends to an intersection with the John Long Canyon trail. Turn right to drop into the upper reaches of Pole Bridge Canyon. Forest fires have thinned the timber here: a few old patriarchs that survived the blaze provided seeds for the thicket of young saplings that blanket the understory. Gaps in the canopy reveal fine views of Chiricahua Peak and the eroded spires that surround the head of the canyon. These pinnacles rise through the trees like stalagmites brought out of some great cave to dry in the sunlight. In fact, they are the exact opposite: while stalagmites are built by dripping water that deposits limestone, the spires seen here are the result of the erosive subtraction of the surrounding rock.

The trail soon drops to the canyon floor, where it enters a stand of large evergreen oaks and Apache pines. This latter tree species can be identified readily by its puffballs of foot-long needles. The streambed is bordered by low cliffs in places, and pleasant waterfalls fall in several spots during the rainy season. The trail emerges from the mouth of Pole Bridge Canyon to return to the Turkey Creek Road 1.2 miles below the Morse Canyon trailhead.

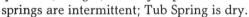

6   CHIRICAHUA CREST

General description: A backpacking trail from Rustler Park to Sentinel Peak, 10.3 miles.
Best season: March-November.
Difficulty: Moderate.
Water availability: Ojo Agua Fria, Bear Wallow, Booger, and Anita springs are reliable; Headquarters, Eagle, and Juniper springs are intermittent; Tub Spring is dry.

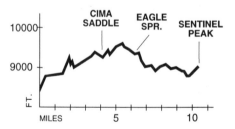

Elevation gain: 2,145 feet.
Elevation loss: 1,544 feet.
Maximum elevation: 9,796 feet (summit of Chiricahua Peak).
Topo maps: Rustler Park, Chiricahua Peak, Portal Peak, *Chiricahua Mountains*.
Jurisdiction: Chiricahua Wilderness, Douglas Ranger District, Coronado National Forest.

Sentinel Peak overlooks the pinnacles of Cave Creek.

Finding the trailhead: Take the Pinery Canyon Road (Forest Road 42) west from Portal or east from Chiricahua National Monument to reach Onion Saddle at the top of the range. Here, turn south on FR 42D to reach the Rustler Park campground. The trail begins here.

0.0	Trail leaves Rustler Park campground.
0.4	Junction with old Bootlegger trail. Keep going straight.
1.5	Bootlegger Saddle. Junction with cutoff trail from Long Park. Keep going straight.
2.5	Saddle north of Flys Peak. Trails to Long Park, Bear Wallow Spring, and Flys Peak depart. Bear right for fastest route.
3.0	Junction with Saulsbury Canyon trail. Keep going straight.
3.4	Round Park. Trails join from Flys Peak and Bear Wallow Spring.
4.2	Cima Saddle. Greenhouse trail joins. Keep going straight.
4.4	Junction with Mormon Ridge cutoff trail. Bear left.
4.9	Junction with Anita Park spur trail. Keep going straight.
5.0	Junction Saddle. Trails depart to Chiricahua Saddle and mountaintop to the north. Bear left for fastest route.
5.1	Junction with Chiricahua Peak trail. Bear left.

5.5	Trails join from Chiricahua Peak and Ojo Agua Fria. Keep going straight.
5.7	Trail joins from Chiricahua Saddle. Keep going straight.
5.8	Junction with cutoff trail to Snowshed Peak. Bear right.
6.2	Eagle Spring.
6.6	Snowshed cutoff trail rejoins Crest trail. Keep going straight.
6.7	Juniper Spring.
7.9	Price Canyon trail drops away to the right.
8.8	South Fork Cave Creek trail rises from the left to join Crest trail.
10.3	Summit of Sentinel Peak.

The trail: This long and heavily traveled trail follows the crest of the Chiricahua Mountains from Rustler Park to Sentinel Peak. The alpine forests and meadows along the route were extensively damaged by fire in 1994, and now only patches of unburned vegetation remain. The trail has received a considerable amount of maintenance since the fire, and should be easy to follow along its entire length. Numerous developed springs supply water for extended trips; backpackers need only bring a water purifier. Hikers seeking solitude may have to travel away from the crest to get it; this trail is undoubtedly the most popular trail in the Chiricahua Wilderness.

The trail departs from the upper end of the Rustler Park campground, and begins by climbing through coniferous forest. After passing the old Bootlegger trail junction, the Crest trail runs along the foot of a massive wall of stone. Gaps in the trees allow glimpses of Rustler Park before the path wanders south again. The footpath joins an old roadbed and receives a cutoff trail from Long Park before entering the charred country of the 1994 Chiricahua burn. As the track crosses a west-facing slope, the low pinnacles of Rhyolite Canyon can be seen through a latticework of charred snags.

Just after entering the Chiricahua Wilderness, the trail arrives at a complicated intersection in Flys Saddle. The Long Park trail rises into the saddle from the northeast, while the Crest trail splits into three forks. The most direct route crosses the burn on the western slope of Flys Peak, receiving the Saulsbury trail along the way. The central trail climbs directly over the summit of Flys Peak, with views to the east through the trees. (The lookout that once stood here was on stilts.) The left-hand path circles far to the east, taking in a number of attractions. First, it angles southeast through a mixed forest of Douglas-fir, quaking aspen, and Englemann spruce. It passes Tub Spring, which only seeps from the ground above an old, dry catch basin. It then rises steadily to a ridgetop, where a spur trail runs onto Centella Point. The main trail turns southeast here, passing Bear Wallow Spring before completing its trek through scorched forest. The three forks converge again at Round Park, a lush meadow set in the midst of the pines. It provides an idyllic contrast to the burned country on the western slopes of Flys Peak.

From the eastern fork of the Crest trail, the Centella Point trail follows a flat ridgetop for a mile, crossing through an old burn area from 1987. Centella (pronounced "sen-TAY-uh") is Spanish for thunderbolt, and, sure enough, this fire was the result of a lightning strike. Near the end of the ridge, flat swards

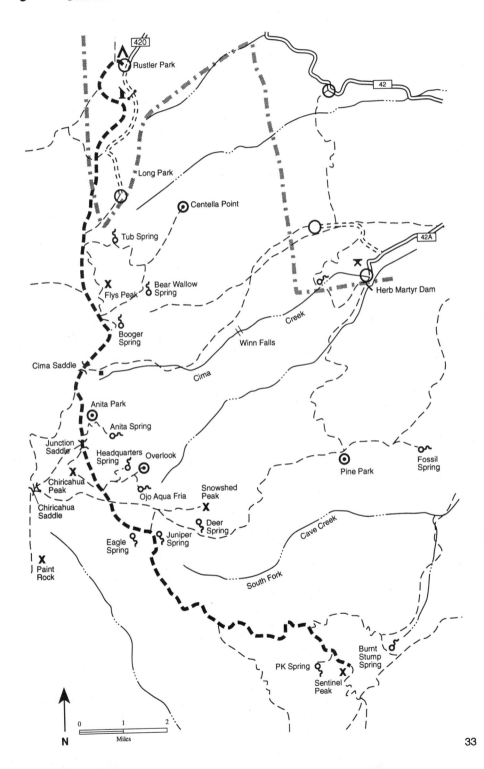

420

Rustler Park

42

Long Park

Centella Point

Tub Spring

42A

Bear Wallow
Spring

Flys Peak

Herb Martyr Dam

Booger
Spring

Creek

Winn Falls

Cima Saddle

Cima

Anita Park

Anita Spring

Junction
Saddle

Headquarters
Spring   Overlook

Fossil
Spring

Pine Park

Chiricahua
Peak

Ojo Aqua Fria   Snowshed
Peak

Chiricahua
Saddle

Deer
Spring   Cave Creek

Eagle
Spring   Juniper
Spring

Paint
Rock

South Fork

Burnt
Stump
Spring

PK Spring

Sentinel
Peak

0   1   2

N   Miles

33

of grass look out over the Cave Creek basin. The tower-studded massifs of Silver and Portal peaks rise beyond this wooded depression. The trail continues to a bald knob at the end of the ridge, which offers views of Cochise Head. Most hikers stop here, but a faint path continues to drop a short distance to reach the rocky promontory of Centella Point itself, with its stone towers that lean out over the abyss.

The Crest trail continues southward, passing to the east of the next mountaintop, where an old-growth stand of firs and aspens soars to astonishing heights. An unmarked spur trail descends to Booger Spring, and the main trail makes its way onto a rounded, south-facing slope where the pines are no strangers to fire. A gradual descent leads to Cima Saddle, where the Greenhouse trail rises to meet the ridgetop in a glade the size of a postage stamp. The Crest trail strikes a level course across the mountainside, passing through a burned stand where a cutoff trail to Mormon Ridge drops into the Turkey Creek drainage. Living trees return in a forest interrupted by shady swards of grass, and a spur path doglegs back to the north on its way to Anita Park. A charming ridgetop meadow here is bordered by graceful aspens, ponderosa pines, and Douglas-firs. A trail descends steeply from the east side of the clearing to access Anita Spring, where a rock catch basin holds a reliable supply of water.

Meanwhile, the Crest trail covers the remaining distance to aptly named Junction Saddle. Here, a spur path climbs the knob to the north, and the Crest trail once again splits into three parts.

The little-used right-hand fork runs southwest through burn and aspen forest to reach Chiricahua Saddle, where it meets the Raspberry Ridge trail. It then zigzags up stony slopes covered in Douglas-fir and aspen. Nearing the top of the ridge, the trail passes through chaotic boulders, which contrast sharply with the orderly ranks of white aspen trunks rising from their midst. The path then begins its descent through pines and eventually crosses a heavily burned slope. Across the valley, the convoluted fins of Paint Rock rise from the crest of Raspberry Ridge.

The left-hand trail is the most direct route, and it follows the contours of the mountain through heavy timber as it rounds its eastern side. The central trail climbs over Chiricahua Peak, which at 9,796 feet is the loftiest summit in the range. Along the way, it ascends through a mature stand of Englemann spruces, which grow here at the extreme southern limit of their range. A small clearing at the summit of Chiricahua Peak is surrounded by tall trees, blocking the view. The path descends through the pines of the south face to rejoin the other trails.

The right- and left-hand trails converge to the south of Chiricahua Peak, and the Crest trail proceeds southward as a single path. Just before it reaches the next saddle, a spur path descends a finger ridge to the east on its way to several springs and an overlook. Before it gets very far, the Headquarters Spring trail branches off to the north and drops through a spruce swamp to reach a murky and undependable pool. The ridgetop route drops to the southern slope of the finger ridge, then follows its crest through the pines. A short spur ascends to Headquarters Overlook, a viewpoint allowing glimpses of Portal Peak. Meanwhile, the main path drops into the ravine to reach Ojo Agua Fria Spring, one of the strongest and clearest flows in the range.

The Crest trail follows ridgetops southward from the junction and splits to negotiate the next mountaintop. The trail winding around the east side of the point is faint as it crosses sidehills through a dense forest. It drops to Snowshed Saddle (where it meets the Snowshed trail) before turning southwest to rejoin the main trail above Juniper Spring. Meanwhile, the more heavily trodden track runs to the west of the aforementioned mountaintop, crossing burned slopes that allow fine views of Paint Rock and the massive cliffs buttressing lower Chiricahua Peak. The trail soon passes Eagle Spring, which rises from a rock outcrop commanding a sweeping vista of peaks to the south. This trail receives the eastern branch of the trail just above the trough at Juniper Spring, and the freshly united route zigzags down into the next saddle.

The forest here is dominated by a doghair growth of pine and Douglas-fir that popped up in the wake of a forest fire that occurred decades ago. This stand of trees was only lightly damaged in 1994 because most of the fuel in the understory had already been consumed by the earlier fire. Intervening ridges block the view of Rucker Canyon as the trail drops into a heavily burned saddle that tantalizes travelers with glimpses of the gravity-defying rock formations in the Portal area. The more primitive Price Canyon trail drops away to the right, providing access to Sage Peak and the Rucker recreation area. The Crest trail rounds the head of Price Canyon, then works its way across burned hillsides to meet the South Fork Cave Creek trail.

The pathway then rounds one last point to reach a bald saddle at the base of Sentinel Peak. To the north, stone towers that rise from Silver and Portal peaks loom above the Cave Creek basin. The trail switchbacks up the slopes of Sentinel Peak, avoiding the extensive talus slopes on its western face. A trail junction near the summit offers the final path to the top. Here, an old lookout site once sat amid firs and aspens. These were killed by the blaze of 1994 and the summit will soon be bare. This point encompasses some of the most sweeping views in the Chiricahuas. To the southeast, the Peloncillo Range rises beyond the tawny expanse of the San Bernardino Valley. The Mule Mountains occupy the southwestern horizon, and visitors can look beyond the southerly Swisshelm Mountains to see deep into Mexico. Travelers who wish to connect with trails to the south can follow the steep path down the southeastern face of Sentinel Peak to reach a trail junction at the base of Jones Peak.

7   MORMON RIDGE

General description: A day hike or backpack from Turkey Creek to the Chiricahua Crest trail, 4.5 miles.
Best seasons: September-November; March-May.
Difficulty: Moderately strenuous.
Water availability: None.
Elevation gain: 2,995 feet.
Maximum elevation: 9,150 feet.
Topo maps: Chiricahua Peak, Chiricahua Mountains.

Jurisdiction: Chiricahua Wilderness, Douglas Ranger District, Coronado National Forest.

Finding the trailhead: From Arizona Highway 181 east of Sunizona, take the Turkey Creek Road (Forest Road 41) 10 miles to the Mormon Ridge trailhead.

0.0	Trailhead
4.0	Junction with old Mormon Canyon trail (abandoned). Keep going straight.
4.5	Trail joins Chiricahua Crest trail at Chiricahua Saddle.

The trail: This trail offers the most direct route from the Turkey Creek basin to Chiricahua Crest. It climbs a bare ridgetop that offers good views in all directions. Because the route has southern exposure and lacks shade, the best time to hike it is early morning before the sun gets high in the sky. There is no water along the trail, and the nearest water source along the Crest trail is upper Cima Creek below Cima Saddle.

At the outset, the trail fords Turkey Creek just above its confluence with Ward Creek. The pines of the bottomlands disappear as the trail climbs the toe of Mormon Ridge, which divides the two drainages. Scrubby oaks become the

7   Mormon Ridge

8   Saulsbury Canyon

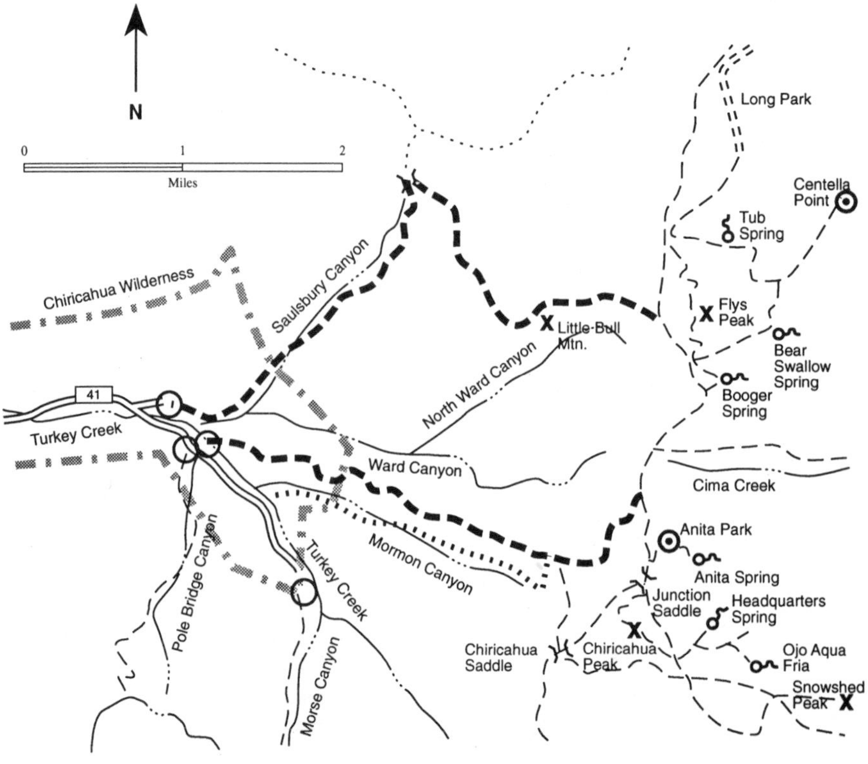

dominant trees as the trail gains elevation, and the sunny understory is dotted with yuccas and agaves. The ascent is steady for the first mile or so, and the rolling ridgetop commands views of the climax coniferous forest that cloaks the north-facing slopes of the Turkey Creek valley.

The ridge steepens sharply and the trail makes its first major ascent, zigzagging upward at a dogged pace. The next two saddles offer increasingly spectacular views of North Ward Canyon, which is guarded by a thicket of rocky spires. Flys Peak can be seen above the head of this valley. After a brief sojourn onto the northern slope of the ridge, the trail resumes its switchbacking ascent on the south side. Look backward to catch a glimpse of the weathered spires projecting from the lower flanks of Mormon Ridge. Across Mormon Canyon, a southern spur of Chiricahua Peak is cloaked in Douglas-fir and aspen and is crowned by a solitary miter of bedrock.

Soon after crossing the wilderness boundary, the trail passes below another high saddle. Here, a short jog to the ridgetop rewards the traveler with a sweeping vista that includes the distant peaks of the Dos Cabezas Range rising above the tawny plains of the Sulphur Springs Valley. The trail continues to climb; it reaches a junction with the abandoned Mormon Canyon trail at the next saddle.

The Mormon Ridge trail splits into two forks at this point. The left-hand route climbs through burned timber to intersect the Chiricahua Crest trail just south of Cima Saddle. The right-hand fork runs southward through a lush forest of aspen and fir, passing several picturesque talus slopes on its way to meet the Crest trail at Chiricahua Saddle.

8 *SAULSBURY CANYON*

General description: A day hike or backpack from Turkey Creek to the Chiricahua Crest trail, 6.4 miles.
Best season: March-November.
Difficulty: Moderately strenuous*.
Water availability: None.
Elevation gain: 3,141 feet.
Elevation loss: 45 feet.
Maximum elevation: 9,160 feet.
Topo maps: Chiricahua Peak, Rustler Park, Chiricahua Mountains.
Jurisdiction: Chiricahua Wilderness, Douglas Ranger District, Coronado National Forest.

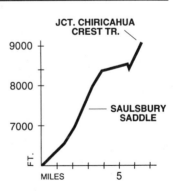

Finding the trailhead: From Arizona Highway 181 east of Sunizona, take the Turkey Creek Road (Forest Road 41) 9 miles to the Saulsbury Canyon trailhead.

0.0   Trailhead
0.3   Old road ends and trail begins.

2.5	Saulsbury Saddle. Junction with Rock Creek cutoff trail. Turn right.
5.3	Little Bull Mountain.
6.4	Junction with Chiricahua Crest trail.

The trail: This trail runs eastward from the Turkey Creek Valley as it climbs to join the Chiricahua Crest trail on the slopes of Flys Peak. The upper portions of the route burned during the 1994 Chiricahua Fire, but the trailbed remains mostly intact and can be followed with a little effort.

The hike begins on a jeep trail that follows Ward Creek as far as the mouth of Saulsbury Canyon. This latter ravine is quite shallow and is cloaked in pines and evergreen oaks. Check dams have been built across the wash to retain rainwater and stall floods. In the upper reaches of the canyon, the trail follows the western edge of the 1994 Chiricahua burn. Immediately after the blaze, a dense carpet of lupines covered the scorched soil to the east of the trail. A nameless butte rises at the head of the canyon, and its cliffs of yellow stone dominate the landscape.

The trail moves east of this butte for the final climb to Saulsbury Saddle, where it reaches a marked intersection. Here, a short connector trail runs down to Rock Creek on the far side of the divide, while the Saulsbury trail turns east to climb toward Little Bull Mountain. As it zigzags upward, it first passes onto the semi-arid south slope of the ridge and then onto the meadowy north slope. The trail can be faint in spots; watch for cairns and old rock cribbing to mark the path. The craggy face of Cochise Head looms far to the north, while the tree-clad summit of Ida Peak and the stone palisade of Barfoot Peak rise in the foreground. Ahead, Little Bull Mountain manifests itself as a conical point rising high above the ridgeline. The trail drops from the ridgetop for a steady descent across its northern face.

After the trail crosses a low saddle, upward progress resumes through patches of forest that were completely razed by the 1994 blaze. A backward look reveals Little Bull as a rounded dome with cliffs across its eastern face. Delicate spires of rock can be seen on its southern slope as the path climbs the slopes of Flys Peak. The trail meets the Chiricahua Crest route on the western slope of this rounded summit, just a short distance north of Round Park.

---

9   *RASPBERRY RIDGE*

General description: A backpack from Rucker Canyon to the Chiricahua Crest trail, 5.7 miles.
Best season: March-November.
Difficulty: Moderately strenuous*.
Water availability: None.
Elevation gain: 3,332 feet.
Elevation loss: 322 feet.
Maximum elevation: 9,255 feet.
Topo maps: Chiricahua Peak, Chiricahua Mountains.

Jurisdiction: Chiricahua Wilderness, Douglas Ranger District, Coronado National Forest.

Finding the trailhead: From U.S. Highway 191 north of Elfrida, take the Rucker Canyon Road (Forest Road 74) into the Chiricahuas. Turn north on FR 74E at signs for the Rucker Canyon Recreation Area. Follow this road 16 miles to the trailhead at its end.

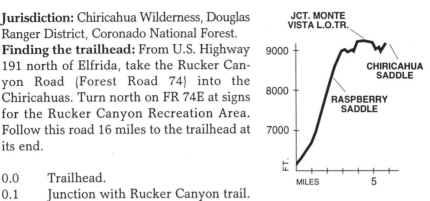

0.0	Trailhead.
0.1	Junction with Rucker Canyon trail. Turn left.
2.2	Raspberry Saddle. Trail leaves Bear Canyon.
4.3	Junction with Monte Vista Lookout trail. Bear right.
4.9	Paint Rock.
5.7	Chiricahua Saddle. Trail joins Chiricahua Crest trail.

The trail: This trail forms the most direct link between the Rucker Canyon area and the Chiricahua Crest trail. It climbs Bear Canyon, then follows a

Looking south from Raspberry Saddle.

39

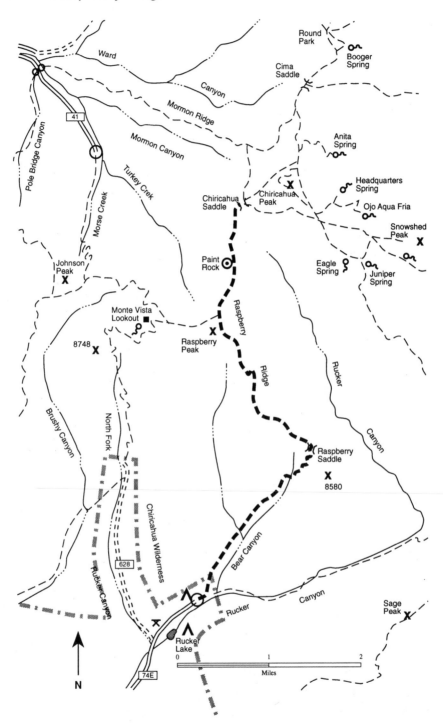

heavily burned ridgetop to meet the Crest trail at Chiricahua Saddle. Because of the burn, the trail was already difficult to follow before the winter rains of 1994-1995, and the wet season was expected to further erode the trail tread. Check with the Douglas Ranger District for current trail conditions and expect some map-and-compass route-finding above the head of Bear Canyon. And note: once the trail reaches Chiricahua Saddle, the nearest water source is Eagle Spring, 0.6 mile southeast of Chiricahua Saddle.

The trail begins on an old jeep trail ascending Rucker Canyon from Camp Rucker. After a few yards, the Raspberry Ridge trail turns off to the left to Bear Canyon. As the path ascends the wooded canyon, startling towers of buff-colored stone can be glimpsed through branches of evergreen oaks. These stone pillars are scattered across the surrounding slopes like broken teeth, and they watch over travelers during the entire ascent of the Bear Canyon bottoms. Upon reaching the head of the canyon, the path zigzags up its eastern wall, offering vistas of the surrounding pinnacles as well as a broad panorama of distant ranges to the southwest.

The trail reaches the ridgetop at Raspberry Saddle, on the pine-girt divide between Bear and Rucker canyons. From the saddle, the trail vigorously follows the ridgeline upward. It finally levels atop a stony crest that offers views into the upper drainage of Rucker Canyon, as well as a backward glimpse of Rucker Lake in its wooded basin to the south. The trail then follows a gently rolling ridgetop through country that sustained varying levels of fire damage during the 1994 blaze. In protected pockets, ground fires left some of the pines standing. In other areas, the fire "crowned out," or jumped into the forest canopy, to burn with an intensity that left little but charred snags and mineral soil. On several occasions, the trail drops onto the eastern slope of the ridge to avoid rocky points, then climbs steeply to regain the mountaintop.

The junction with the trail to Monte Vista Lookout survived the fire in fine shape, as did the remainder of the trail running northeast to Chiricahua Saddle. In between patches of charred country, the path makes frequent dips into the surviving fir-aspen forest on the north slope of the ridge. Paint Rock soon rises from the hilltop, its thin vertical walls dappled in reds, yellows, and ochre greens. This formation offers several fine overlooks that highlight the cliffy flanks of Chiricahua Peak. The trail descends past several lesser rock formations to reach a low divide, then climbs a brief pitch to its endpoint at Chiricahua Saddle, where it links up with the Chiricahua Crest trail.

10   RUCKER CANYON

General description: A day hike to an overlook above Rucker Canyon, 3.9 miles. See map on page 46.
Best season: Year-round.
Difficulty: Moderate.
Water availability: Rucker Canyon contains water seasonally.
Elevation gain: 1,490 feet.

Elevation loss: 30 feet.
Maximum elevation: 7,630 feet.
Topo maps: Chiricahua Peak, Chiricahua Mountains.
Jurisdiction: Chiricahua Wilderness, Douglas Ranger District, Coronado National Forest.

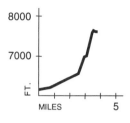

Finding the trailhead: From U.S. Highway 191 north of Elfrida, take the Rucker Canyon Road (Forest Road 74) into the Chiricahuas. Turn north on FR 74E at signs for the Rucker Canyon recreation area. Follow this road 16 miles to the trailhead at its end.

0.0	Trailhead.
0.1	Junction with Raspberry Ridge trail. Keep going straight.
0.8	Old road ends; trail becomes a footpath.
2.6	Trail begins climb out of Rucker Canyon.
3.5	Junction with Sage Peak/Red Rock Canyon trail. Bear left.
3.9	Overlook point.

The trail: This trail makes an outstanding day hike from the end of the Rucker Canyon Road (Forest Road 74E). The bottomland forests along the lower part of the trail make excellent bird and deer habitat, and the upper segment of the trail offers spectacular views of multicolored rock formations flanking upper Rucker Canyon. At its upper end, the trail links up with the Red Rock Canyon trail via Sage Peak, and a primitive track also runs up Price Canyon to meet the Chiricahua Crest trail. There may be water in the wash of Rucker Canyon seasonally, but there are no springs along the route.

The trail begins as an old two-rut road that follows Rucker Creek eastward through a bottomland dominated by evergreen oaks and ponderosa pines. The oaks soon fall away, and Apache pines replace the ponderosas as the dominant overstory trees. Arizona cypress, a member of the cedar family, grows along the stream banks where its roots can tap underground water sources. This graceful tree looks like a spruce, but has bark that is ribbed in long smooth strips.

A band of grayish bedrock soon bars the valley. The creek has carved a swirling channel through the stone. Beyond this point, grassy glades interrupt the forest, allowing views of rocky knobs protruding from the valley walls. These knobs resolve themselves into cliffs of reddish rhyolite that can be glimpsed through gaps in the thickening forest. The trail crosses the streamcourse more frequently in its upper basin, and Arizona sycamore becomes a prominent member of the riparian forest.

As the valley makes a sharp bend north, the trail passes among a scattering of large boulders, then climbs the south wall of the valley. As the path makes its way upward, stone walls and pinnacles above the opposite slope of the valley appear in reds, yellows, and oranges like flames frozen into stone. Above the trail, towers of naked rock rise like ruined castles, and piñon pines grow in gnarled forms from clefts in the bedrock. This sublime spectacle is re-

Towers of stone guard Rucker Canyon.

vealed bit by bit as the traveler gains elevation, until the thickening pine forest blocks the views.

The trail then zigzags upward along a rocky scarp to reach the crest of the ridge. Here, it meets the Red Rock Canyon trail at the foot of an immense overhang. Turn north, following a rocky ridgeline covered with wind-sculpted manzanita, juniper, and piñon. The effect is not unlike that of a well-tended Japanese garden. After 0.8 mile of ridgetop travel, the trail reaches an overlook that allows close inspection of some of the upper formations guarding Rucker Canyon. The path that leads onward from this point drops into Price Canyon, where an indistinct trail can be traced up to the crest of the Chiricahua Range or down to a primitive road in the foothills.

11   RED ROCK CANYON (G)

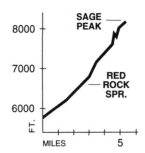

General description: A long day hike to Sage Peak, 5.4 miles.
Best season: Year-round.
Difficulty: Moderately strenuous*.
Water availability: Red Rock Spring is dependable.
Elevation gain: 2,654 feet.
Elevation loss: 80 feet.
Maximum elevation: 8,360 feet.
Topo maps: Chiricahua Peak, Chiricahua Mountains.
Jurisdiction: Chiricahua Wilderness, Douglas Ranger District, Coronado National Forest.
Finding the trailhead: From U.S. Highway 191 north of Elfrida, take the Rucker Canyon Road (Forest Road 74) into the Chiricahuas. Turn north on FR 74E at signs for the Rucker Canyon recreation area. After 8.5 miles, turn right on Forest Road 354. The jeep trail to Red Rock Canyon splits off to the west after 1 mile.

0.0	Red Rock Canyon jeep road splits away from FR 354.
0.1	Jeep trail forks. Turn left.
0.6	Jeep track enters Red Rock Canyon.
2.3	Red Rock Spring. Trail enters Chiricahua Wilderness.
4.5	Trail begins climb out of Red Rock Canyon.
4.8	Junction with abandoned cutoff trail to Rucker Canyon. Bear right.
5.4	Sage Peak.

The trail: This trek follows a jeep trail to Red Rock Spring, then enters the Chiricahua Wilderness and becomes a footpath running all the way to the summit of Sage Peak. The trail goes beyond the peak for hikers who wish to connect with the Rucker Canyon trail. It features some fantastic stone

Dobson Peak dominates the view from Sage Peak.

pinnacles along the way, and typically receives less traffic than other trails in the Rucker Canyon Recreation Area.

From Forest Road 354, turn east onto a jeep trail marked with signs for Red Rock Canyon. Bear left as a jeep track bound for Coal Pit Tank splits away to the southeast. The Red Rock Canyon trail runs eastward from this intersection, crossing flat savannahs of live oak. This area is a favorite haunt of Coues white-tailed deer. Low foothills define the mouth of Red Rock Canyon, and rocky palisades adorn the peaks beyond.

The trail soon passes beneath a corrugated wall of rhyolite, livid with splashes of red and orange. Spires and pinnacles of the same stone surround the cliff. Just beyond this point, the valley jogs north at the site of Red Rock Spring, which drips fitfully into a concrete retaining tank. The wilderness area boundary lies just beyond the spring.

The jeep trail soon forks into two branches. Follow the valley-bottom track, which crosses the wash frequently as it goes up the floor of the canyon. The rock formations in this part of the canyon take on a pink hue, and rise in bulky blocks from the wooded hillsides. To the south, the pale gray formations of Erickson Peak rise high above the valley. Near the head of the drainage, the rock takes on a chalky white appearance, and pine savannahs replace the live

10   Rucker Canyon
11   Red Rock Canyon

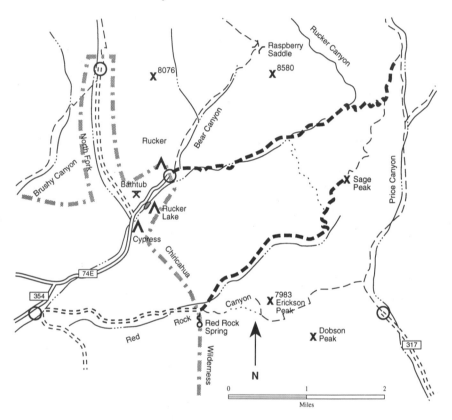

oak woodlands of the lower canyon. The trail fades here and frequently occupies the streambed for short distances. The pine forest thickens, and groves of aspen grow along the banks of the wash. As the valley arcs northward, the trail climbs sharply, then levels to return to the floor of the drainage.

A signpost marks the spot where the path crooks west to begin its ascent to Sage Peak. It zigzags upward, crossing an arid slope that rises to the north of the valley. At the crest, one can look south for fine views of Erickson and Dobson peaks, as well as grassy basins and hazy hills in the distance. The trail makes a brief drop onto the northern side of the ridge, then climbs to a saddle where it meets an abandoned cutoff trail that descends into Rucker Canyon.

The Sage Peak trail climbs steadily up the ridgeline to the east through a loose forest of mature pines. The saddle just before the peak offers unobstructed views of the Chiricahua massif, guarded by its sheer buttresses of stone. The trail climbs just south of the summit, which can be reached with a 30-yard bushwhack. From Sage Peak, there are good views of upper Rucker Canyon through gaps in the ragged pines. A marker atop the peak commemorates the death of a former fire lookout who served here. Meanwhile, the main trail continues northeastward, descending steadily for 1.6 miles to reach a junction with the Rucker Canyon trail.

12 GREENHOUSE TRAIL

General description: A day hike or backpack from the Cave Creek basin to the Chiricahua Crest trail, 5.6 miles. See map on page 50.

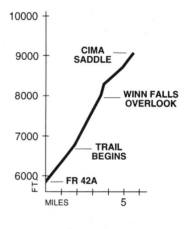

Best season: March-November.
Difficulty: Moderately strenuous.
Water availability: Cima Creek is perennial in its upper reaches.
Elevation gain: 3,420 feet.
Maximum elevation: 9,250 feet.
Topo maps: Portal, Chiricahua Peak, Rustler Park, Chiricahua Mountains.
Jurisdiction: Chiricahua Wilderness, Douglas Ranger District, Coronado National Forest.

Finding the trailhead: Take Forest Road 42 west from Portal to the Southwestern Research Station. Here, turn south on FR 42A. The primitive road to the Greenhouse trailhead departs from FR 42A 0.4 mile before the Herb Martyr Picnic Area.

0.0   Primitive road leaves FR 42A.
1.5   Greenhouse trail departs from end of primitive road.
3.0   Winn Falls overlook.
3.7   Administrative cabins.
5.6   Cima Saddle. Trail joins Chiricahua Crest trail.

The trail: This trail provides a brief but vigorous climb to the crest of the Chiricahua Range from the Cave Creek Basin. Along the way, it visits Winn Falls, a towering cataract that spills year-round over the brink of a cliff. There are also scenic views of Portal Peak from the lower slopes of the grade, which burned in 1994. The upper basin remained untouched during the blaze, and still offers a taste of the virgin forest that once prevailed in the higher parts of the range. The Greenhouse trail links up with the Chiricahua Crest trail at Cima Saddle.

The trek begins on a primitive jeep road that leaves Forest Road 42A near the Herb Martyr Picnic Area and crosses the Cave Creek basin on a northwesterly course. The southern segment of the Basin trail soon takes off to the left, while the road bends north to strike a major tributary. The northern section of the Basin trail then peels away to the right, and hills crowd the creek as the road ends. The trail narrows to a footpath as it ascends with the valley floor.

Looking across the Cave Creek basin at Portal Peak.

It passes tall Douglas-firs that survived the 1994 fire with the help of their thick, corky bark.

The path soon leaves the streamcourse in favor of a dry gulch to the south. It begins a steady slog upward through heavily burned timber. Then it passes behind a rocky point to reach a saddle overlooking Winn Falls. Here, a tiny rivulet pours intermittently over a cliff that is more than 400 feet tall, flanked by palisades of stone that are even more impressive. As the trail resumes its ascent, Portal Peak becomes visible to the south, ornamented with many stone towers and pinnacles.

After reaching a much higher saddle, the trail enters the upper valley of Cima Creek, which gives rise to Winn Falls. Its steep, forested walls block long views for the remainder of the trek. Englemann spruce becomes increasingly prevalent as the trail follows the valley upward. These graceful conifers were able to survive the blaze because the cool, moist pocket that they occupy is not as fire-prone as the drier forests surrounding it. The trail passes a pair of administrative cabins owned by the Forest Service, and Cima Creek provides a year-round supply of water here. The trail then climbs the final pitch to a junction with the Chiricahua Crest trail at Cima Saddle, about halfway between Flys and Chiricahua peaks.

13   SNOWSHED PEAK

General description: A long day hike or backpack from the Cave Creek basin to the Chiricahua Crest trail, 6 miles.

Best season: September-November; March-May.

Difficulty: Moderately strenuous*.

Water availability: Cave Creek usually has water; Deer Spring is intermittent.

Elevation gain: 3,937 feet.

Elevation loss: 80 feet.

Maximum elevation: 9,657 feet.

Topo maps: Portal Peak, Chiricahua Peak, Chiricahua Mountains.

Jurisdiction: Chiricahua Wilderness, Douglas Ranger District, Coronado National Forest.

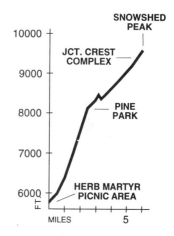

Finding the trailhead: Take Forest Road 42 west from Portal to the Southwestern Research Station. Here, turn south on FR 42A. Follow this improved dirt road to its end at the Herb Martyr Picnic Area.

0.0	Herb Martyr Picnic Area. Follow the Herb Martyr trail.
0.1	Junction with the Basin trail. Turn left.
2.4	Trail meets the Snowshed trail. Turn right.
2.5	Pine Park.
5.0	Deer Spring.
5.5	Trail meets the eastern lobe of the Chiricahua Crest trail at Snowshed Saddle. Turn right for Snowshed Peak.
6.0	Summit of Snowshed Peak.

The trail: This trip combines the Herb Martyr and Snowshed trails, linking the Cave Creek basin with an eastern lobe of the Chiricahua Crest trail. There are good camping spots at Pine Park; backpackers looking for a tent site along Chiricahua Crest will have to venture some distance from the end of this trail to find unburned country. The upper part of this route was heavily burned in 1994, and the trail had began to erode by the following fall. Winter rains may have done further damage to the newly exposed slopes, erasing the trail tread. Check with the district ranger station for current trail conditions.

From the Herb Martyr Picnic Area, take the Basin trail into a gulch that drains into Cave Creek. The Basin trail soon splits away to the right, running north to Ash Spring and the Greenhouse trail. Travelers bound for Snowshed Peak should bear left at this junction, following the Herb Martyr trail up the south bank of Cave Creek. This country was once covered in evergreen oaks, but the fire killed most of the trees and cleared the underbrush. As the path wanders onto the bluffs above the stream, there are good view of Sanders Peak

12   Greenhouse Trail
13   Snowshed Peak

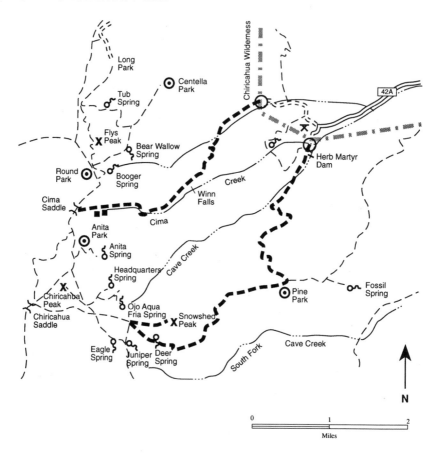

and its sharp palisades of rock, as well as the massive dome of Snowshed Peak rising above the headwaters. The trail takes a side trip up a dry ravine running parallel to Cave Creek, then returns streamside.

The path then turns southward, leaving Cave Creek to climb the fire-scarred slopes above it. It zigzags up through blackened snags that frame eastward views of Silver Peak's twin-humped mass. The trail soon strikes the crest of a finger ridge, which it follows south toward a much higher divide. Upon reaching the base of the divide, the trail crosses a level bench that makes a good camp spot, then winds east and upward across spurs and gullies. Keep an eye out for Arizona madrone, which grows sporadically on unburned ridgetops in this area. This unusual tree has white bark that peels away toward the ends of its branches to reveal a smooth, red inner bark. Pines cloaking the north-facing slopes here have for the most part survived the fire and provide welcome shade for the final climb.

Near the ridgetop, the Herb Martyr trail meets the Snowshed trail. Turn west, following this path through a loose collection of enormous boulders to reach Pine Park. This shallow ridgetop depression is filled with wide-spaced ponderosa pines, and is surrounded by low hillocks. Shafts of sunshine beam through gaps in the canopy, dappling the forest floor with pools of light. Upon leaving this basin, the trail works its way across the heavily burned southern slope of the ridge. A few rock pinnacles lean out over the South Fork Cave Creek valley. Agaves and dagger yuccas eke out a marginal existence in spots that were too rocky to carry a flame during the 1994 fire.

The trail maintains a straight and gentle uphill grade as it makes for the head of the valley. As the trail rounds an east-facing slope, travelers can see Portal Peak with its many towers of stone. The trail makes a single set of switchbacks to avoid a rock outcrop, and soon thereafter passes beneath the concrete trough of Deer Spring. It then rounds the western slope of Snowshed Peak, where it joins an eastern lobe of the Crest trail at Snowshed Saddle.

A spur trail climbs from the saddle onto the western slopes of Snowshed Peak, bound for the summit. It is faint at first, but gains definition as it zigzags upward through talus and snags. Atop the peak, a growth of Douglas-firs and aspens survived the flames to form a forest oasis in the heart of the burn. The trail ends at the summit, where the slopes drop away to the east and charred snags obscure views of Portal Peak. Snowshed Peak was one of the first fire lookout sites in the Chiricahuas, and lookouts used to climb high into a ponderosa pine outfitted with spikes for footholds. From this treetop perch, they kept watch over the surrounding valleys, and reported any signs of smoke or flame.

14 SOUTH FORK OF CAVE CREEK

General description: A long day hike or backpack from South Fork Picnic Area to the Chiricahua Crest trail, 6.8 miles.
Best seasons: Year-round (lower); March-November (upper).
Difficulty: Easy along the South Fork; moderately strenuous** beyond.
Water availability: The South Fork of Cave Creek contains water year-round; Burnt Stump Spring is intermittent.
Elevation gain: 3,560 feet.
Elevation loss: 30 feet.

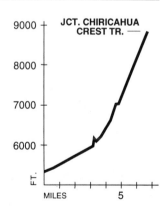

Maximum elevation: 8,830 feet.
Topo maps: Portal Peak (inc.), Chiricahua Mountains.
Jurisdiction: Chiricahua Wilderness, Douglas Ranger District, Coronado National Forest.
Finding the trailhead: From Portal, drive west on Forest Road 42 to reach the South Fork Cave Creek Road (Forest Road 42E). The trail departs from the picnic area at its end.

0.0	South Fork Cave Creek Picnic Area.
1.8	Junction with Horseshoe Pass trail. Keep going straight.
3.6	Trail leaves the South Fork of Cave Creek and ascends side canyon.
5.3	Junction with cutoff trail to Burnt Stump Spring and Horseshoe Ridge trail. Bear right.
6.8	Junction with Chiricahua Crest trail.

The trail: This popular trail is readily followed as it runs along the South Fork, but becomes increasingly tricky to find as it climbs toward its junction with the Chiricahua Crest trail. The last several miles cross heavily burned country where the trailbed was damaged by heavy erosion in the wake of the 1994 fire. The lower canyon is noted for its diversity of both plants and birds, including the rare, elegant trogon and the blue-throated hummingbird. It provides spectacular displays of fall color in late October.

The trail begins in rich bottomland forest below soaring towers of multicolored rhyolite. Mountain trees such as Chihuahua and ponderosa pines and evergreen oaks mix with water-loving trees such as cypresses and sycamores. As the path ascends the valley, bigtooth maples become prevalent. A scattering of yuccas reminds the traveler that the Chiricahuas are a desert range.

The trail frequently crosses the streamcourse as the water splashes through

Magnificent spires and outcrops rise above the South Fork of Cave Creek.

14   South Fork of Cave Creek
15   Horseshoe Pass

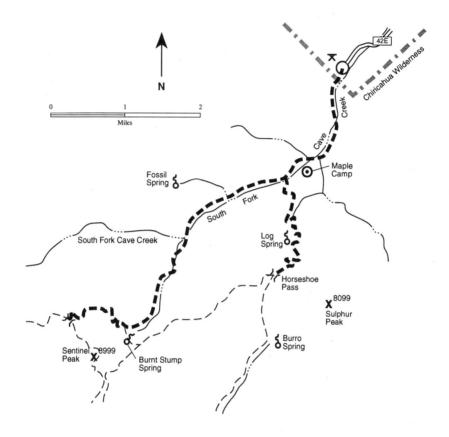

stony runs and quiet pools. The trail junction at Maple Camp is difficult to spot; look for a broad track that ascends the far bank of the stream at the foot of a steep slope. Beyond this point, the trees become smaller and sparser, and cliff walls rise to remote heights on either side of the valley.

As the trail progresses up the canyon, these cliffs give way to a scattering of isolated towers and pointed spires. Straight ahead, a colossal castle of stone marks a split in the valley. The main branch of the stream lies up the western canyon; the trail swings into the lesser gulch to the south. Here, a small rill splashes across sills of bedrock and into quiet pools. Water ouzels can sometimes be spotted among streamside boulders.

This entire basin was burned by a low-intensity ground fire during the summer of 1994. Larger pines survived by virtue of their thick bark, but many younger trees were girdled by the flames. The trail passes through a mixed stand of aspen and fir, then climbs into a shallow basin. Here, the valley forks into three steep ravines and the faint Burnt Stump cutoff trail strikes off to the east. The main path initially climbs the northernmost gulch, then zigzags up the hillside immediately south of it. After returning to the northern draw, the track fades as it crosses the floor of the ravine, which has been buried in a layer of alluvial rubble. The trail ultimately climbs back onto the slopes for the final ascent. Fine views of Portal Peak and Cathedral Rock appear just before the trail meets the Chiricahua Crest route at a signpost atop the ridgeline.

15 HORSESHOE PASS

General description: A day hike from the South Fork Picnic Area to Horseshoe Pass, 4.8 miles.
Best season: Year-round.
Difficulty: Moderately strenuous*.
Water availability: The South Fork of Cave Creek contains water year-round; Log Spring is intermittent.
Elevation gain: 2,395 feet.
Elevation loss: 485 feet.
Maximum elevation: 7,210 feet.

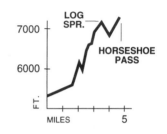

Silver Peak.

Topo maps: Portal Peak, Chiricahua Mountains.
Jurisdiction: Chiricahua Wilderness, Douglas Ranger District, Coronado National Forest.
Finding the trailhead: From Portal, drive west on Forest Road 42 to reach the South Fork Cave Creek Road (Forest Road 42E). The trail departs from the picnic area at its end.

0.0	South Fork Cave Creek Picnic Area. Follow the South Fork Cave Creek trail.
1.8	Junction with Horseshoe Pass trail. Turn left and cross streamcourse.
3.6	Spur trail descends to Log Spring.
4.8	Horseshoe Pass.

The trail: This trail makes a fantastic day trip from the South Fork Cave Creek Picnic Area, offering outstanding views of the stone towers above the Cave Creek basin. The first part of this trek is discussed at length under Trail 14 (South Fork of Cave Creek) in this book. The second part of the journey begins on the South Fork Cave Creek trail, which ascends gradually through a rich riparian forest below colorful pillars of stone. After passing the first canyon that enters from the east, the trail goes into a nebulous area known as Maple Camp. The trail to Horseshoe Pass (also known as the Burro trail) takes off from an unmarked junction here; look for a well-used horse ford on the stream just above a low wall of pink stone that has been undercut by water.

The trail zigzags up a slope facing an enormous butte of orange and yellow rhyolite, its sheer walls capped by a rounded toupee of forest. The path crests the ridgetop behind a lesser knob of the same rock, then works its way into the side canyon to the east. The vegetation here is typical arid scrubland, with piñon pine and alligator juniper scattered among low-growing live oaks. Agaves and dagger yuccas grow amid swards of bunchgrasses between the trees. The side canyon soon divides into a series of steep-sided ravines, and the trail works its way upward through this maze of slopes and gullies.

The path breaks out onto a flattened, gradually sloping ridgetop clad in Chihuahua and Apache pines. It follows this angled bench upward as the steep country returns. A broken signpost beside a pile of rocks marks an overgrown spur path that drops a few yards to Log Spring. The main trail keeps ascending, crossing the draw and climbing onto a north-facing slope. Openings in the scrub allow jaw-dropping vistas of Silver Peak, its cliffs and spires soaring from wooded slopes like petrified wings.

Excellent views accompany travelers for the remainder of the ascent to Horseshoe Pass. This open saddle overlooks Horseshoe Canyon, and trails depart from it, bound for the floor of Horseshoe Canyon and for Sentinel Peak on the tail end of the Chiricahua Crest trail.

THE BORDER RANGES

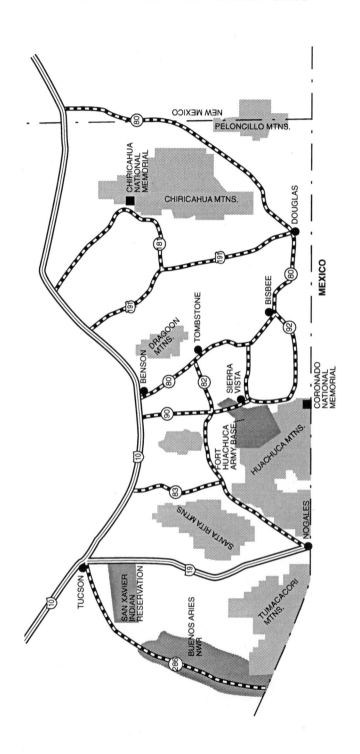

This section covers a smattering of isolated ranges that rise near the U.S.-Mexican border. With the exception of the Santa Rita Mountains, none of them has a well-developed trail system, but each offers one or two first-rate hiking trails. The Chiricahua and Huachuca mountains, also in the border region, are covered in their own chapter. Wilderness designation protects parts of the Pajarita and Santa Rita ranges, and the Peloncillo Mountains are classed as a wilderness study area, which may attain protected status in the near future. Forest Service ranger stations at Douglas and Nogales disburse information about these ranges.

The Peloncillo Mountains straddle the Arizona–New Mexico border and are only a short drive from Douglas. Peloncillo means "little sugar loaf" in Spanish. Hispanic pioneers were inspired to name these mountains after their similarity to the rounded cakes of sugar that they carried. The range is low and arid, although pine forests are present at its heart. Public access roads to this range typically run across private lands, and hikers should get permission to cross—locals are suspicious due to past problems with the smuggling of drugs and illegal aliens through this region. A network of primitive trails crisscrosses the range, but this area is a low priority for trail maintenance, and travelers who penetrate the backcountry will be challenged to find trail routes.

The Dragoon Mountains were a bastion for Apaches, who sallied forth from this mountain enclave to hunt and gather in the surrounding basins. The Dragoon Range is located between Benson and Willcox, and has good road access from the eastern side. There are few trails here, but there is a heavily developed campground at Cochise Stronghold. The Amerind Museum, located off the Dragoon Road exit on Interstate Highway 10, presents a fascinating collection of archaeological relics and displays highlighting the cultural history of Arizona's native people.

The Santa Rita Range rises between Tucson and Nogales, and has an extensive system of trails covering its length and breadth. Most hikers begin from the popular Madera Canyon area, where an entrance fee may be charged during the peak season for visitors. Madera Canyon is built up with summer cottages, but even so it is a popular area with birders during nesting season. The canyon has a Forest Service campground near Bog Springs. Trails originating on the eastern side of the range are accessed by primitive roads, and four-wheel-drive is recommended. The crest of the range is protected as the Mount Wrightson Wilderness, but the hand of man is apparent everywhere, from water pipes beside the trails to the Smithsonian Institution's observatory atop Mount Hopkins. The remote southern and eastern parts of the range saw heavy mining activity during the early 1900s.

To the east of Nogales, the tiny Patagonia–Sonoita Creek Preserve offers opportunities for hiking and birding in a low basin bottomland. The Tumacacori Mountains and the smaller Pajaritas rise to the west of Nogales. These arid ranges reach craggy heights in the midst of rolling oak woodlands. Forest Road 39 (which begins as Arizona Highway 289) runs through the heart of this area, providing an access route suitable for passenger cars. Peña Blanca Reservoir is the most popular recreation site in the area, and it offers opportunities for camping, fishing, and boating.

General description: A day hike up Skeleton Canyon in the Peloncillo Mountains, 3.4 miles.

Best season: Year-round.

Difficulty: Easy.

Water availability: None.

Elevation gain: 163 feet.

Maximum elevation: 4,840 feet.

Topo map: Skeleton Canyon.

Jurisdiction: Peloncillo Wilderness Study Area, Douglas Ranger District, Coronado National Forest.

Finding the trailhead: Take U.S. Highway 80 north from Douglas to the settlement of Apache. Here, turn east on the improved Skeleton Canyon Road. After 8.5 miles, the road is gated at the Snure Ranch. Ask permission before passing through, and park inside the national forest boundary.

0.0   Jeep track crosses Skeleton Canyon wash.

0.1   Geronimo surrender site. Junction with South Skeleton Canyon jeep trail. Turn left.

Low cliff walls guard Skeleton Canyon.

0.6   Devil's Kitchen.
1.4   Trail crosses Arizona–New Mexico state line.
2.0   Pony Canyon joins Skeleton Canyon from the south.
2.7   Pine Canyon trail takes off to the south.
3.4   End of jeep road.

The trail: This trek follows an active jeep trail deep into the Peloncillo Mountains. It follows Skeleton Canyon, which has been an important travel route through the range since pre-Columbian times. According to legend, a band of travelers was waylaid and massacred in the canyon in the late 1800s, and coins and human bones turned up in the wash for years after the event. The Peloncillo Mountains are currently under study for inclusion in the national system of wilderness areas. The area was being heavily grazed by cattle when this book was written, and it is likely that grazing permits will remain unaffected by wilderness designation if and when it occurs.

From the national forest boundary, hike southward on the primitive road to reach the convergence of Skeleton and South Skeleton canyons. This spot was where the Apache warrior Geronimo finally surrendered to U.S. Army forces in 1886 after a long and bitter campaign. Geronimo was incarcerated in a Florida prison, and his Chiricahua Apaches were deported to Oklahoma.

The road splits here; follow the left-hand track eastward along the main fork of Skeleton Canyon. Widely spaced walnuts, oaks, and junipers stand amid grassy bottomlands that are heavily grazed by cattle, and white-barked Arizona

16   Skeleton Canyon

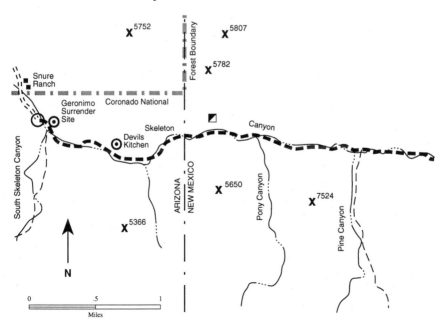

sycamores guard the banks of the watercourse. The track soon passes a formation known as the Devil's Kitchen, where two slabs of yellow bedrock vertically enclose a flat-bottomed alcove. To the south, cone-shaped hills cluster amid upright pillars of stone, creating the effect of an overcrowded cemetery. The low-slung formations that guard the north side of the canyon are breached by wide openings that reveal a cliff-crested peak to the north. Fiery bands of bedrock seam its craggy countenance in hues of red and orange.

The canyon widens, and a gate marks the crossing into New Mexico. A short distance farther, the concrete ruins of a herder's jacal squat against the base of the cliff to the north of the track. The jacal was built into a natural overhang in the rock, and a check dam in the cliff above it once provided a supply of water.

Just beyond this ruin, Pony Canyon wanders up from the south to join Skeleton Canyon in a grove of live oaks. A massive butte looms to the southeast, while the northern side of the canyon is guarded by a low palisade of cliffs ornamented with finely carved pillars and spires. These fascinating formations persist as far as Pine Canyon, where a marked trail runs southward into the heart of the Peloncillos.

Beyond this point, the cliffs are transformed into a low mass of solid stone, and the mountains devolve into arid foothills. The jeep trail ends at the site of an old ranger station, a short distance farther on. The wash of Skeleton Canyon is easily navigable above this point, following a wilderness route marked with cairns. This route ultimately links up with another jeep trail in the Animas Valley of New Mexico.

17   COCHISE STRONGHOLD

General description: A day hike into the Dragoon Mountains, 4.5 miles.
Best season: Year-round.
Difficulty: Moderately strenuous*.
Water availability: Cochise Spring and Half Moon Tank may be dry.
Elevation gain: 1,075 feet.
Elevation loss: 680 feet.
Maximum elevation: 5,975 feet.
Topo map: Cochise Stronghold.
Jurisdiction: Douglas Ranger District, Coronado National Forest.
Finding the trailhead: From the north end of Sunsites, take Ironwood Road (Forest Road 84) west then south for 12 miles to reach Cochise Stronghold Campground. For the west trailhead, drive north from Tombstone on U.S. Highway 80, turning right on Middlemarch Road after 1 mile. Turn left onto Forest Road 687 at the national forest boundary. Then turn right on Forest Road 688 and follow this four-wheel-drive road to the trailhead at its end.

Pinnacles of granite soar above West Stronghold Canyon.

0.0	Route leaves Cochise Stronghold Campground on nature trail.
0.2	Junction with equestrian trail. Turn right.
0.8	Junction with old Middlemarch Canyon trail. Bear right.
1.0	Cochise Spring.
2.1	Halfmoon Tank.
2.9	Stronghold Divide. Trail begins descent into West Stronghold Canyon.
4.5	West Stronghold Canyon trailhead.

The trail: In the lore of southwestern deserts, few Indian leaders were as renowned and respected as the Apache warrior Cochise. His band, known as the Chokonen or "Tall Cliffs People," used the rocky mazes of the southern Dragoons as a natural fortress. Here they were secure from attack and had commanding views of the surrounding country. This fantastic formation of jumbled granite is known today as Cochise Stronghold, and the fabled warrior whose name it bears is said to be buried in a secret chasm deep within these rocks.

The hike begins on an interpretive nature trail; follow the left fork for quickest access to the Cochise Stronghold trail. A path leaves the nature loop to cross the wash of East Stronghold Canyon, then climbs the opposite bank to link up with an equestrian trail arriving from the north. Turn right at this junction.

17   Cochise Stronghold

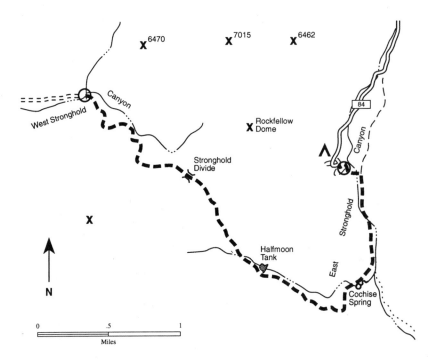

Follow the wash southward through a woodland of oak and juniper. Early on, there are good views of the massive granite slabs that form the backbone of the stronghold, but these spires soon disappear behind rounded foothills. The valley widens into a broad basin as the trail curves westward. A faint track runs south toward Middlemarch Canyon; bear right at this junction.

The first clumps of weathered granite soon rise to the north of the path, which skirts the edge of the Stronghold formation. The trail passes Cochise Spring at the 1 mile mark, then continues upward through a woodland of montane plants such as piñon pine and lechuguilla. The rock formations rise impressively as the trail climbs, resembling orderly stacks of tilted stone that were arranged by some forgotten giant. Half Moon Tank offers the last water on the trail; be sure to treat it before drinking.

The path then climbs steadily to the top of a rounded prominence, where inspiring views of the Sulphur Springs Valley can be observed through a gap in the rocks. The most massive peaks of Cochise Stronghold appear as the trail approaches Stronghold Divide, but views from the pass itself are largely blocked by an intervening hillock.

Beyond this point, the trail commences a sustained downhill grade into West Stronghold Canyon, where views are even more impressive. Mighty peaks of naked stone rise north of the canyon, seamed with fissures and adorned with pillars and spires. As the trail descends, Rockfellow Dome emerges to the east like an enormous whale's head breaching the surface of the sea. Centuries of wind erosion have weathered this massive monolith into soft curves and rounded ribs. The scale of the peaks increases to awe-inspiring proportions as the path approaches the broad floor of the basin. Here, a sheer peak of granite soars unexpectedly to the south of the canyon. The trail becomes an old jeep track as it crosses the basin to reach the end of Forest Road 688 at the confluence of two streamcourses.

18 MOUNT WRIGHTSON SUPER TRAIL

General description: A long day hike or backpack to the summit of the tallest peak in the Santa Rita Range, 8.1 miles.
Best season: March-December.
Difficulty: Moderate.
Water availability: Sprung Spring is dependable; Baldy Spring may be dry.
Elevation gain: 4,043 feet.
Maximum elevation: 9,453 feet.
Topo maps: Mount Wrightson, *Santa Rita Mountains.*
Jurisdiction: Mount Wrightson Wilderness, Nogales Ranger District, Coronado National Forest.

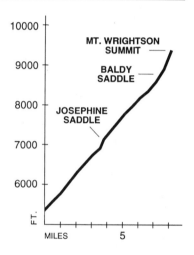

Finding the trailhead: Take I-19 south from Tucson, and get off at the Continental exit. Follow the road east across the Santa Cruz River, and take the first major right (White House Road). Follow this paved road 11.6 miles to the head of Madera Canyon. There may be a fee charged for admission into the Madera Canyon area.

0.0	Madera Canyon trailhead.
3.1	Sprung Spring.
3.7	Josephine Saddle trail junction. Turn left.
3.8	Junction with Temporal Canyon trail. Bear left.
3.9	Junction with Old Baldy trail. Turn right.
5.4	Riley Saddle.
6.4	Junction with Gardner Canyon trail. Keep going straight.
7.0	Baldy Spring.
7.2	Baldy Saddle. Junction with Old Baldy and Santa Rita Crest trails. Turn left.
8.1	Summit of Mount Wrightson.

The trail: The Super Trail was built in 1966 to supplant the Old Baldy trail, a steep and erosion-prone route to the summit of Mount Wrightson. The

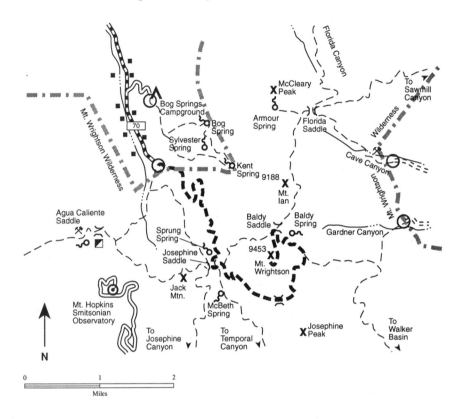

new grade is so gentle and well-cleared that Forest Service officials recommend it as a nice sunset trail or moonlight hike during a full moon. This trail is also unique in that it offers one of the few treks above 8,000 feet that is generally passable year-round. It doesn't pay to get complacent about the local weather, though—three Boy Scouts died of hypothermia along this route in November 1953. The more strenuous Old Baldy trail is still maintained, and some folks like to combine the two trails for a loop trip. The Super Trail can also be combined with the Crest trail (see Trail 19, Florida Canyon) for one-way trips along the top of the Santa Rita Range.

The trek begins by ascending a draw wooded densely in evergreen oaks, with alligator junipers and Arizona sycamores scattered along the bottoms. The path climbs onto the east wall of the draw as openings in the woods allow a first view of Mount Hopkins, to the west. As the trail ascends, the lush oak woodlands are sprinkled with Arizona madrones and Apache pines. Watch for Coues white-tailed deer along the knolls and ridgetops. The trail ultimately crests the ridge and runs along a high divide, revealing fine views of the pale, slanted strata of Mount Ian and Mount Wrightson, farther south. A southward course runs toward Josephine Saddle; the trail passes Sprung Spring just before reaching it. At Josephine Saddle, the Super Trail is joined by the Old Baldy route and a host of other trails, and a memorial honors the Boy Scouts who died here.

Bear east from the saddle, following signs for Mount Wrightson. The rocky crest of this peak rises straight ahead and can be glimpsed through gaps in the foliage. As the path climbs, it splits again into the Old Baldy and Super trails. Bear right as the route turns southward to skirt the slopes of the mountain. Openings in the oaks allow views of the intricate hills surrounding Copper Canyon. The oaks become progressively shorter as the trail rounds the south slope of Mount Wrightson, climbing to Riley Saddle. The major peak rising just to the south of this pass is Mount Josephine. The path then winds onto an east-facing slope that looks out over the herringbone cañoncitos that border the town of Patagonia. From this angle, Mount Wrightson's stony summit takes the form of a rounded whale back.

Pines close in as the trail approaches the Gardner Canyon trail. The pines soon give way to a solid stand of Douglas-firs as the trail gradually gains altitude. The path winds onto the north slope of the peak to reach Baldy Spring, then climbs to Baldy Saddle atop the crest of the range. Here, it meets the Old Baldy and Crest trails before turning south for the final ascent of Mount Wrightson. It climbs southward across this lofty miter of stone, then switchbacks up the final pitch to the summit.

The isolation of the Santa Rita Range allows vistas for hundreds of miles in all directions. Baboquivari Peak guards the western skyline, the Rincons and Santa Catalinas rise to the north, and Mount Graham crowns the Pinaleño Mountains far to the northeast. Closer at hand, the Patagonia, Whetstone, and Huachuca mountains crowd the southeastern horizon.

19   FLORIDA CANYON

General description: A backpack to the crest of the Santa Rita Mountains, 7.4 miles.

Best season: Year-round.

Difficulty: Strenuous.

Water availability: Robinson and Armour springs may be dry; there is no water at the source of Florida Spring.

Elevation gain: 3,495 feet (to Florida Saddle); 4,840 feet (to Baldy Saddle).

Elevation loss: 375 feet (to Baldy Saddle).

Maximum elevation: 7,820 feet (Florida Saddle); 9,040 feet (to Baldy Saddle).

Topo maps: Helvetia, Mount Wrightson, *Santa Rita Mountains.*

Jurisdiction: Mount Wrightson Wilderness, Nogales Ranger District, Coronado National Forest.

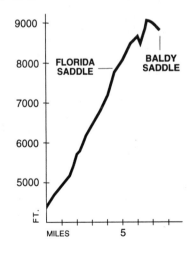

Mt. Wrightson from the Crest trail.

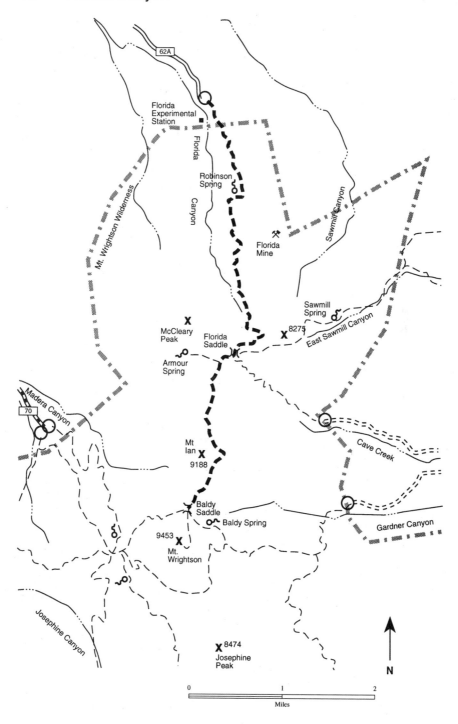

Finding the trailhead: Take I-19 south from Tucson and get off at the Continental exit. Follow the road east across the Santa Cruz River and take the first major right (White House Road). Follow this paved road 5.5 miles to a marked junction indicating the Florida Experimental Range Station. Drive straight ahead onto the gravel road and turn right at Forest Road 62A. The trailhead is just before the experiment station.

0.0   Florida Canyon trailhead.
1.3   Robinson Spring.
4.7   Florida Saddle. Junction with Sawmill Canyon and Santa Rita Crest trails. Description continues with Crest trail.
5.0   Junction with Armour Spring trail. Turn left.
7.4   Baldy Saddle. Junction with Old Baldy and Mount Wrightson Super trails.

The trail: From its beginnings at the north end of the range, the Florida Canyon trail climbs aggressively to reach the crest of the Santa Ritas. Florida Canyon is pronounced "floh-REE-duh," and is Spanish for "flowered." An optional trek along the Santa Rita Crest trail leads to Baldy Saddle, providing an alternate route to the summit of Mount Wrightson. The route up Florida Canyon has northern exposure, and its final pitch is shaded by climax coniferous forest. As a result, this trail offers one of the cooler routes to the high country at the top of the Santa Ritas.

The trail begins by skirting the Florida Experimental Station, a center for range management studies. It passes through a grassland dotted with mesquite and prickly pear, then ascends the grassy draw to the east of Florida Canyon. The mesquites give way to a savannah dotted with isolated clumps of live oak. Pause for a moment to watch the light play across the grassy hills trailing away to the north. The oaks close in to form an arid woodland as the trail approaches Robinson Spring. The old Florida Mine site lies straight up the draw from the spring, but the trail veers southwest in pursuit of a ridgetop overlooking Florida Canyon.

The trail reaches the ridgeline at a clearing that offers an excellent view of Mount McCleary. Far below, angular rock outcrops guard the floor of Florida Canyon, and these shards of stone are heavily encrusted with greenish lichens. The trail climbs straight up the ridgetop, setting an unrelenting pace in its quest for Florida Saddle. The path ultimately winds onto a second ridgetop, ascending along its crest for a time, then dropping into the draw. As it resumes the climb, the trail passes Florida Spring, which is now buried. This spring site marks the beginning of a dense stand of Douglas-firs, some of which have grown to old-growth proportions. The trail zigzags relentlessly up the steep, fir-clad slope, crossing soft duff scented with the lingering essence of resin. The trail tops out at Florida Saddle, where a number of trails converge amid a stand of full-grown pines.

SANTA RITA CREST OPTION

Hikers bound for Mount Wrightson should follow the Crest trail westward from Florida Saddle. This track climbs vigorously up the hillside to a junction with the 0.4-mile spur trail to Armour Spring. This spring emerges below a cliff at the base of Mount McCleary, and offers an intermittent supply of water. Bear left at this trail junction as the main trail runs onto the eastern slope of the Santa Rita crest. Openings in the pines allow sweeping views of the Sonoita Creek basin, which is bounded by the Mustang, Whetstone, and Patagonia mountains. Far to the southeast, the Huachuca Mountains dominate the skyline.

The trail climbs steadily, and after a mile it rounds a spur ridge to reveal Mount Ian rising straight ahead. The path climbs to a saddle at its base, where a lightning fire in 1993 opened up the trees to allow a glimpse of Elephant's Head far below on the western edge of the range. The path then skirts to the west of Mount Ian, climbing stiffly to attain the ridgetop beyond it. The landscape found here is a rugged alpine environment, with twisted pines eking out a marginal existence amid ribs and promontories of metamorphic rock. Mount Wrightson rises immediately to the north, a lone fang of stone rising from forested folds. The trail makes a long and steep descent to reach Baldy Saddle, where the Mount Wrightson trail can be picked up for the final ascent of the peak.

20   SONOITA CREEK LOOP

General description: A day loop in the bottomlands of Sonoita Creek, 1.6 miles round-trip.
Best season: Year-round.
Difficulty: Easy.
Water availability: Sonoita Creek is silty, but runs year-round.
Maximum elevation: 1,450 feet.
Map: A map of the preserve trails is available at the information station.
Jurisdiction: Patagonia-Sonoita Creek Preserve (The Nature Conservancy).
Finding the trailhead: From downtown Patagonia, turn west on Fourth Avenue, then south on Pennsylvania. Cross the creek and drive about 0.7 mile farther to the preserve entrance.

The trail: This loop trail follows an old railroad bed while traversing floodplain and riparian habitat that is well-known for its diverse birdlife. The preserve is home to the gray hawk and green kingfisher, among other rare species of birds. Although it is located on the outskirts of the town of Patagonia, this nature preserve has retained much of its wild character, and represents

Arizona gray squirrels thrive under the protection provided by the Patagonia-Sonoita Preserve.

one of the few riparian ecosystems that has survived in the Arizona lowlands. The preserve is open to visitors Wednesday through Sunday from 7:30 a.m. to 3:30 p.m. There is no entrance fee for the preserve, but a $5 donation is requested to help fund the management of the area.

The hike begins by following the old New Mexico & Arizona Railroad bed southwest from the preserve's entrance. This railway was an ill-fated venture. It was intended to link mining and trading communities in the southwestern deserts with the Mexican port of Guaymas. The railway had a colorful history of holdups and robberies before it was abandoned in the early 1900s.

Enormous Fremont cottonwoods rear their gnarled branches above the floodplain here; these are some of the largest individuals of their species. Canyon hackberry and black walnut grow from the railbed itself. Openings in the trees allow glimpses to the south of Red Mountain in the Patagonia Range.

The Cienega trail loops to the west, visiting an isolated wetland that represents one of the most endangered plant communities in southern Arizona. *Cienegas*, or wetlands, were once common here, but irrigation, livestock, and municipal development have drawn down the aquifers in this desert state, eliminating most of the free-flowing rivers and drying up the desert wetlands.

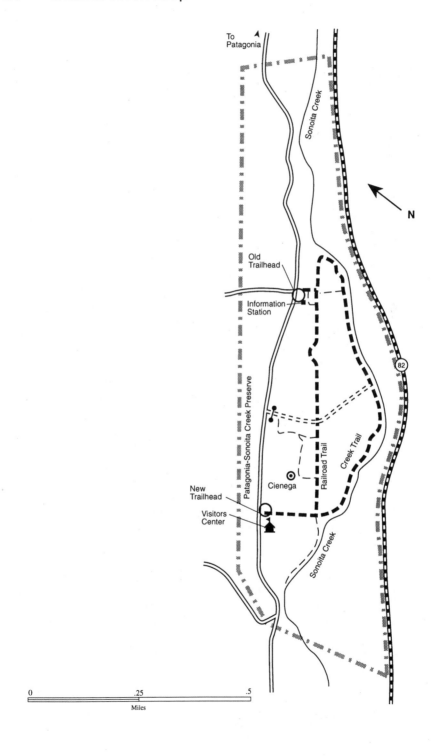

The Railroad trail continues south to an intersection with the Creek trail. A short spur continues southward from this point, passing an old bridge abutment before following Sonoita Creek to the preserve boundary.

To complete the loop, turn east onto the Creek trail. This trail tracks Sonoita Creek through a riparian community of willows and cottonwoods. The enclosure in the center of the preserve is being grazed by horses in an effort to rid it of exotic Johnson grass. Note the depauperate appearance of overgrazed land when compared to the rich riparian community beside it. The path continues to follow Sonoita Creek, which is home to four endemic species of fish, including the speckled dace. At an old railway bridge, the loop returns to the railbed, which carries the traveler back to the starting point of the hike.

21   ATASCOSA LOOKOUT

General description: A day hike to a fire lookout in the southern end of the Tumacacori Mountains, 2.4 miles.

Best season: Year-round.

Difficulty: Moderately strenuous.

Water availability: None.

Elevation gain: 1,549 feet.

Maximum elevation: 6,249 feet.

Topo map: Ruby.

Jurisdiction: Nogales Ranger District, Coronado National Forest.

Finding the trailhead: Take I-19 north from Nogales to the exit for Arizona Highway 289. After 9 miles, this paved road reaches Peña Blanca Reservoir and becomes the improved gravel Forest Road 39. Follow this road another 5 miles to a parking area atop a bald knob to the south of the road. The trail departs to the north.

0.0	Trailhead.
0.3	Trail crosses saddle above Atascosa Trail Tank.
2.4	Atascosa fire lookout.

The trail: This well-groomed trail provides an outstanding day hike to an old fire lookout high in the southern Tumacacori Mountains near Nogales. The hike begins in grassy foothills, bearing north as it makes a gradual ascent. Upon reaching the hilltops, a blocky butte rises ahead, and a glittering stock tank nestles among live oaks in a hollow to the east. The arid Patagonia Range dominates the eastern horizon, mounting ridge upon sunbaked ridge toward the desert sky. The high grasslands traversed by the trail make ideal hunting grounds for the American kestrel, a songbird-sized raptor that makes its living on grasshoppers and an occasional smaller bird.

Looking southward into Mexico from the Atascosa lookout trail.

21   Atascosa Lookout

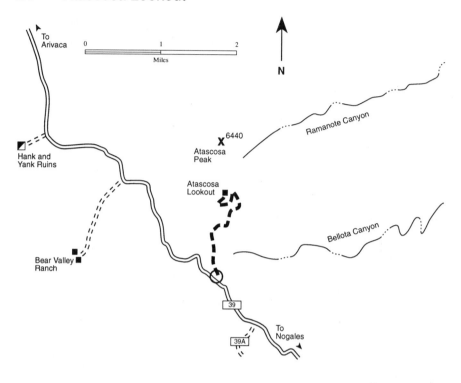

As the trail passes to the east, the blocky butte resolves itself into a long mesa palisaded by cliffs of buff-colored stone. The path climbs along its eastern slope, then zigzags upward through gaps in the cliffs. To the northeast, the Santa Rita Mountains are framed by the closer crags of the Tumacacori Range. The scattering of live oaks soon gives way to a rather solid forest of piñon pine and juniper. Numerous openings allow panoramic views of the surrounding country, featuring the cliffs that gird the mesa. To the south, an ocean of burnt hills stretches away into Mexico.

The path turns north along the crest of the mesa, climbing vigorously to top the pinnacle that bears the old Atascosa fire lookout. Sweeping vistas stretch in all directions; even the outhouse has a view. The most prominent feature visible from the lookout is Atascosa Peak, which spreads its soaring bands of stone to the north. Folded uplands to the south sprawl like a choppy sea of arid savannah. Far to the west, the sacred spire of Baboquivari rises on the edge of the Tohono O'odham Indian Reservation.

General description: A wilderness route along a permanent stream that penetrates the Pajarita Mountains, 5.8 miles.

Best season: Year-round.

Difficulty: Moderate**.

Water availability: Sycamore Canyon carries water year-round.

Elevation loss: 550 feet.

Maximum elevation: 4,000 feet.

Topo map: Ruby.

Jurisdiction: Pajarita Wilderness, Nogales Ranger District, Coronado National Forest.

Finding the trailhead: Take I-19 north from Nogales to the exit for Arizona Highway 289. Turn left. After 9 miles, this paved road reaches Peña Blanca Reservoir and becomes improved gravel Forest Road 39. Follow this road another 9.2 miles to reach the Sycamore Canyon Road (Forest Road 218). This primitive road crosses the wash for the final 0.5 mile to reach Hank and Yank Ruins; hikers who love their cars should not attempt to cross the streambed.

Striated cliffs above Sycamore Canyon.

1.4	Streamcourse enters a narrow slot.
2.0	Peñasco Canyon enters from the east.
2.7	Route enters narrow bottleneck.
5.8	U.S.-Mexican border.

The trail: This wilderness route follows Sycamore Canyon downstream into the heart of the Pajarita Wilderness. It involves travel along gravel bars and frequent crossings of a permanent stream. A little rock scrambling may be required in some tight spots for travelers who want to keep their feet dry; this route does place a premium on agility. Clumsier hikers need not worry, however. They can always slog through the water when the going gets tricky.

The hike begins at the Hank and Yank Ruins, which are the remains of an unsuccessful ranching attempt by mountain men Hank Hewitt and Yank Bartlett in the 1880s. The ranch was established by this pair of seasoned trappers, but a determined attack by local Indians drove them out; they were lucky to escape with their lives. A track wanders past crumbled adobe walls and down to the streamcourse, which carries the traveler southward through gently rolling savannahs dotted with clumps of oak. Hikers who venture onto stonier

22   Sycamore Canyon

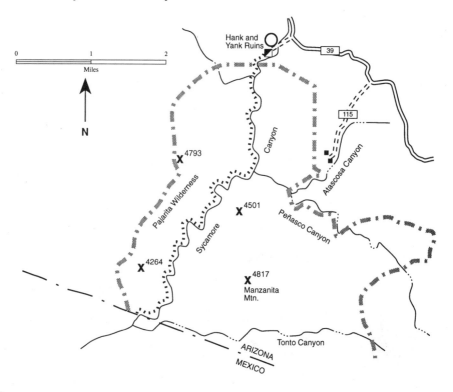

gently rolling savannahs dotted with clumps of oak. Hikers who venture onto stonier ground may discover delicate specimens of pincushion cactus growing amid the grass.

After a short distance, ragged cliffs and pinnacles rear up on either side of the stream. The hillsides become densely wooded with evergreen oaks as the stream approaches a long stretch of cliff-girt narrows. A hairpin curve announces the beginning of the slot, and hikers may have to scramble over a narrow neck of land to get around the curve. Sheer walls of slickrock rise above the canyon on either side, crowding the water and forcing numerous stream crossings. The rock has been sculpted into curvaceous hollows by wind and water, but a sharp tilt of the parent rock is revealed by the well-layered bedding of the stone. Two more spots may require climbing to gain a dry passage through the slot. Sharp pinnacles of stone rise on every side to distract the climber.

The white-barked sycamores that give the canyon its name appear near the lower end of the narrows, sending stout columns upward from intricate root webs that anchor the great trees to their tenuous footholds in the shifting gravel of the streambed. Beyond this narrow passage, the canyon broadens into a valley; the traveling is easy for the next mile or so. A gap in the gentle hills admits the wash of Peñasco Canyon, entering from the east. The main streamcourse takes a sharp westward bend and enters another group of sheer peaks, which augur difficult traveling ahead. Sure enough, there is a bottleneck as the stream returns to its southward course. Some fancy footwork is required to negotiate it. The craggy peaks then recede from the stream, allowing ready passage along streamside bars of loose gravel.

Sycamores grow in long rows down the center of the streamcourse, deflecting the flow of the current. Once a large tree becomes established in midstream, the eddy behind it builds a long gravel bar on the downstream side. This bar offers suitable purchase for another seedling, and thus the row of trees progresses down the streambed, with water flowing on either side.

A magnificent crag looms ahead, and the canyon jogs west to avoid it. The live oaks have been replaced by thorn scrub on the slopes above the wash, and saguaros dot the hillsides. A long southward reach leads out of the Pajarita Mountains, and low foothills surround the stream as it makes another jog to the west. A barbed-wire fence stretched across the stream marks the international border with Mexico, and travelers must retrace their steps at this point or follow a little-used border track eastward to reach an alternate trailhead on the Skyline Road (Forest Road 39A).

THE HUACHUCA MOUNTAINS

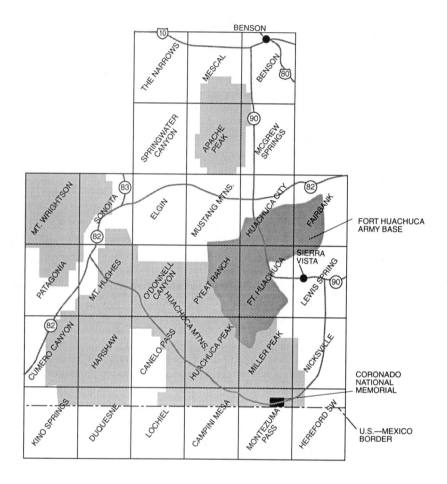

The lofty, pine-clad Huachuca Mountains rise from the grassy borderlands near Sierra Vista. They are made up of a confusing hodgepodge of metamorphic and sedimentary rock, some of which is limestone that was laid down when this entire area lay at the bottom of a shallow sea. Fingerlike intrusions of magma, called dikes, later seeped into fissures in this jumble of uplifted bedrock. The igneous dikes had enough metal to tantalize miners, who prospected the Huachucas extensively in the late 1800s and early 1900s. Despite a profusion of mines, only small quantities of copper, silver, lead, and tungsten were extracted, and the mines ultimately fell silent.

Today, a network of hiking trails provides access throughout the range. Many of these trails visit old mineshafts and ruins. These historic sites represent an unrenewable cultural resource, and hikers should leave them untouched. Since mineshaft openings can be unstable, and abandoned tunnels are prone to cave-ins, hikers should give these shafts a wide berth.

Trails on the east side of the Huachucas receive the greatest amount of maintenance, while those on the western side of the range are accessed by old jeep trails that have lapsed into hiking routes. These western trails may be unmaintained and/or poorly marked, and route-finding skills are a must. Trails within Coronado National Memorial are well-maintained, while trails on Fort Huachuca are, with a few exceptions, neglected.

The central part of the range is administered by the Forest Service, and the higher elevations fall within the Miller Peak Wilderness Area. There is a developed campground on a high shelf beneath Carr Peak, near the site of the old Reef Mine. To the west of the range, Parker Canyon Lake offers trout fishing and boating (with electric trolling motors or human power). The northern part of the range falls within the Fort Huachuca military reservation. Its trails are open for day hiking, but a visitor pass must be obtained (free of charge) at the main gate. Coronado National Memorial encompasses the southern edge of the range. This National Park Service site commemorates the explorations of Francisco Vásquez de Coronado, a Spanish conquistador who traveled through the San Pedro Valley long before the *Mayflower* was even a dream in a shipbuilder's head.

23   *CORONADO PEAK–JOE'S CANYON*

General description: A day hike along an arid ridgetop in the southern Huachucas, 3.1 miles.
Best season: September-May.
Difficulty: Moderate west to east; moderately strenuous east to west.
Water availability: None.
Elevation gain: 90 feet (Joe's Canyon); 304 feet (Coronado Peak).
Elevation loss: 1,291 feet (Joe's Canyon).
Maximum elevation: 6,864 feet (Coronado Peak).
Topo map: *Hiker's Map of the Huachuca Mountains.*
Jurisdiction: Coronado National Memorial (NPS).

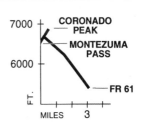

Finding the trailhead: Drive 13 miles south from Sierra Vista on Arizona Highway 92 to reach the Coronado National Memorial Road (Forest Road 61). Turn right on this road and follow it 8.5 miles to the parking area atop Montezuma Pass. The trail departs to the south.

0.0   Montezuma Pass parking area.
0.1   Trail splits into Coronado Peak trail (0.3 mile, moderate) and Joe's Canyon trail. Turn left for Joe's Canyon.
1.7   Trail descends into head of Joe's Canyon.
3.1   Trail returns to Montezuma Canyon Road.

Looking down Smuggler's Ridge at San Jose Peak.

The trails: These two trails offer day hiking opportunities along a hogback known as "Smuggler's Ridge," which runs along the Mexican border in the southern foothills of the Huachucas. Both trails begin as one from a trailhead on Montezuma Pass. The short Coronado Peak spur soon splits away to the right, ascending the rounded summit to the south. Interpretive plaques line the path en route to the summit, describing various aspects of the Coronado expedition. According to his journals, Coronado first passed through the San Pedro Valley (the great, grassy basin to the east) in the year 1540 on his quest for the fabled Seven Cities of Cibola. He mentioned San Jose Peak, just across the present-day Mexican border, as an important landmark along his route.

A covered ramada stands atop the summit and looks over an impressive panorama of the San Pedro Valley. For visitors who think of the Mexican interior as a desert wasteland, the grassy altiplano stretching south will be a revelation. The distant and solitary tooth of San Jose Peak and the closer mass of Montezuma Peak at the south end of the Huachucas dominate the scene. To the southwest, the great cordillera of the Sierra Madre guards the approaches to the Sea of Cortez.

The Joe's Canyon trail heads eastward down the ridgeline, bearing toward the distinctive spire of San Jose Peak. Massive cliffs on Montezuma Peak rise to imposing heights on the far side of Montezuma Canyon, while to the south lie the distant ranges of old Mexico. The lush grassland community found along

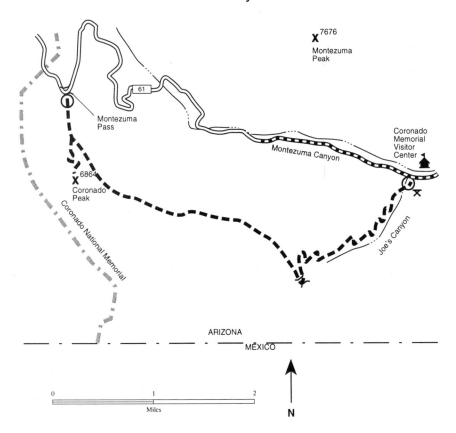

the ridge is home to Coues white-tailed deer—as well as its largest predator, the mountain lion. Upon reaching a broad saddle on the ridgetop, the trail drops northward into the head of Joe's Canyon. This defile is not much more than a steep-sided ravine, where picturesque copses of live oak, juniper, and piñon pine frame views of the distant Mule Mountains. As the trail nears the rocky mouth of Joe's Canyon, striking views of Montezuma Peak unfold to the north. The trail then drops to meet the road at a picnic ground just above the Coronado National Memorial Visitor Center.

24 *MILLER PEAK*

General description: A day hike or backpack from Montezuma Pass to the summit of Miller Peak, 5.3 miles.
Best season: March-December.
Difficulty: Moderately strenuous.
Water availability: Bond Spring may be dry.

Elevation gain: 2,906 feet.
Maximum elevation: 9,466 feet.
Topo maps: Montezuma Pass, Miller Peak (inc.); *Hiker's Map of the Huachuca Mountains.*
Jurisdiction: Coronado National Memorial (NPS); Miller Peak Wilderness, Sierra Vista Ranger District, Coronado National Forest.
Finding the trailhead: Drive 13 miles south from Sierra Vista on Arizona Highway 92 to reach the Coronado National Memorial Road (Forest Road 61). Turn right on this road and follow it 8.5 miles to the parking area atop Montezuma Pass. The trail departs to the north.

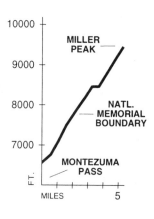

0.0	Montezuma Pass trailhead. Hike north on Huachuca Crest trail.
1.5	Mine shafts.
1.8	Mine shafts.
2.0	Trail leaves Coronado National Memorial.
4.1	Junction with Lutz Canyon trail. Bear left.
4.2	Junction with Bond Spring spur trail. Keep going straight.
4.8	Junction with Miller Peak spur trail. Turn right.
5.3	Summit of Miller Peak.

Looking southeast to San Jose Peak, which lies just across the border in Mexico

24   Miller Peak

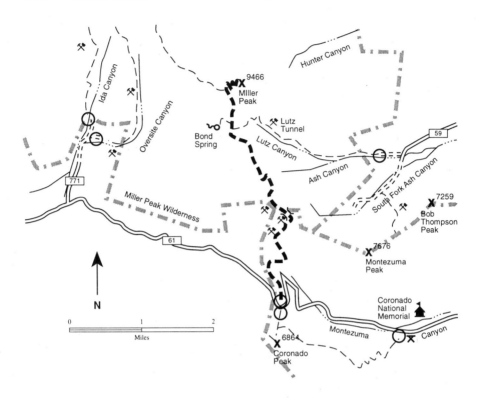

The trail: This trek uses the southern leg of the Huachuca Crest trail, which follows the top of the range to reach Miller Peak. There are a large number of old mine and prospect sites along this well-maintained trail, and the sweeping views of the surrounding country never stop. Miller Peak is the highest point in the Huachuca Mountains, and from its summit hikers can get a 360-degree view that encompasses most of south-central Arizona.

The trail begins at Coronado National Memorial and traverses northward across the grassy slopes bordering Montezuma Pass. Scattered live oaks interrupt the grasslands, providing pockets of shade along the route. The path makes a brief sojourn on the ridgetop, where it reveals views of the Sierra Madres, to the southwest. To the east San Jose Peak is framed by the sloping walls of Montezuma Canyon. Both of these massifs rise south of the Mexican border.

The path continues to climb as it crosses the grassy slopes, and before long several gray mounds of mine tailings can be spotted in a draw to the north. The path first passes the shafts of the Alto Mine, hidden in a gully to the west. It then turns east across a rocky head to reach a second group of tunnels. Both of these mine groups produced copper, zinc, and silver in the early 1900s.

The trail then climbs to the crest of the ridge behind Montezuma Peak, and here it leaves the memorial and enters Coronado National Forest. There are several protected tent sites in ridgetop swales near this point. The path turns northwest across the head of Ash Canyon; Miller Peak rises ahead like a great wave cast in stone. Looking east across the San Pedro Valley, travelers will see the diminutive Mule Mountains sprawl across the horizon like the remains of some great beast. The trail climbs vigorously toward a pinnacle of gray limestone, then crosses the ridgetop to run along the western slope of the Huachucas. The Patagonia Mountains rise just beyond the San Rafael Valley, and the distant tooth of Baboquivari Peak stands sentinel over the western horizon.

The path passes an arid saddle filled with agave, then works its way around the next point to enter a shady forest of Douglas-fir. The next saddle holds a junction where the Lutz Canyon trail rises to meet the Huachuca Crest route. A spur path to Bond Spring drops away to the west a short distance farther on, and the main trail runs onto the western slope of Miller Peak. The path clings precariously to the steep face of the mountain, weaving and dodging as it negotiates a maze of sheer stone outcrops. Douglas-firs and storm-wracked aspens grow from clefts in the rock.

After crossing the western slope of the peak, the Crest trail reaches a high saddle where the spur trail to Miller Peak climbs toward the summit. This path switchbacks upward at a steady pace, climbing the northwestern slope of the peak to avoid the outcrops along its crest. At the summit, an old lookout site commands views deep into Mexico, and most of the ranges in southern Arizona can be spotted from here on a clear day.

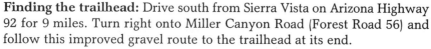

25   MILLER CANYON

General description: A day hike or backpack to the Huachuca Crest trail, 3.9 miles.
Best season: March-December.
Difficulty: Moderately strenuous.
Water availability: Miller Canyon may carry water in the winter; Tub Spring is reliable.
Elevation gain: 2,790 feet.
Maximum elevation: 8,550 feet.
Topo maps: Miller Peak; *Hiker's Map of the Huachuca Mountains.*
Jurisdiction: Miller Peak Wilderness, Sierra Vista Ranger District, Coronado National Forest.

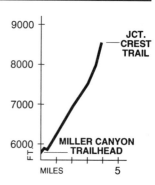

Finding the trailhead: Drive south from Sierra Vista on Arizona Highway 92 for 9 miles. Turn right onto Miller Canyon Road (Forest Road 56) and follow this improved gravel route to the trailhead at its end.

0.0	Miller Canyon trailhead.
0.2	Junction with Clark Spring trail. Turn left.
0.6	Junction with trail to Hunter Canyon. Bear right.
3.9	Tub Spring. Junction with Huachuca Crest trail.

The trail: This trail offers hikers an alternate route to Miller Peak and the southern end of the Huachuca Crest trail. The hike begins with a brief climb to a junction with the Clark Spring trail. Turn left at the junction.

The Miller Canyon trail crosses sidehills above a private ranch before seeking the wooded floor of the canyon. Beyond the ranch, the trail adopts an old road grade that wanders up the valley in the shade of full-grown oak trees. The road grade soon splits, marking a junction with a trail running over the divide to the south and into Hunter Canyon. Stay right to follow the Miller Canyon route, which soon reveals rocky wings of stone rising along the flanks of Carr Peak.

The old jeep track then swings to the south side of the canyon, passing groves of sycamores before climbing into a stand of Douglas-firs. These conifers, which dominate Pacific Northwest timberlands, occupy a "frost pocket" in these desert mountains. Here, cold night air sinks and pools on the canyon floor, creating local growing conditions that are too cold in winter for most desert plants. The track passes some prospect diggings before returning to the north side of the canyon, where it becomes a narrow footpath.

This footpath climbs vigorously onto warmer slopes above the canyon, entering a scrubland of live oak. As it traces these higher, drier slopes, openings in the woods unveil fine views down canyon. Agaves and yuccas take advantage of these openings to gain a foothold in the sunshine. The valley splits near its head, and the trail initially ascends the intervening ridge between the two ravines. It then swings into the northern draw before climbing high onto slopes that burned in 1977. A few old pines survived the blaze and stand amid a riot of regenerating manzanita and live oak. The openness of this plant com-

25　Miller Canyon
26　Clark Spring

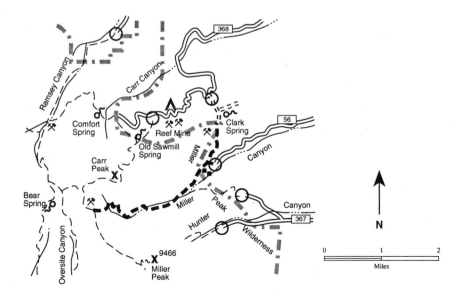

munity allows distant views of the ranges to the east, as well as a good look at the summit of Miller Peak, rising above the south wall of the canyon.

The path passes several old glory holes as it climbs onto a flattened ridgetop, harking back to the hardscrabble heyday of mining activity. The trail then swings southwest around the head of the canyon to meet the Huachuca Crest trail at Tub Spring. This spring was built by a reclusive prospector named Max Baumkirchner who had a cabin here and tried his hand at mining in 1908. He hauled a cast-iron tub all the way up to the site of his cabin by pack mule; this tub was set into the ground as a catch basin for spring water.

Hikers can venture south along the Crest trail for 1.6 miles to reach the base of Miller Peak, or turn north at this point to access the equally lofty summit of Carr Peak.

26   CLARK SPRING

General description: A short day hike along the eastern edge of the Huachucas, 1.7 miles.
Best season: Year-round.
Difficulty: Moderate.
Water availability: Clark Spring is likely to be dry.
Elevation gain: 350 feet.
Elevation loss: 85 feet.
Maximum elevation: 6,110 feet.
Topo map: *Hiker's Map of the Huachuca Mountains.*
Jurisdiction: Miller Peak Wilderness, Sierra Vista Ranger District, Coronado National Forest.
Finding the trailhead: Drive south from Sierra Vista on Arizona Highway 92 for 9 miles. Turn right onto Miller Canyon Road (Forest Road 56) and follow this improved gravel route to the trailhead at its end.

0.0	Miller Canyon trailhead.
0.2	Junction with Miller Canyon trail. Turn right.
1.2	Clark Spring.
1.3	Junction with old jeep trail. Bear left.
1.7	Trail emerges on Carr Canyon Road.

The trail: This short trail makes a pleasant day hike along the eastern edge of the Huachuca Mountains. It begins by jogging westward for a short distance to a junction with the Miller Canyon trail. Turn right at the intersection as the Clark Spring trail begins a modest climb through a loose-knit woodland of live oak. A craggy palisade of sandstone known locally as "The Reef" rises above the trail. This promontory is actually an eastern buttress of Carr Peak, one of the loftiest summits in the Huachucas. Sweeping views of the San Pedro Valley are bounded to the east by the Mule Mountains. The trail passes a prospect hole as it approaches a substantial finger ridge

A spur of Carr Peak known as "The Reef" overlooks the Clark Spring trail.

projecting eastward from the main mass of the mountain. Hopeful miners excavated this pit as they followed a vein of quartz tinged with red, which is a field indicator of metal-bearing ores.

Clark Spring lies just beyond this glory hole, and here an abundance of groundwater allows the trees to attain a much taller stature. The path adopts an old jeep trail at this point and climbs gently through a gate to a ridgetop intersection. A spur track leads eastward along the crest of the finger ridge, while the main track continues northward across a steep hillside. The oak trees grow more vigorously on this north-facing slope, because less sunshine means less evaporation, and this leads to more moisture in the soil. The jeep trail descends to an unmarked and rather inconspicuous trailhead at a hairpin turn on the Carr Canyon Road (Forest Road 368).

27 RAMSEY CANYON LOOP

General description: A long day loop that visits the crest of the Huachuca Range, 10.1 miles round-trip.
Best season: March-December.
Difficulty: Moderately strenuous (*beyond Hamburg Meadow).
Water availability: Ramsey Canyon has a permanent flow of water.
Elevation gain: 3,300 feet.

Elevation loss: 3,300 feet.

Maximum elevation: 8,530 feet.

Topo map: *Hiker's Map of the Huachuca Mountains.*

Jurisdiction: Ramsey Canyon Preserve (The Nature Conservancy); Miller Peak Wilderness, Sierra Vista Ranger District, Coronado National Forest.

Finding the trailhead: From Sierra Vista, take Arizona Highway 92 south for 6 miles to the Ramsey Canyon Road. Follow this paved route for 3.8 miles to reach the Nature Conservancy trailhead.

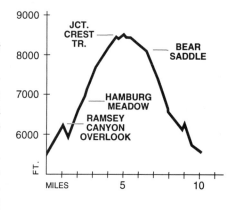

0.0	Ramsey Canyon trailhead.
1.1	Ramsey Canyon Overlook.
1.3	Trail reaches bottoms of Ramsey Canyon.
1.5	Junction with Brown Canyon trail. Keep going straight.
2.1	Junction with cutoff trail from Carr Canyon. Keep going straight.
2.2	Hamburg Meadow. Former site of Hamburg mining town.
2.3	Trail splits into Wisconsin Canyon and Pat Scott Canyon trails. Turn right to begin the loop.
4.5	Junction with Huachuca Crest trail. Turn left.
4.6	Junction with Copper Glance trail. Keep going straight.
6.5	Bear Saddle trail junction. Turn left onto Wisconsin Canyon trail.
7.8	Trail rejoins Pat Scott Canyon trail.
10.1	Trail returns to Ramsey Canyon trailhead.

The trail: This trek begins on land owned by The Nature Conservancy, then climbs into Coronado National Forest on its way to the crest of the Huachuca Mountains. The trailhead is only open from 8 a.m. to 5 p.m., and all hikers must carry a permit that is available free of charge at the Ramsey Canyon Nature Preserve headquarters. Parking is limited to thirteen spaces; when they filled up, the preserve turns visitors away. Some summer cabins on preserve property are rented out to visitors; these cabins tend to be booked several years in advance during the spring birding season. The upper reaches of Ramsey Canyon are nesting habitat for the rare eared trogon, and hikers are asked to wear muted colors to avoid disturbing these birds while passing through their territories. In addition to the rich assemblage of birds found here, visitors may encounter Coues whitetailed deer, black bears, and even troops of coatis. Because the trailhead is closed overnight, backpackers should access the route from the Carr Canyon trailhead. Ramsey Canyon can also be reached via Brown Canyon, but the beginning of this trail is quite difficult to locate.

The hike begins by following the closed road past a collection of ramshackle summer cabins. At road's end, a nature trail bears to the right, but hikers on

Ramsey Peak rises above Pat Scott Canyon.

their way up Ramsey Canyon should turn left at a sign for the Hamburg trail. This well-maintained footpath climbs the slopes to the south, crossing and re-crossing the old mining road that once ran up the canyon to the settlement of Hamburg. The path tops out at the Ramsey Canyon overlook, which offers good views of the cliffs that hem in the upper reaches of the canyon. The path then drops to the streamcourse and crosses it at a picturesque waterfall.

As the track turns south to follow the valley floor, a strip of grassy meadow adorns the stream bank. Swards of moisture-loving horsetail grow in the dampest spots. This primitive, leafless plant contains tiny granules of silica, and pioneers used it to scour their pots and dishes. A stand of Douglas-firs crowds the valley floor as the Brown Canyon trail joins up from the north. After 0.9 mile of woodland traveling, the track is met by a cutoff trail descending from Carr Canyon. Hamburg Meadow lies a few yards beyond this junction. The silent shafts of the Hamburg Mine litter the hillside above in mute testimony to silver and copper mining in the canyon. This spot was once a bustling mining community, but was leveled by an explosion in the early 1900s.

Just above this sunny glade, Ramsey Canyon splits into Wisconsin and Pat Scott canyons. The loop trip can be completed by hiking up either of these gulches; this description covers the gentler Pat Scott trail first. This track climbs steadily up the northern draw, passing a tailings heap that fills half the gulch.

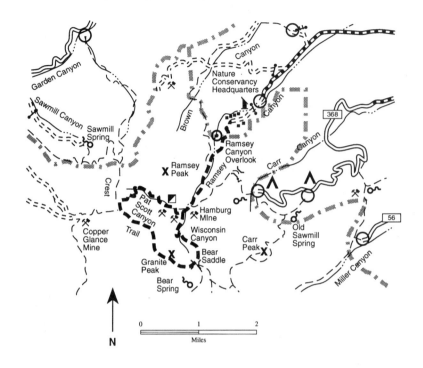

A 0.25 mile farther, two abandoned shafts and ruins of a stone shed mark the uppermost limits of mining activity in Pat Scott Canyon. The trail follows the streamcourse upward, passing a sill of resistant bedrock that holds falls and pools during the rainy season. At the top of this geological formation, the trail enters the Pat Scott Canyon burn of 1983. The path continues along the bottom of the draw, then zigzags upward along the northern fringe of the burn. Chihuahua and ponderosa pines frame views of Ramsey Peak and its rounded band of cliffs, which rise across the valley.

The trail ultimately bends southwest to meet the Huachuca Crest trail in a sun-splashed saddle. Turn south onto the Crest trail, which crosses ponderosa pine savannahs on the western slope of the divide. The junction with the Copper Glance trail is passed in short order; the main track soon finds its way onto a grassy spot on the crest of the ridge. Carr Peak looms ahead, while to the west is a panorama highlighted by the Sierra Madre and the Patagonia Mountains.

The trend of the trail is downward from this point on, and it alternates between Douglas-fir forests on the eastern slopes and open pine woodlands that face westward. A growth of evergreen oaks covers the western face of Granite Peak. After traversing these arid slopes, the trail drops into Bear Saddle.

A confusing assortment of trails comes together at Bear Saddle. To complete the loop, turn eastward to the Wisconsin Canyon trail. This path descends steadily across pine-clad slopes, keeping high above the floor of the gulch. From these slopes, travelers can peer through the branches to view Ramsey Peak from a different perspective. After a considerable eastward trek, the trail drops to the floor of Wisconsin Canyon, following the streamcourse through dense timber to reach the trail junction above Hamburg Meadow. From here, hikers can retrace their steps for the 2.3-mile return trip to the Ramsey Canyon trailhead.

28   OVERSITE CANYON LOOP

General description: A long day hike or backpack up the western slope of the Huachuca Mountains, 6.7 miles overall.
Best season: March-December.
Difficulty: Moderately strenuous* (clockwise); strenuous* (counterclockwise).
Water availability: Bear Spring may be dry.
Elevation gain: 2,255 feet.
Elevation loss: 1,975 feet.
Maximum elevation: 8,165 feet.
Topo map: *Hiker's Map of the Huachuca Mountains.*
Jurisdiction: Miller Peak Wilderness, Sierra Vista Ranger District, Coronado National Forest.
Finding the trailhead: Drive 13 miles south from Sierra Vista on Arizona Highway 92 to the Coronado National Memorial Road (Forest Road 61). Turn right on this road and follow it 11.7 miles, over Montezuma Pass, to a junction with Forest Road 771. Follow this primitive road 0.9 mile, bearing right at the first fork. The second split is between Ida and Oversite canyons; park at the split and hike the route either way.

0.0	Ida Canyon trailhead.
0.3	Trail climbs out of Ida Canyon.
2.0	Abandoned mine site.
2.4	Trail enters Bear Canyon.
2.8	Bear Spring.
3.5	Bear Saddle. Turn right onto Huachuca Crest trail.
3.8	Junction with Oversite Canyon trail. Turn right.
5.3	Trail reaches Oversite Canyon floor at old mine site.
6.7	Oversite Canyon trailhead.

The trail: This trek combines the Oversite and Ida canyon trails with a short section of the Huachuca Crest trail to form a loop. The grade is gentler and the trail is easier to find when the loop is approached in a clockwise direction, as described here. The hike traverses the steep country on the western side of the Huachucas, and level tent spots are hard to find along the route. Bear Spring occupies a level bench; it represents the best destination for backpackers.

The trek begins with a hike up the Ida Canyon road. This jeep track is blocked at the wilderness boundary, beyond which it is only open to foot and stock traffic. Soon after the track crosses the main wash, a signpost indicates the spot where the trail abandons the old roadbed and climbs onto the slopes to the west. This path zigzags upward through a loose collection of live oak, juniper, and piñon pine. The swards of grass between the trees are punctuated with yuccas and agaves, two desert succulents that do well in the uplands of the Huachucas. As the trail gains altitude, some of the lesser peaks of the Huachuca Range appear to the east.

After a long and steady ascent, the trail reaches the abandoned site of the Ida Mine. This mine was active in the early 1900s, and produced small quantities of lead, silver, tungsten, and copper ore before it shut down. Several shafts are sunk deep into the mountainside. The remains of an old power hoist, once used for hauling ore buckets to the surface, stands rusting at the mouth of one of the mineshafts. These shafts pose a deadly hazard to any animal that strays close to their yawning mouths; hikers should stay clear of the openings.

28   Oversite Canyon Loop

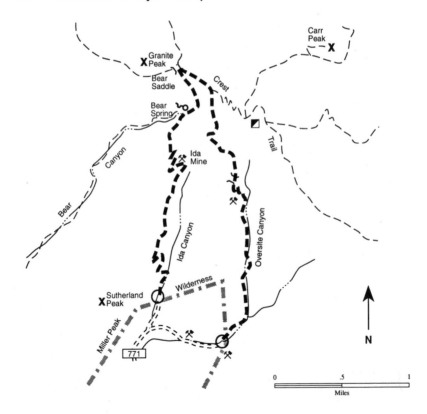

Beyond the mine site, the trail completes its zigzagging climb to the top of the ridge, then drops onto the western face. The trail takes a northwesterly bearing, passing through a mixed woodland. Openings in the trees afford views of the San Rafael Valley, with the Patagonia Mountains rising beyond. Farther south, the blue Sierra Madre trails away into the heart of Mexico.

The trail rises and falls gently as it crosses a pine-clad draw, then rounds the next finger ridge to emerge high above Bear Canyon. The path crosses sidehills toward the canyon's head, and the valley floor rises to meet it. The trail reaches the floor of the valley at Bear Spring, where water bubbles up from the ground in a grove of tall ponderosas. There is a good tent pad nearby; it is the campsite of choice for travelers who plan an overnight trip. An old trail once ran up Bear Canyon to meet the Ida Canyon trail here, but it has been swallowed by forest. The main trail swings northward across the head of Bear Canyon. It tops out at Bear Saddle, a pine-clad pass holding an intersection with the Huachuca Crest and Wisconsin Canyon trails.

To complete the loop, follow the Crest trail southward from Bear Saddle. This trail soon reaches yet another intersection, where the Oversite Canyon trail sidehills southward while the Crest trail climbs to the left. Follow the Oversite trail as it traverses high slopes clad in Douglas-fir. The path climbs over a spur ridge, then scrambles above a sheer outcrop of gray stone looming over the head of Ida Canyon. The open stand of hardwoods beyond this point offers some of the finest views of the loop, highlighted by the distant spire of Baboquivari Peak rising from the western skyline.

The path descends onto the next major spur ridge, then drops into Oversite Canyon. A steep and tortuous descent leads to the floor of this ravine, where the trail encounters a second mine site. A rusting ore cart lies overturned near the shafts. The trail fades as it follows the canyon downward through a dense woodland of live oaks. It ventures onto the western slopes of the valley from time to time before descending to the wash to complete the journey. Stick to the streamcourse if the trail disappears, and look for an old jeep track leading out of the hills. This track crosses the wilderness boundary and passes more evidence of mining activity on its way back to the starting point of the trip.

29   SCHEELITE CANYON LOOP

General description: A long day hike in the northern end of the Huachuca Mountains, 7.2 miles overall.
Best season: March-December.
Difficulty: Strenuous*.
Water availability: Sawmill Spring may be dry.
Elevation gain: 2,830 feet.
Elevation loss: 2,100 feet.

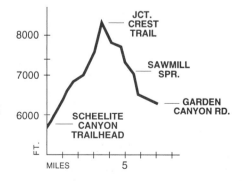

29   Scheelite Canyon Loop

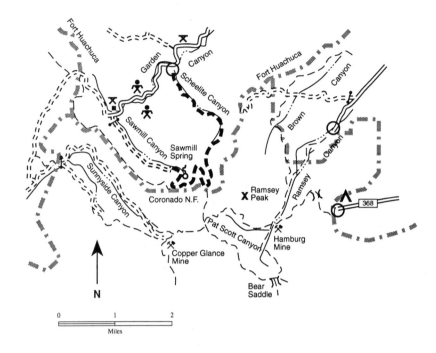

Maximum elevation: 8,350 feet.
Topo map: *Hiker's Map of the Huachuca Mountains.*
Jurisdiction: Fort Huachuca (U.S. Army base)
Finding the trailhead: Enter the main gate of Fort Huachuca. Stay on the main road for 9.5 miles, following signs for the Garden Canyon Road at intersections. The Scheelite Canyon trail departs from a pullout on the left side of the road, 0.7 mile beyond the end of the pavement.

0.0	Scheelite Canyon trailhead.
0.5	Canyon splits into two forks. Trail follows the eastern one.
3.6	Junction with Huachuca Crest trail. Turn right to complete the loop.
5.0	Junction with Sawmill Canyon trail. Turn right.
5.5	Sawmill Spring.
5.9	Trail follows old Sawmill Canyon road.
7.2	Trail meets Garden Canyon Road.

The trail: This trail forms a challenging loop trip in the northern part of the Huachuca Mountains. It lies within the bounds of the Fort Huachuca army base, and a visitor permit is required. The trail is faint in the upper reaches of Scheelite Canyon, so it is safer to approach it from a clockwise direction to avoid getting lost at the top of the range.

The trek begins on a well-defined path that follows steep-sided Scheelite Canyon up through groves of live oak and bigtooth maple. After half a mile, sheer walls of limestone close in around the wash, and travelers will scramble as the track surmounts boulders and stone outcrops. Buff-colored cliffs of granite rise from the slopes high above the canyon as it splits in two.

The trail initially climbs the intervening ridge, then swings into the eastern canyon. Here, steep pitches are interspersed with tiny, pine-clad basins that provide a breather between bouts of climbing. The cliffs fall away entirely as the draw bends to the south; the track alternates between the streamcourse and the slope above it. The shady floor of this north-facing canyon provides ideal growing conditions for Douglas-firs, while the drier slopes above it are a live oak woodland. Steep slopes crowd the head of the canyon, where the wash splits into a fan-shaped array of steep ravines. Here, the path abandons the canyon floor and ascends to the west at a calf-burning pace. As the path zigzags upward, the forest alternates between dense stands of Douglas-fir and an open pine woodland thinned by forest fires. A few isolated stands of aspen are scattered among conifers near the top of the grade.

The path tops out at Fort Huachuca Gate Number 2, where it intersects the Huachuca Crest trail. To complete the loop, follow this trail northwest down a long finger ridge. The terrain becomes barren and windswept, allowing views of Huachuca Peak to the north and of the Santa Rita and Patagonia mountains to the west. The trail soon drops from the ridgetop to zigzag down wooded slopes, then doglegs back to the southwest and levels off. The open slopes found here offer sweeping vistas. The Crest trail soon drops onto a low finger ridge, and upon reaching a broad saddle intersects the Sawmill Canyon trail.

Turn right onto this well-defined path, which drops into the pines as it enters the head of Sawmill Canyon. The trail sidehills across the head of this valley to reach Sawmill Spring, where a pipe pours water into an ancient catch basin. The trail then drops to the canyon floor, where it meets the Sawmill Canyon Road (which has been closed permanently). In contrast to Scheelite Canyon, Sawmill Canyon is broad and gentle, with sunny savannahs of mature pines. The road follows the canyon to its confluence with the Garden Canyon Road. Travelers who complete the loop afoot will notice two footbridges on the way back to Scheelite Canyon. Each of these bridges leads to a group of Apache petroglyphs that adorn the sheer rock walls of Garden Canyon.

30 HUACHUCA PEAK

General description: A day hike from theend of a jeep road to the summit of HuachucaPeak, 2.1 miles.
Best season: Year-round.
Difficulty: Strenuous*.
Water availability: None.
Elevation gain: 1,810 feet.
Maximum elevation: 8,410 feet.
Topo map: Hiker's Map of the Huachuca Mountains.

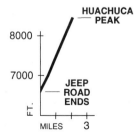

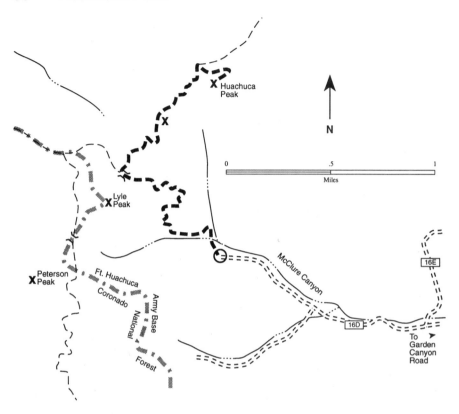

Jurisdiction: Fort Huachuca (U.S. Army base).

Finding the trailhead: Enter the main gate of Fort Huachuca. Stay on the main road for 9 miles, following signs for the Garden Canyon Road at intersections. The pavement ends beyond the second picnic area; turn right at the next road (#16D,E). Follow this road to its end, bearing left at all splits, to reach the trail.

0.0	End of jeep road #16.
1.2	Junction with cutoff to Huachuca Crest trail. Turn right.
1.8	Junction with trail to Huachuca Canyon. Turn right.
2.1	Summit of Huachuca Peak.

The trail: This short but strenuous route climbs to the summit of Huachuca Peak for excellent views of the Whetstone Mountains and the surrounding lowland basins. The route lies within the bounds of Fort Huachuca, so all hikers will need a visitor permit. The road to the trailhead is a jeep track that is completely impassable at its upper end; visitors should plan on hiking at least part of this road.

The trail begins by climbing through the rocky cleft that is the head of McClure Canyon. Its walls of jointed stone are ornamented with twisted junipers and oaks, and the wash has hollowed a curvaceous channel through the rock. The trail soon turns west, climbing aggressively onto slopes covered by live oaks. Openings in the trees afford fine southward views of Ramsey Peak. The trail finds itself tracking a westward-running draw, which teases travelers by always seeming to be on the verge of cresting the ridgeline. Each time a pass seems imminent, however, the path jogs into a side ravine and the brutal climb swings northward. The trail finally tops the ridge at a saddle just north of Lyle Peak, which is really no more than a wooded hump on the crest of the range.

Here, a cutoff route drops westward to meet the Huachuca Crest trail, while the Huachuca Peak route turns north up the ridgeline. Scattered pines allow occasional glimpses of the Santa Rita Mountains as the ascent slows to a more reasonable pace. The trail passes to the west of the next high point, crossing slopes with mature pines. As the path ascends onto the western slope of Huachuca Peak, the pines give way to a stunted growth of deciduous shrubs. The trail tops out on the ridge behind the peak, then drops a short distance to meet the spur trail running eastward to the summit. This windswept aerie commands an outstanding panorama of the surrounding country, with its island ranges rising like ocean swells from the tawny basins that surround them. Prominent among the peaks are the southern Huachucas, dominated by Carr Peak, and the low but rugged Whetstone Range rising to the north.

THE ARAVAIPA COUNTRY

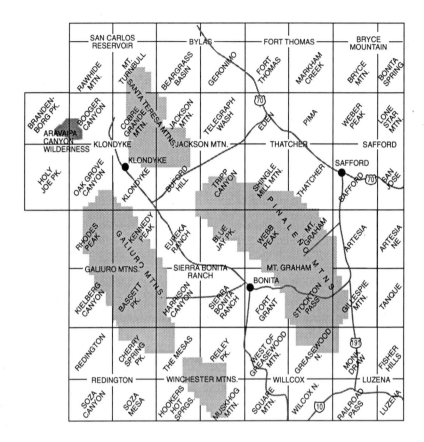

Aravaipa Creek is one of the last free-flowing streams in Arizona. It is older than the mountains that surround its upper basin, and its free-flowing middle reaches have cut a deep gorge through the Galiuro Mountains that rivals the Grand Canyon in scenic beauty. The tilted strata of the Galiuros force groundwater to the surface at the eastern end of the canyon, creating a permanent watercourse that is inhabited by seven species of indigenous fish. This canyon is one of the premier hiking areas in Arizona, and the Bureau of Land Management has secured wilderness status for the canyon and surrounding lands.

Improved gravel roads lead up to Aravaipa Canyon from both sides, but they may be washed out some distance from the trailheads. Brandenburg Camp is located 3 miles from the west trailhead. On the east side, visitors can camp at Fourmile Canyon Campground, 10 miles from the trailhead, or can practice dispersed camping along the road running up Turkey Creek from the east trailhead.

Desert bighorn in Hell Hole.

The upper reaches of Aravaipa Creek drain a broad valley between the Galiuro, Santa Teresa, and Pinaleño mountains. This remote basin is accessible only via gravel roads, which wash out from time to time and can be extremely muddy following rainstorms. The communities of Klondyke and Aravaipa were once thriving boomtowns that served surrounding mines, but are now ghosts of their former glory. The Pinaleños are discussed in their own chapter, while the most accessible routes in the Galiuros and Santa Teresas are discussed here.

Both the Galiuros and Santa Teresas have old trail systems that were built by the Civilian Conservation Corps (CCC) in the 1930s. These trails have received little maintenance by the Forest Service since that time, and most have lapsed into map-and-compass routes overgrown with brush. The result is a wilderness experience that places a high premium on self-reliance and route-finding skills. Both the Santa Teresas and the Galiuros have the protection of wilderness status, but cattle grazing is still allowed within the wilderness boundaries.

The Galiuros form a long, unbroken scarp between the San Pedro and Sulphur Springs valleys, and were called the Sierra del Aravaipa as late as the nineteenth century. There is little public access from the western side of the range, and many of the roads that approach it from the east require four-wheel-drive. Access to the southwest corner of the range runs through The Nature Conservancy's Muleshoe Ranch property. The Muleshoe Ranch includes Hooker Hot Springs and seven permanently flowing streams, and offers primitive hiking as well as four-wheel-drive access to the Jackson Cabin on national forest lands. The Santa Teresas are even more remote and, in many cases, the roads leading to them are blocked by locked gates on private land. The northern part of this range is surrounded by the San Carlos Apache Reservation, and access requires special permission from the tribe.

31 ARAVAIPA CANYON

General description: A wilderness route through Aravaipa Canyon, 10.8 miles one way.
Best seasons: March-May; September-November.
Difficulty: Moderate**.
Water availability: Aravaipa Creek runs year-round; there may be pools in all of the side canyons except Hell Hole.
Elevation gain: 465 feet.
Elevation loss: 80 feet.
Maximum elevation: 3,065 feet.
Topo maps: Brandenburg Mountain, Booger Canyon.
Jurisdiction: Aravaipa Canyon Wilderness, Safford District, Bureau of Land Management.
Finding the trailhead: To reach the west trailhead, leave Arizona Highway 77 some 11 miles north of Mammoth at the signs for Central Arizona College. This is the Aravaipa Road, and after 4.5 miles the pavement gives way to an improved gravel surface. The trailhead is 12 miles from the highway, at the end of the road. The east trailhead can be reached from Klondyke by traveling northwest on the Klondyke–Aravaipa Road. This road departs U.S. Highway 70, 15 miles west of Safford.

0.0	West trailhead. Follow path down to the streamcourse.
0.2	Trail reaches Aravaipa Creek and becomes a route.
1.1	Route enters Aravaipa Canyon Wilderness.
2.0	Hell's Half Acre Canyon joins from the south.
2.3	Painted Cave Canyon enters from the north.
3.4	Javelina Canyon enters from the north.
4.5	Virgus Canyon enters from the south.
4.9	Horse Camp Canyon enters from the north.
6.4	Booger Canyon enters from the north.
7.1	Paisano Canyon enters from the north.
8.4	Hell Hole enters from the north.

9.0   Parsons Canyon enters from the south.

10.8   Turkey Creek enters from the south. East trailhead.

The trail: Aravaipa Canyon is ranked among the great scenic wonders of the state of Arizona. Here, the rushing waters of Aravaipa Creek cut through volcanic stone as the Galiuro Mountains rose around it. The erosion of the water cut faster than the land rose, and the result was a steep-walled canyon chiseled through the heart of the mountains. Vanished tribes left cliff dwellings and cave paintings here, and later this rocky channel was an important travel corridor for the Aravaipa Apaches, who were among the last of their tribe to submit to reservations. A permanent stream runs through the canyon, forming one of the last wetland ecosystems in Arizona. One of the healthiest desert bighorn populations in the state roams these canyon walls. Because of its rare species and wild character, Aravaipa Canyon is now protected under the Wilderness Act, which forbids motor travel in the canyon.

Horses are allowed for day trips only, and all visitors must obtain a permit in advance (by phone or mail) from the Safford District of the Bureau of Land Management. Permits are limited, and visitors apply up to thirteen weeks in advance for more popular weekends. The trek requires map and compass

31   Aravaipa Canyon

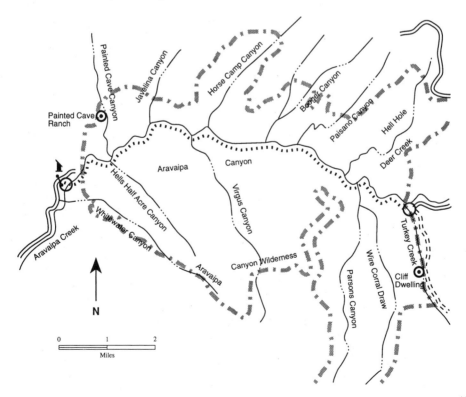

Cliff walls below the mouth of Painted Cave Canyon.

navigation and frequent stream crossings; the canyon is prone to heavy flooding and is completely impassable following rains.

Contamination from human wastes is probably the greatest threat to this wetland ecosystem. Visitors should practice minimum-impact techniques when relieving themselves and pack out solid wastes. When this book was written, the western access road was washed out at Brandenburg Campground (3 miles from the trailhead), and the eastern access road was impassable 8 miles from the eastern trailhead. These roads may be repaired in the near future. The trail description given here covers the canyon upstream from west to east, and discusses side canyons individually at the end. The side canyons often require scrambling, and visitors should be especially wary of rattlesnakes while exploring them.

The trek begins by following a dirt road toward the ranger station. A path splits off to the right, and hikers should follow this track down to Aravaipa Creek. From this point on, the trek consists of travel along gravel bars and wading up the stream itself. Visitors are asked to stick to the creekbed since the route crosses private lands owned by The Nature Conservancy. Great blue herons, belted kingfishers, and water ouzels are a few of the birds that can be spotted along the stream, and songbirds congregate among the saguaros and cottonwoods that line its banks.

Just beyond the wilderness boundary, cliffs loom above the north bank of Aravaipa Creek. Their bottom layers consist of a chocolate brown stratum of volcanic conglomerate topped by a chalky band of tuff. High above a massive band of welded tuff forms the upper palisade of the canyon. The streamcourse bends sharply to the southeast, and the massive buttes surrounding Hell's Half Acre Canyon rise ahead. Saguaros dot the gentle slopes to the left, and cottonwoods and willows grow from benches of alluvial gravel beside the stream. Aravaipa Canyon bends to resume an easterly course, and the narrow cleft of Hell's Half Acre Canyon enters from the south. The canyon walls constrict the stream above this point, and periodic floods have scoured the canyon floor of all vegetation. The mortised walls hemming in the watercourse are composed of highly resistant rhyolite, shot through with veins of quartz.

Painted Cave Canyon enters from the left, providing a bit of an opening that allows views to the north. There are several boulder-choked passages above this point, and sheer walls and enormous prows of stone rise almost a thousand feet on all sides. Javelina Canyon is the next major cleft to join Aravaipa Canyon, and it does so in a brush-choked alluvial fan that is guarded by gigantic points of stone. The inspiring scenery continues as the trek makes its way to Virgus Canyon, which enters from the south and is the largest feeder canyon in the wilderness area. Just beyond it is a long, elevated bench of grass and shrubs along the south bank of the stream. A couple more twists and the hiker arrives at Horse Camp Canyon, which interrupts the solid cliffs to the north. This is a good place to look for bighorn sheep.

Beyond Horse Camp Canyon, Aravaipa widens as the cliffs recede to create an air of spaciousness. The width of the canyon floor permits greater accumulation of sand and gravel here, and Fremont cottonwoods and Arizona sycamores rise along the stream above dense brakes of their younger cousins. This wooded bottomland provides excellent habitat for birds and mammals, and offers a diverse selection of camp spots. Following the streamcourse upward, stout bastions of stone loom from the north wall of the canyon like the turrets of some long-forgotten castle. The alcoves between them have been scooped out by the wind, and there is at least one cave here that provides a roosting spot for bats.

Around Booger Canyon, the walls of the main canyon are broken into irregular buttes and ridges. The slopes beneath them support an especially dense growth of saguaros, although the stream bottoms are still densely wooded with water-loving hardwoods. The welded tuff found here shows deep vertical jointing, which makes it more susceptible to weathering. Just beyond Paisano Canyon, the cliffs devolve into well-weathered foothills covered in desert scrub.

A natural arch graces a northern promontory as the creek rounds a headland to reveal sheer walls of sedimentary origin. These sandstones and conglomerates were once old valley fill, and they mark the entrance of Hell Hole. Deer Creek enters Aravaipa Canyon here, and the ruins of a turn-of-the-century ranch stand abandoned in brush near the confluence. The main canyon jogs south then east again to the narrow mouth of Parsons Canyon, where the sheer walls of the Hell Hole conglomerate close around Aravaipa Creek. These cliffs have been weathered into washboards, overhangs, and knobs that are intriguing in their complexity. The stream scours the narrow bottoms from time to time, and there are no elevated benches for camping above Parsons Canyon. Tall cliffs accompany travelers all the way to Turkey Creek, where the wilderness ends at the eastern trailhead. For visitors who want to do extra exploring, a cliff dwelling built by the ancient Salado people is 1.5 miles up Turkey Creek on the western side of the canyon. Please be sure to leave this cultural resource as you found it.

HELL'S HALF ACRE CANYON

This narrow chasm provides easy walking for the first 100 yards, then deadends as a stack of three immense boulders neatly corks the opening. Sheer walls confine its wash to a narrow channel and create an atmosphere that is at once inspiring and claustrophobic.

PAINTED CAVE CANYON

This canyon is wide at its mouth, and offers easy walking up a gravel wash for the first 0.5 mile. Low cliffs of breccia constrict the streamcourse, and an enormous boulder forms the first obstacle to progress. It can be negotiated with some scrambling, and the walking is easy beyond it as the streamcourse runs across a solid bed of rhyolite. Two headwalls with deep plunge pools soon bar the way; travel beyond this point should only be attempted by experienced climbers who are willing to get wet. Beyond the larger headwall is a second rockfall, followed by a narrow passage where the water is often quite deep. The route dead-ends at a 30-foot overhang that offers little in the way of toeholds.

JAVELINA CANYON

This tributary is passable only for the first few hundred yards of extremely steep and dangerous boulder climbing. Beyond this point, sheer headwalls block passage to all but seasoned mountaineers. Along the way are several hanging gardens where ferns and mosses grow among willowy tamarisks and gnarled specimens of cottonwood and sycamore. The slopes above provide a contrasting vegetation dominated by full-grown saguaro and beavertail cacti.

VIRGUS CANYON

The entrance to this canyon is blocked by a jumble of huge boulders that compels the explorer to seek passage through the thorny jungle cloaking the higher ground. Expect slow going for the first 100 yards, and watch for a substantial bat cave that opens like a cathedral nave in the rock of the east wall. Travelers who make it past the boulders will find the traveling easier beyond them, although periodic rockfalls will require some scrambling. The watercourse has cut grooves and whorls into the bedrock of the canyon floor, and there will be some friction pitches to negotiate where this stone forms sills. This bedrock has large pores that held volatile gases when it was formed, and is called "vuggy." The bouldering becomes more technical as the canyon approaches the 0.5-mile point. Here, the sheer walls close around the wash, and a deep basin necessitates some wading when water levels are up. Just beyond this pool is a jumble of boulders so large and sheer as to block passage to all except well-equipped rock climbers.

HORSE CAMP CANYON

Beyond its boulder-choked mouth, this canyon has been swept clean of debris by water. Initially, the streamcourse is composed of porous vuggy, a volcanic rock. A headwall soon blocks the way, and a waterfall graces its rounded face following wet weather. Hikers can scramble up the east side of this face to gain the next level of the canyon. Here, the stream has cut through a layer of welded tuff, whittling channels and potholes deep into the stone. These natural water pockets, or tinajas, reflect the towering walls looming on both sides of the canyon. Traveling gets trickier as the gradient steepens, with occasional bands of resistant bedrock barring the way. About 0.5 mile into the canyon, travel along the streamcourse is blocked by a large pool surrounded by vertical walls. It is possible to climb high into the thorn scrub on the eastern slope and thereby gain passage beyond the pool, but the slopes are steep and unstable; attempting them is not recommended.

BOOGER CANYON

The initial pitch of this canyon is steep and strewn with boulders, forcing travelers to pick a perilous course among fallen rocks and over a series of low headwalls. Visitors skilled in the scrambling arts should be able to wind through to an upper valley, where the stream grade eases but the problematic boulder jams remain. The canyon is bordered by ragged peaks of stone rather than continuous walls, and thorn scrub covers the gentler slopes. The canyon soon splits into two forks of about equal size. The left fork is a box canyon that contains a fairly dependable spring. The right fork is the main canyon. It narrows into pools surrounded by sheer walls. Travelers who decide to go on should be prepared to engage in water sports, since the narrow cleft winds through deep pools for another 0.6 mile before opening into rolling desert.

PAISANO CANYON

This canyon offers a brief but strenuous boulder course before ending at a steep headwall. Skilled rock climbers might be able to find a passage past this chokepoint and onto the rolling desert beyond, but hikers should turn back here.

HELL HOLE

This canyon may appear impassable at first glance, but in fact it provides easy traveling along a smooth bed of gravel for its entire length. It begins as a tight chasm between towering walls of conglomerate stone. The canyon makes a seemingly impossible series of hairpin turns, causing the traveler to lose all sense of direction. There are two spots where the sheer walls are broken into wind-sculpted obelisks and spires, and between these clusters of pinnacles is a wonderland of overhangs, keyholes, and grottos. While traversing this area, watch for a superb natural arch high on the left wall of the canyon. Sunlight rarely reaches the canyon floor here, and the cool microclimate allows pockets of brilliant vegetation to grow in seepy areas.

The trek progresses past an area where the stream has cut deep into the rock on the outsides of the curves, and the canyon soon widens out into a pocket valley. Here, a typical desert canyon vegetation of live oak and sycamore thrives in the abundant sunlight. This condition persists for almost a mile, after which the vertical walls of stone again crowd the streamcourse. Watch for a weeping wall on the right side of the canyon that supports a hanging garden of moisture-loving plants. A rockfall of enormous size marks the end of the cliffs, but its huge boulders can be surmounted without difficulty. Beyond it, the canyon devolves into a series of beehive-shaped domes punctuated by an occasional butte. This arid landscape accompanies the traveler to the wilderness boundary.

PARSONS CANYON

Beyond its tree-screened entrance, this canyon offers boulder-hopping between massive sandstone walls. After 200 yards, a boulder jam and plunge pool block further progress when water levels are high. Beyond this chokepoint the cliff walls give way to sloping foothills covered in desert scrub.

32   THE TORTILLA TRAIL

General description: A backpack to a historic ranch in the northern Galiuro Mountains, 8.5 miles.

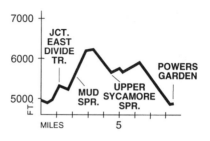

Best season: Year-round.
Difficulty: Moderate* east to west; moderately strenuous* west to east.
Water availability: Mud Spring is reliable, but Upper Sycamore Spring may be dry; there is also a reliable spring in Rattlesnake Canyon just above Powers Garden.
Elevation gain: 1,769 feet.
Elevation loss: 1,840 feet.
Maximum elevation: 5,950 feet.
Topo map: Kennedy Peak.
Jurisdiction: Galiuro Wilderness, Safford Ranger District, Coronado National Forest.
Finding the trailhead: Drive northeast from Bonita for 19 miles on the Aravaipa Road. Turn west on Forest Road 253, following signs for Deer Creek. Follow this primitive road for 8.5 miles to reach the trailhead.

0.0	Begin the hike from Deer Creek Road.
0.8	Deer Creek Cabin (leave gates closed).
1.2	Junction with East Divide trail. Go straight on Tortilla trail.
1.8	Trail crosses Oak Creek wash.
2.1	Mud Spring. Junction with Sycamore Canyon trail. Turn left.
3.3	Trail crosses saddle to enter Sycamore Canyon.
3.6	Sycamore Canyon trail rejoins Tortilla trail.
4.5	Upper Sycamore Spring. Trail starts climbing.
6.6	Trail crosses pass above Horse Canyon.
7.2	Trail reaches floor of Horse Canyon.
8.2	Junction with Rattlesnake Creek trail. Turn left for Powers Garden.
8.5	Powers Garden ranch site.

The trail: This trek follows the Tortilla trail across mostly open country as it penetrates deep into the northern Galiuros. It ends at Powers Garden, an abandoned ranch in the valley of Rattlesnake Creek. The ranch has a colorful history, having once been owned by the notorious Power family. The two Power sons, Tom and John, had refused to register for the draft during World War I. On February, 9, 1918, a party of lawmen tried to arrest the Power men at their mine property far to the south of Powers Garden. A shootout

The old ranch house at Powers Garden.

ensued, and a sheriff and two deputies, as well as the Power patriarch, were killed. The fugitives fled into Mexico where they were finally apprehended by an army patrol that had crossed the border in pursuit. Powers Garden was the main ranch of the Power family, and its buildings still stand intact. Backcountry travelers can stay in the ranch house.

The trek begins on a primitive, closed road that runs through the Deer Creek administrative site. Pass through the corrals (and be sure to close the gates) and follow the rocky path that climbs to the Deer Creek-Oak Creek divide. There is a marked junction here; the East Divide trail takes off to the left while the trail to Powers Garden runs straight ahead through a gate. The path is well-worn as it descends into the rolling Oak Creek basin, but it nonetheless can be a bit tricky to follow. It makes a beeline westward, crossing the several draws of the Oak Creek drainage and climbing the slopes beyond. The rolling grasslands of the basin are dotted with oaks. They are bounded to the north by the conical summit of China Peak, to the south by the wooded slopes and rocky palisades of Kennedy Peak.

The trail enters the Galiuro Wilderness at a marked trail junction below Mud Spring. The faint Sycamore Canyon trail runs to the north, while the Tortilla trail jogs southward on its way to Powers Garden. It soon climbs vigorously to a ridgetop and follows it southwest until bands of cliffs block the way. The path bends northward to avoid them, rounding the point to a saddle above the headwaters of Sycamore Canyon. The trail drops rapidly to the valley floor,

32 Tortilla Trail (Powers Garden)
33 Corral Canyon

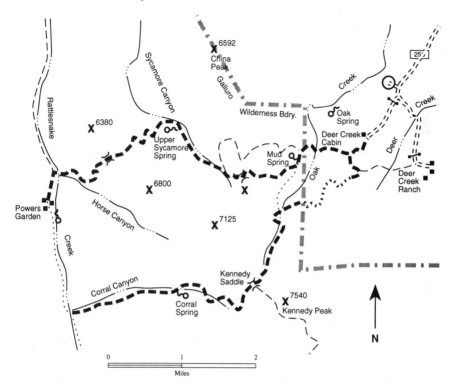

rejoining the Sycamore Canyon trail along the way. The route then follows the heavily wooded valley bottom for 0.8 mile to reach Upper Sycamore Spring. The trail levels off at this point then begins a gentle climb along the western wall of the valley. The valley floor drops away, and the trail is soon several hundred feet above the watercourse. Stark cliffs of red stone guard the opposite slope of the canyon.

The path weaves across folds of the hill as the ascent continues, crossing several high saddles and overlooks that command views of the Rattlesnake Creek watershed. After topping a final high pass, the trail makes a foot-pounding descent into Horse Canyon. Groves of tall pines shade its bottoms, and the trail follows its watercourse down. It passes through a band of resistant stone as it descends. Blade-shaped pinnacles and undercut cliffs tower above both sides of the wash. The trail then runs out into the wide basin of Rattlesnake Canyon, where it joins the Rattlesnake Creek trail. Follow this trail southward to reach the historic ranch buildings of Powers Garden.

33   CORRAL CANYON

General description: A backpack from Deer Creek to the Rattlesnake Creek route, 8.7 miles.

Best season: March-December.

Difficulty: Strenuous**.

Water availability: Corral Spring is reliable.

Elevation gain: 2,169 feet.

Elevation loss: 2,060 feet.

Maximum elevation: 7,160 feet.

Topo map: Kennedy Peak (inc.).

Jurisdiction: Galiuro Wilderness, Safford Ranger District, Coronado National Forest.

Finding the trailhead: Drive northeast from Bonita for 19 miles on the Aravaipa Road. Turn west on Forest Road 253, following signs for Deer Creek. Follow this primitive road for 8.5 miles. Park here.

0.0	Begin the hike on Deer Creek Road.
0.8	Deer Creek Cabin (leave gates closed).
1.2	Junction of Tortilla and East Divide trails. Turn left onto East Divide trail.
1.5	Junction with trail from Deer Creek Ranch. Turn right.
3.3	Junction with Mud Spring cutoff trail. Keep going straight.
4.9	Kennedy Saddle. Junction with Corral Canyon trail. Turn right.
7.0	Corral Spring.
8.7	Junction with Rattlesnake Creek trail.

The trail: This route runs to the crest of the East Divide near Kennedy Peak, then drops down Corral Canyon to reach the upper reaches of Rattlesnake Creek. After following a closed road to the Deer Creek Cabin, the trek begins with a stony 0.4-mile climb across grassy slopes to reach the divide above Oak Creek. Turn left at the ridgetop signpost and follow the East Divide trail southward along the rounded ridgetop. There are fine views of the buttes that guard the eastern approaches to the range; the rolling savannahs of the Oak Creek basin stretch away toward China Peak. The trail rounds a hillock, then meets a track that rises from the Deer Creek Ranch. Turn right and climb through the low saddle marked by a fence gate. Beyond the gate, the trail becomes sketchy as it rounds the skirts of the nearest butte. Watch for cairns marking the route across an arid grassland dotted with junipers. To the south, great bluffs of stone rise from the wooded flanks of Kennedy Peak.

The track crosses the heads of two minor ravines, then follows the bluffs

Rugged buttes of rhyolite guard the eastern approaches to the Galiuro Mountains.

rising above the east bank of Oak Creek. Looking across the valley, one can see several curious walls of stone that jut vertically from the hillside. The Oak Creek draw soon becomes steep and wooded, and the trail becomes distinct again before joining a cutoff trail from Mud Spring. A brutal slog carries the traveler up the north slope of Kennedy Peak, and openings in the pine-oak woodland allow views of China Peak, the distant Santa Teresas, and the ragged cliffs on nearby slopes. The trail tops out at Kennedy Saddle, which is protected from the wind by enormous and gnarled piñon pines. The summit of Kennedy Peak lies just to the south, while travelers bound for Corral Canyon should follow the trail that runs due west from the saddle.

This path crosses a lobe of Douglas Canyon, and Bassett Peak rises to a sharp point far to the south. The trail then follows a ridgetop screened by pine, juniper, and manzanita. At the end of the ridge, the path breaks out onto open slopes above the head of Corral Canyon. Looking northwest, Rhodes Peak and the nameless summits trailing away to the south of it form the West Divide of the Galiuro Mountains.

The trail is tricky to follow as it descends across arid grasslands interrupted by slabs of bedrock. At the bottom of the draw, tall ponderosa pines shade the trail, which follows the streamcourse downward. A sheer drop through vertical walls soon bars the way, and the path wanders northward onto a grassy shoulder that affords views of ragged buttes above the canyon. A zigzagging descent leads to Corral Spring, where a fence encloses the water source. This spot was once used by cowboys as a natural trap for half-wild cattle. The trail then follows the streamcourse the rest of the way to Rattlesnake Creek, fading in and out through a shaded riparian woodland. The trail ends at a signpost on the east bank of Rattlesnake Creek, 1.3 miles south of Powers Garden.

34 BASSETT PEAK

General description: A long day hike to the summit of the tallest peak in the Galiuro Mountains, 5.5 miles.
Best season: March-December.
Difficulty: Moderately strenuous**.
Water availability: Upper Ash Creek Spring may be dry.
Elevation gain: 2,768 feet.
Elevation loss: 75 feet.
Maximum elevation: 7,663 feet.
Topo maps: Harrison Canyon, Bassett Peak.
Jurisdiction: Galiuro Wilderness, Safford Ranger District, Coronado National Forest.

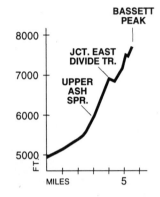

Finding the trailhead: From Bonita, take the Sunset Road west for 13 miles. This fair-weather road then turns south, becoming Forest Road 651. Follow it for another 3.5 miles to a junction with the Ash Mesas Road (Forest Road 659) and follow this until it turns south. Continue west on the primitive Forest Road 660 for the remaining 2.3 miles to the trailhead.

0.0	Trailhead.
1.7	Lower Ash Spring water troughs.
2.5	Trail enters Galiuro Wilderness.
3.0	Upper Ash Spring.
4.1	Trail joins East Divide trail. Turn left and follow it southward.
5.3	Saddle behind Bassett Peak.
5.5	Bassett Peak summit.

The trail: This route ascends along the North Fork of Ash Creek, then climbs strenuously to the top of the highest summit in the Galiuros. The trek begins by following a jeep trail up the wooded bottomlands of Ash Creek's North Fork. There are numerous crossings of the streamcourse as the track wanders into the foothills of the Galiuro Mountains. A pair of water storage tanks marks the end of the jeep road and the beginning of the trail, and ponderosa pines overtop the more numerous evergreen oaks. There is a second set of water troughs just before the wilderness boundary. Above them, bigtooth maples crowd the streamcourse and offer a brilliant display of fall colors as the canyon splits into two gulches. The trail ascends

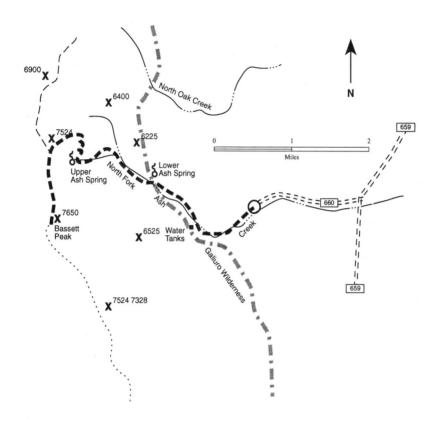

the more southerly one, where the trees fall away as the gradient steepens. A series of intermittent cascades leads to Upper Ash Spring, which is located in a grove of tall aspens.

At this watering trough, the trail leaves the bottoms and begins a rigorous ascent along the north wall of the canyon. Twisted spires of rock crowd the canyon's head. A look downstream reveals the grass-clad Ash Creek Black Hills rising on the edge of the Sulphur Springs Valley. The trail crests the ridge and turns west to follow its crest. A rocky peak soon looms ahead. The path swings south to avoid it, then climbs to a ridgetop junction behind the peak. Turn left along the East Divide trail to get to Bassett Peak. The trail may be overgrown as it follows the ridgetop southward, with phenomenal views all along the way. The path passes beneath several outcrops that have been sculpted into intriguing shapes by wind and water.

Upon reaching the eastern slopes of Bassett Peak, the path zigzags upward across brushy slopes dotted with young Douglas-firs. There is no established trail to the top of the peak, but a good route can be had by following the main trail to a saddle south of the peak, then bushwhacking up the ridgeline to the summit. A trail register is located atop this tallest peak of the Galiuros, and magnificent views spread in all directions. The Winchester Mountains rise directly to the southeast, while the long chain of the Galiuros stretches away to the north, uninterrupted for 50 miles. The Rincons and Santa Catalinas are clearly visible to the west, while the Pinaleños crowd the eastern horizon.

35   COTTONWOOD MOUNTAIN

General description: A day hike to a mountaintop in the Santa Teresa Mountains, 3.5 miles.
Best season: Year-round.
Difficulty: Moderately strenuous*.
Water availability: Cottonwood Canyon has water in the wet months.
Elevation gain: 1,960 feet.
Maximum elevation: 7,260 feet.
Topo maps: Buford Hill, Jackson Mountain.

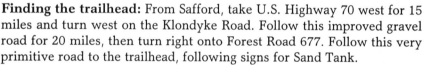

Jurisdiction: Santa Teresa Wilderness, Safford Ranger District, Coronado National Forest.
Finding the trailhead: From Safford, take U.S. Highway 70 west for 15 miles and turn west on the Klondyke Road. Follow this improved gravel road for 20 miles, then turn right onto Forest Road 677. Follow this very primitive road to the trailhead, following signs for Sand Tank.

0.0	Sand Tank trailhead.
0.1	Sand Tank (dry).
1.5	Trail leaves Cottonwood Creek to begin ascent.
3.3	Trail crosses crest of Cottonwood Mountain.
3.4	Route leaves established trail.
3.5	Cottonwood Mountain overlook point.

The trail: As of this writing, the Cottonwood Mountain trail was the only cleared pathway into the wild and remote Santa Teresa Mountains. The entire south slope of this range burned in 1994, and the trail traverses recovering grasslands and upland shrub communities. From the trailhead, follow a faint jeep track to the dry bed of Sand Tank. The track disappears amid the sycamores and alluvial debris of Cottonwood Wash; follow the streamcourse upward and the trail will soon reappear on its western bank. When the valley takes a sharp bend to the east, the trail drops to the streambed and follows it closely, with several crossings. Low walls of bedrock rise out of the hillsides at odd intervals, and the path ultimately has to make a steep climb to avoid a solid band of rock. Here, an unusual waterfall has worn a diagonal slit, following a joint in the stone. Rounded hills surround the watercourse above this point, and the trail climbs away to the north as it begins its ascent of Cottonwood Mountain.

35 ● Cottonwood Mountain

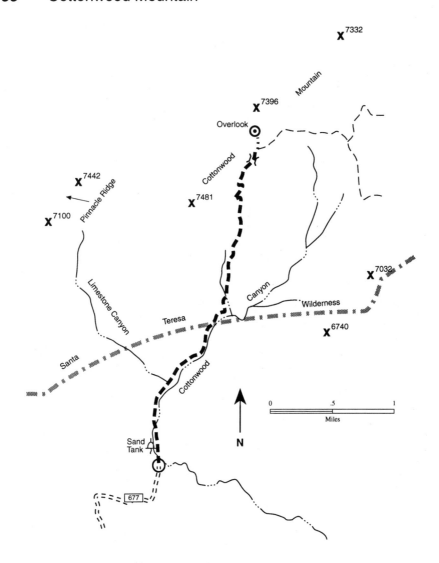

X 7332

Mountain

X 7396

Overlook ◉

Cottonwood

X 7442

Pinnacle Ridge

X 7481

X 7100

X 7032

Limestone Canyon

Canyon

Wilderness

Teresa

X 6740

Santa

Cottonwood

Sand Tank

677

0   .5   1
Miles

N

Cottonwood Mountain commands sweeping views of Pinnacle Ridge and the heart of the Santa Teresas.

The trail splits early in the ascent; hikers can select either track because they come together again 50 yards uphill. The path then makes a beeline up the slope, followed by numerous switchbacks as the mountainside steepens. The trail tops out on the crest of the ridge amid a once and future forest of ponderosa and Chihuahua pines that has received a temporary setback by the fire. The burn spared few of the trees, and grasses are beginning to take advantage of the newly available sunlight to create temporary meadows among the snags. For better views, follow the trail northward along a spur ridge. This path soon turns west and descends; leave the path here and travel 100 yards farther north to sheer outcrops of stone that command impressive views into the Santa Teresas. The jagged monoliths of Pinnacle Ridge dominate the scene, and the northern tail of the Galiuro Mountains rises in the distance.

THE PINALEÑO MOUNTAINS

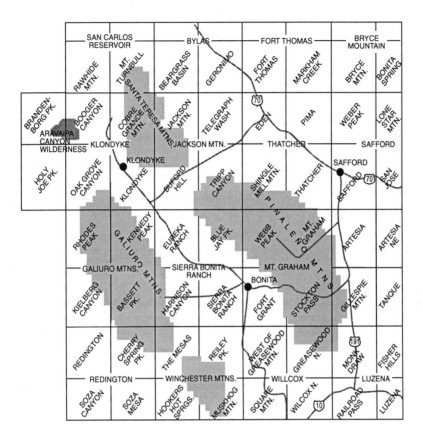

The mighty Pinaleño Range towers above the Gila Valley and culminates in Mount Graham, which at 10,720 feet is the tallest peak in southern Arizona. The range represents a great uplift of metamorphic stone, an origin shared by the Rincons and Santa Catalinas. This island range has a plant assemblage similar to that of the southern Rocky Mountains in New Mexico, highlighted by Douglas-firs, ponderosa pines, and quaking aspens. It has a least one unique animal: an endemic subspecies of squirrel inhabits the high-altitude forests of Mount Graham and its surroundings. The area has been set aside as a preserve for this particular squirrel, and has been closed to all human entry. Black bears, Coues white-tailed deer, and cougars are some of the larger inhabitants of the Pinaleños that may be spotted by hikers.

The surroundings were used by humans as well as the various wildlife species within them. Heliograph Peak was once used by the U.S. Army Signal Corps to flash mirror signals during the Apache Wars. The Pinaleño Mountains were the site of logging operations in the late 1800s and early 1900s, and a

Civilian Conservation Corps (CCC) camp at Old Columbine in the 1930s provided the labor force that built much of the Swift Trail and the hiking routes that descend from it.

The trail system in the Pinaleños is quite extensive, but the Safford Ranger District receives little funding for trail maintenance; thus, most of the less popular trails in this range have lapsed into neglect. The Swift Trail (Arizona Highway 366) is paved to Shannon Park and provides gravel access down the crest of the range to Riggs Lake. In winter months, November 15 to April 15 and possibly later, the route is closed beyond Shannon Park. There are improved campgrounds along this road at Arcadia, Shannon Park, Hospital Flat, Soldier Creek, and Riggs Lake. An improved dry weather road runs most of the way up to the West Peak lookout on the northern end of the range. The northeastern flanks of the range are served by a network of primitive roads. Arizona Highway 266 provides access to the Righthand Canyon and Shake trails, while the western slopes and southern tail of the range are accessible only by jeep trails.

36   ROUND THE MOUNTAIN TRAIL

General description: A backpack along the northeast slope of the Pinaleño Mountains, 14.4 miles.
Best season: April-October.
Difficulty: Moderately strenuous*.
Water availability: Round the Mountain Spring is reliable; Marijilda, Gibson, Deadman, and Frye canyons usually have water.
Elevation gain: 7,220 feet.
Elevation loss: 3,360 feet.
Maximum elevation: 9,160 feet.
Topo maps: Mount Graham, Webb Peak.
Jurisdiction: Safford Ranger District, Coronado National Forest
Finding the trailhead: From Safford, drive south on U.S. Highway 191 and turn onto the Swift Trail (Arizona Highway 366). Go west for 8 miles to reach the lower trailhead, which is just beyond the Noon Creek Picnic Area. To reach the upper trailhead, drive 21 miles farther up this road to the Columbine Ranger Station, and take a right onto the Southern Arizona Bible Camp Road. The upper trail begins at the end of this road.

0.0	Round the Mountain trailhead.
0.1	Trail crosses Noon Creek.
0.8	Junction with Noon Creek Ridge trail. Turn right.
1.9	Trail crosses pass into Marijilda Canyon.
3.2	Trail crosses Marijilda Creek.
4.0	Trail crosses Gibson Creek.
4.3	Junction with upper Gibson Canyon trail. Bear left.
4.5	Junction with lower Gibson Canyon trail. Bear right.

The trail: This trail offers one of the longer backpacking routes in southern Arizona, traversing the high and wild country beneath the crest of the Pinaleño Mountains. The trail is well-maintained and fairly easy to follow, but is physically challenging because it continually climbs up and down a series of

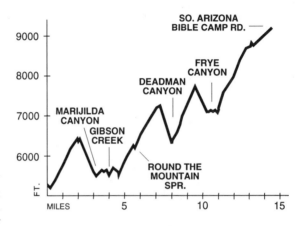

high passes. Round the Mountain Spring provides the only reliable source of water on the trail, although Marijilda and Frye canyons often carry water. Most of the country traversed by the route is quite steep, but camping spots can be found in the bottoms of most of the major canyons.

From the lower (southern) trailhead, the path drops and crosses Noon Creek, then climbs to the rounded top of a low ridge. It turns west and follows the ridgetop upward as the highway falls away, leaving travelers in the silence of the juniper scrubland. Heliograph Peak rises above the head of the valley. Now crowned with radio towers, this summit was once the site of a U.S. Army Signal Corps post; soldiers stationed here used mirrors to communicate over long distances during the Apache Wars of the mid-1800s.

After a time, the trail reaches a T-intersection. The left fork is the Noon Creek Ridge trail; the Round the Mountain trail takes off to the right. The Round the Mountain route climbs steadily to a rocky gap in the hills that overlook Marijilda Canyon. The barren crag to the north is Deadman Peak. Triangular blocks of granite rise to the forested summits of Plain View Peak and Mount Graham to the west.

The trail then zigzags toward the canyon floor, and a scattering of pines and Douglas-firs frames vistas of the Gila Valley and the Blue Mountains that rise beyond it. Agaves and hedgehog cacti grow from chinks in the rock, and juniper trees thrust their twisted limbs toward the desert sky. The path makes

Deadman Peak.

its way into the cool bottoms of Marijilda Canyon, where pines, evergreen oaks, and alligator junipers attain impressive sizes. Velvet ash, canyon grape, and other drought-intolerant plant species also thrive in this riparian area.

After crossing the canyon floor, the trail climbs onto the arid benchlands beyond it. The path makes several minor dips and rises amid a savannah of oak and manzanita. At one narrow draw, the trail fades as it climbs straight up the grassy gully, then turns north across the slopes once more. The route soon drops into the stony cleft of Gibson Canyon, where Arizona sycamores thrive in shade. The path then climbs vigorously onto the next ridge, where it meets the upper leg of the Gibson Canyon trail and an impressive view of Deadman Peak. This is followed by a descent to connect with the lower segment of the Gibson Canyon trail.

This latter junction marks the beginning of a long and arduous ascent across the arid hills above S Canyon. After crossing sun-baked slopes, the trail enters a pine-cloaked fold in the hills. Here, a band of exposed bedrock forces groundwater to the surface. The result is Round the Mountain Spring, which provides a steady source of moisture and creates a miniature wetland amid the arid slopes. The abundance of game trails in the area is a testimony to the importance of such a spring to desert wildlife.

From the spring, the trail runs across the slopes to reach the floor of S

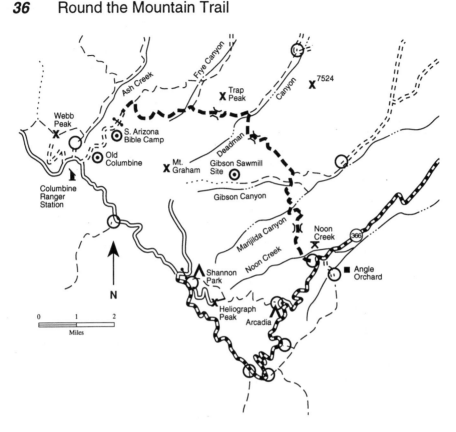

Canyon. It follows the dry wash upstream for a short time before climbing onto a finger ridge to the southwest. When the trail returns to the wash for a final crossing, the canyon floor is transformed into a luxuriant oasis of pines, Gambel oaks, and bigtooth maples.

The trail climbs arid slopes to the top of Deadman Ridge, then drops into the pines on the opposite side. A zigzagging descent leads to the floor of Deadman Canyon, where the Deadman Canyon trail turns northeast to follow the valley downward. The Round the Mountain trail climbs the opposite slope. As the latter trail climbs, a scrub community of oaks and junipers ultimately gives way to a solid stand of pines, and the path grows faint as it crosses a thick mat of needles. The trail crests the divide behind Trap Mountain, and immediately reveals a fine view of eroded pillars on the south face of Hawk Peak. This vista accompanies the traveler throughout the descent into Frye Canyon.

On the valley floor, the trail passes a junction with a faint track that runs down Frye Canyon. The Round the Mountain trail makes its way northwest, crossing the mouths of several ravines that converge to form the main basin. The path follows one of these drainages upward for a time, then climbs onto fir-clad slopes where seeps nourish clumps of moss on the forest floor. The path runs upward through the pines to complete its ascent onto Ash Creek Ridge.

From this point, a spur trail runs northeast along the ridgetop toward The Pinnacles. The main trail sidehills westward across talus slopes dotted with aspens. After rounding a rocky spur, the path descends to a lofty overlook that offers a sweeping panorama of the Ash Creek valley. The trail then runs southward through a fir-dominated forest to reach the end of the Old Columbine Road. Travelers will have to walk 0.8 mile along this road to reach a locked gate that is accessible to vehicles.

37   ARCADIA TRAIL

General description: A day hike from Arcadia Campground to Shannon Park, 5 miles.
Best season: April-October.
Difficulty: Moderate west to east; moderately strenuous east to west.
Water availability: None.
Elevation gain: 500 feet.
Elevation loss: 2,800 feet.
Maximum elevation: 9,500 feet.
Topo map: Mount Graham.
Jurisdiction: Safford Ranger District, Coronado National Forest

Finding the trailhead: Take the Swift Trail (Arizona Highway 366) west for 11.5 miles to reach Shannon Park Campground. The trail leaves from a group site at the upper edge of the campground.

0.0   Shannon Park Campground.
1.0   Junction with Heliograph Peak spur trail. Keep going straight.
2.8   Junction with Noon Creek Ridge trail. Turn left.
4.5   Trail crosses streamcourse of Wet Canyon.
5.0   Arcadia Campground.

The trail: This trail runs from the Shannon Park Campground on the crest of the Pinaleño Mountains down a long and steady descent to reach Arcadia Campground, which is about halfway up the grade on Arizona Highway 366. A 1-mile spur trail runs to the top of Heliograph Peak near the upper end of the trail, offering a panoramic view of the southern Pinaleños amid the radio towers. The trail is well-maintained and is popular with day hikers and even a few hard-core mountain bikers. There is no water along the route, and there are few spots level enough to pitch a tent.

Beginning from the back of Shannon Park Campground, the trail first traverses a grassy basin interspersed with tall ponderosa pines. This is Shannon Park, and it bears the headwaters of Marijilda Canyon. Watch for stumps that indicate the logging activity that occurred here in the early 1900s. Look

Looking down into the Noon Creek Valley.

also for wild raspberries that ripen here in late summer. The trail runs eastward, gaining altitude gradually as the pines are replaced by Douglas-firs. After rounding the mountainside onto an east-facing slope, the trail zigzags upward at a steady clip. Stout aspens and firs tower above the trail, providing a deep shade and cooling the forest floor.

The trail soon reaches a junction with the Heliograph Peak spur trail, which sits atop a high saddle with excellent views of the Gila River basin and the forested ranges beyond it. This intersection marks the beginning of a steady and uninterrupted descent down the slopes of Heliograph Peak. The upper slopes are steep and rocky, and the trail often skirts above sheer dropoffs. Far below lies the canyon of Noon Creek, visible through gaps in the old-growth Douglas-firs. The path resumes its eastward course, descending steadily down a steep slope forested in a dense growth of conifers. A huge boulder split in half interrupts this forest, and a few graceful aspens grow around it. Beyond this, the pines dominate the forest once more.

The path reaches a junction with the Noon Creek Ridge trail, which runs out onto a rocky ridgetop on its way down to the Noon Creek picnic area. The main trail continues down the slopes to the south of it, and offers fine views of rugged outcrops on the south face of the ridge. As the trail loses altitude, live oaks dominate the south-facing slopes; pines and firs cloak those with a northern aspect. The trail finds its way into the moist bottoms of Wet Canyon, which it follows for the remaining distance to reach its endpoint at the Arcadia Campground.

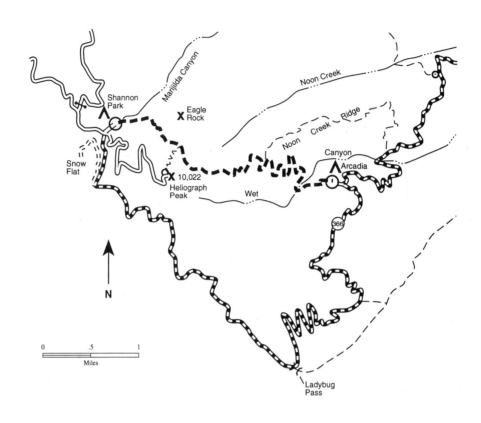

N

0   .5   1
Miles

---

38   *LADYBUG TRAIL*

General description: A day hike from Ladybug Pass to the Angle Orchard Road, 6.3 miles.
Best season: Year-round.
Difficulty: Moderate west to east; moderately strenuous east to west.
Water availability: None.
Elevation gain: 705 feet.
Elevation loss: 4,022 feet.
Maximum elevation: 8,760 feet.
Topo maps: Stockton Pass, Mount Graham.
Jurisdiction: Safford Ranger District, Coronado National Forest.

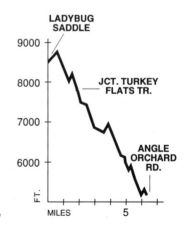

Looking south from Ladybug Peak over the tail of the Pinaleño Mountains.

Finding the trailhead: From U.S. Highway 191, follow Arizona Highway 366 west for 17 miles to the Ladybug Pass trailhead.

0.0	Ladybug Pass trailhead.
0.5	Junction with Ladybug Peak trail. Keep going straight.
0.6	Junction with Dutch Henry trail. Keep going straight.
1.9	Junction with Turkey Flats cutoff trail. Keep going straight.
4.8	Trail leaves the ridgeline and begins descent into Jacobson Canyon.
6.0	Trail crosses Jacobson Wash.
6.2	Junction with Adams Flat trail. Turn right.
6.3	Trail reaches Angle Orchard Road.

The trail: This trail, like the nearby peak, is named for its abundance of ladybug beetles, which cluster here in red and black masses during late spring. Herptophiles should note that there is also an amazing abundance of lizards along the route.

Like the Arcadia trail, this route can be accessed at both its upper and lower ends from Arizona Highway 366. Hikers with two cars can begin the hike at

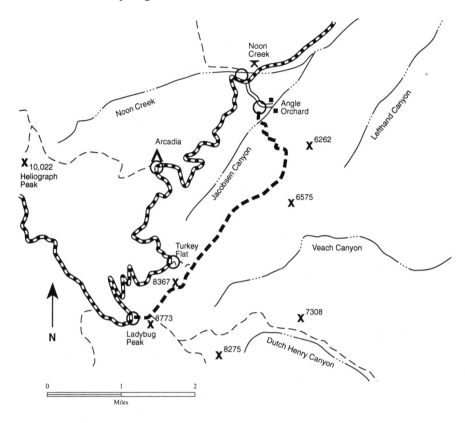

its upper end and run downhill all the way to the floor of Jacobson Wash. The Turkey Flats cutoff trail runs 0.3 mile from the highway to intersect the Ladybug trail near its midpoint, and allows less-ambitious hikers to take on either the upper or lower half of the trail as a day hike. There is no water along the trail, and there are few flat spots suitable for pitching a tent.

From Ladybug Pass, the trail switchbacks up the western slope of Ladybug Peak. It soon finds itself atop a rocky ridge that boasts excellent views to the south. Greasewood Mountain is in plain sight, rising in the midst of the low, arid summits that form the tail end of the Pinaleño Mountains. The trail then moves onto the heavily forested northern slope of Ladybug Peak, and a short spur trail climbs toward the summit. The main trail continues eastward, passing a junction with the Dutch Henry/Bear Canyon trail before beginning a series of downward switchbacks. The descent is arrested by a rocky pinnacle that rises sheer from the ridgetop. As the trail climbs across its northern slope, views of Heliograph Peak and Mount Graham present themselves.

The trail descends rather sharply to reach the next low saddle, where it meets the cutoff trail from Turkey Flats. From this junction, the descent continues down the ridgeline, which is shaded by a forest of Douglas-firs and pines.

Before long, a point of broken bedrock interrupts the ridge. The trail skirts its eastern side, where scattered trees allow excellent views of Veach Canyon and the pointed peaks of Veach Ridge rising beyond it. The Dos Cabezas Mountains rise in the hazy distance, far to the southeast.

The trail then climbs back to the ridgeline to resume its trek through the conifers. As the ridge levels off, the Douglas-firs are replaced by live oaks, with bear grass and manzanita in the understory. The pines are the next trees to fall away, to be replaced by juniper as the climate grows increasingly arid. The trail then climbs onto another rocky point that provides clear views of Heliograph Peak and Mount Graham, as well as the arid crest of Deadman Peak, rising far to the north.

The trail drops into a low saddle guarded by convex semi-domes of bedrock. Curving to the north, it begins to zigzag down through an isolated patch of pines and Douglas-firs. The route then abandons the main ridgeline and instead bears north toward a low nub. Lefthand Canyon is now, ironically, on the right-hand side, and the Angle Orchard can be seen on the floor of Jacobson Canyon, to the left. Upon reaching the nub, the path begins its long descent through the scrub to reach the valley floor. It crosses the shady bottoms of Jacobson Wash, then climbs onto a bare hilltop to meet the Adams Flat spur trail. Bear right to cover the final distance to the trail's terminus on the Angle Orchard Road.

39   DUTCH HENRY CANYON

General description: A day hike or backpack from Ladybug Pass to Dutch Henry Well, 7.5 miles.
Best season: September-May.
Difficulty: Moderately strenuous* west to east; strenuous* east to west.
Water availability: Dutch Henry Canyon may have water during the wet months.
Elevation gain: 425 feet.
Elevation loss: 5,082 feet.
Maximum elevation: 8,760 feet.
Topo maps: Gillespie Mountain, Stockton Pass.
Jurisdiction: Safford Ranger District, Coronado National Forest.
Finding the trailhead: The upper

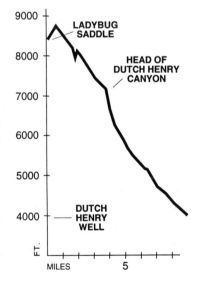

trailhead is at Ladybug Pass (see Trail 38, The Ladybug Trail). To reach the lower trailhead, take U.S. Highway 191 for 2 miles south of Artesia to the Dutch Henry Road (Forest Road 119). Follow the main road; bear left at the first set of corrals and park at the second one. Hike due east to strike the jeep track that leads the final mile to Dutch Henry Well.

0.0	Ladybug Pass. Follow the Ladybug trail.
0.5	Junction with Ladybug Peak trail. Keep going straight.
0.6	Junction with Dutch Henry trail. Turn right.
1.3	Junction with Bear Canyon trail. Bear left.
3.0	Trail crosses pass to enter Dutch Henry Canyon.
7.5	Dutch Henry Well trailhead.

The trail: This trail provides a long and often steep descent from Ladybug Saddle to the *bajadas*, or alluvial hills, at the southeastern edge of the Pinaleño Mountains. The trail is not always obvious as it descends Dutch Henry Canyon, but numerous cairns and splotches of orange paint on the rock mark the route. The lower trailhead is hard to find and requires a four-wheel-drive vehicle with wide tires that can negotiate the sandbars of Stockton Wash. Many hikers accessing the lower trailhead choose to stop at a windmill about a mile east of the trailhead and hike across Stockton Wash to reach Dutch Henry Well.

From Ladybug Pass, follow the Ladybug trail to a marked junction on the eastern slope of Ladybug Peak. Turn right onto the Dutch Henry trail, which

Huge boulders at the mouth of Dutch Henry Canyon.

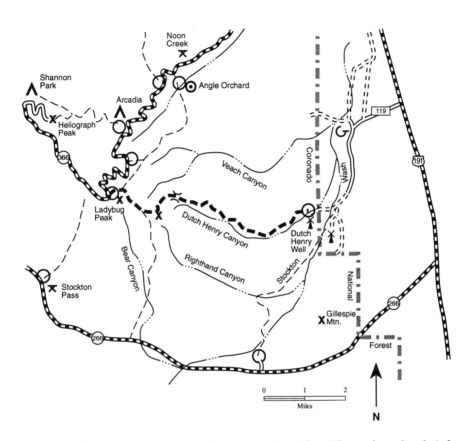

Noon
Creek
X

Shannon
Park

Arcadia

Angle Orchard

Heliograph
Peak

366

Veach Canyon

Coronado

119

191

Ladybug
Peak

G

Dutch Henry Canyon

Dutch
Henry
Well

Wash

Righthand Canyon

Bear Canyon

Stockton

National

Stockton
Pass

Gillespie
X Mtn.

266

266

Forest

0   1   2
Miles

N

descends along the crest of a southeast-running ridge. The path makes brief
forays onto the northern slopes whenever the ridgetop steepens a bit. This ridge
is covered with parklike glades that are dotted by stands of pine, Douglas-fir,
and Gambel oak. After a mile, the trail reaches a second junction at the foot
of a buff-colored outcrop. The Bear Canyon trail drops away to the south, while
the Dutch Henry trail descends onto the north slope of the ridge.

The forest thickens here and is dominated by moisture-loving Douglas-firs.
A damp swale holds a grove of bigtooth maples, after which the trail threads
its way across a slope ribbed with bladelike outcrops of stone. There are good
views across Veach Canyon here, with Deadman Peak and Mount Graham
peeking above its far slopes. Having negotiated the rocks with some steep ups
and downs, the path levels for a short distance. It then zigzags down a precipi-
tous slope to reach a saddle above the head of Dutch Henry Canyon.

The trail drops into the canyon, which is narrow and steep at its upper end.
The canyon floor soon widens out, and the path sidehills onto a bluff top above
the north bank of the streamcourse. Atop this miniature ridge are level
savannahs dotted with ancient oaks spreading canopies. This area is fine habitat for Coues white-tailed deer, and also makes a good camping spot for

travelers on overnight trips. As the trail proceeds eastward, the ridgetop falls away and the path zigzags downward. Prickly pear cacti are abundant in the drier spots, and clumps of bear grass and sotol dot the rocky grasslands. The trail weaves among huge boulders and domes of gneiss, and scrubby oaks are scattered among the stones.

The streamcourse swings northeast upon emerging from the mountains, and the trail follows its north bank. The path becomes well-trodden by local cattle that congregate in the vicinity of Dutch Henry Well. The trek ends as the path crosses the streamcourse beside a windmill marking Dutch Henry Spring.

40   ASH CREEK

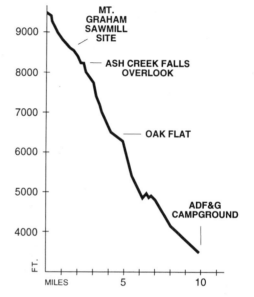

General description: A day hike to Ash Creek Falls, 2.5 miles, or backpack to Cluff Ponds, 9.8 miles. See map on page 134.
Best season: May-October.
Difficulty: Moderately strenuous* south to north; strenuous* north to south.
Water availability: Ash Creek carries water year-round.
Elevation gain: 100 feet.
Elevation loss: 5,990 feet.
Maximum elevation: 9,490 feet.
Topo maps: Webb Peak (inc.), Shingle Mill Mountain, Thatcher.
Jurisdiction: Safford Ranger District, Coronado National Forest.
Finding the trailhead: Take U.S. Highway 191 south from Safford to reach a junction with the Swift Trail (Arizona Highway 366). Follow this road for 29 miles to reach the trailhead, located across the road from the Columbine Ranger Station. To reach the lower trailhead, take Main Street south from downtown Pima; this street ultimately becomes Cluff Ranch Road. After 2 miles, bear left at signs for the Cluff Ranch Wildlife Area, and take another left at the ranch headquarters. The Ash Creek road leaves this road 1 mile past the headquarters, and a trailhead and camping area are 1.2 miles up this road.

0.0   Ash Creek trailhead.
0.5   Junction with Webb Peak trail. Bear right.
1.3   Site of old Mount Graham sawmill.

1.7	Junction with Slick Rock horse detour. Foot traffic bear right.
2.2	Slick Rock.
2.4	Slick Rock horse detour rejoins trail.
2.5	Ash Creek Falls overlook.
3.0	Junction with Shingle Mill trail. Turn right.
4.4	Oak Flat.
7.1	Trail joins old jeep track.
9.8	Jeep track arrives at Department of Fish and Game campground.

The trail: This popular and well-trod trail runs down the northeast side of the Pinaleño Range along one of the few permanent watercourses in southern Arizona. The upper basin is dominated by coniferous forest and is separated from the lower basin by Ash Creek Falls. This 200-foot cascade can be viewed from the trail. It is the largest perennial waterfall in the southern part of the state. There is a lush forest of hardwoods below it, and the bottom part of the trail follows an old jeep road down through mesquite bosque to reach the Cluff Ponds area.

The trail begins by dropping through a narrow gulch cloaked thickly in young Douglas-firs. It passes an old log shanty on its way to the Ash Creek bottoms, where it joins an old roadbed that descends from the Old Columbine

The Pinnacles as seen from Oak Flats.

Civilian Conservation Corps (CCC) camp. Follow this road along the eastern bank of the stream. The trail makes a short-lived crossing to meet the Webb Peak trail, then returns to the east side of Ash Creek.

After making an eastward jog to traverse a side valley, the path drops into the open meadows where the Mount Graham sawmill once stood. This sawmill was a primary source of lumber for the CCC construction projects of the 1930s; it also supplied timber products for surrounding communities. Forested ridges crowd the edges of this narrow vale, through which the brook wanders lazily down a shallow gradient.

After leaving the sawmill site, a detour for horses climbs away to the left to avoid the treacherous Slick Rock formation. A footpath sticks to the streamside, crossing the brook frequently as the ravine narrows. A tiny waterfall drops into a rounded pool, and soon thereafter the stream slides down a tilted scarp of bedrock in a watery sheet. The path is cribbed into the bedrock here with the assistance of metal grates; watch your footing. Just beyond this point, the horse detour rejoins the foot trail. Thus bolstered, the wide track makes its way to a rocky overlook of Ash Creek Falls. This graceful veil of water drops more than 100 feet across cliffs of metamorphic rock.

The trail descends steadily to a saddle at the base of a minor peak, where it meets the Shingle Mill trail. The Ash Creek trail then drops eastward through a series of tortuous curves, descending at a rapid clip to reach the valley floor. It then resumes its streamside wanderings, crossing the creek on numerous occasions as it makes its way through a mix of pines and hardwoods. The pools in this part of the stream are home to the native Apache trout. Cliffs loom above the west bank.

One last stream crossing offers fine views of The Pinnacles before the creek shoots through a tight spot and runs onto Oak Flats. The surface water disappears here, and numerous copses of Gambel oak interrupt the pines. The trail fades as it wanders through hardwood bottomlands bordered by stony heights. A sheer face of metamorphic rock soon rises to the east, marking the lower end of Oak Flats as the valley narrows and steepens.

As a rocky gorge blocks the way, the trail climbs eastward onto a rounded ridgetop covered in oak scrub. The path drops into a side valley for a time, then switchbacks down a foot-pounding grade that lands the traveler on the valley floor. Here, a cairn marks its intersection with a jeep trail that runs the rest of the way to the Cluff Ponds. The mountains turn to foothills, and these in turn degenerate into a series of sloping mesas covered in mesquite and prickly pear cactus. Look backward for majestic parting views of the Pinaleños, which appear particularly jagged from this angle. The trek ends at a camping area about a mile above the Cluff Ponds, in the Cluff Ranch State Wildlife Preserve.

General description: A backpack from the Gila Valley to the Ash Creek trail, 8.4 miles.

Best season: Year-round.

Difficulty: Moderately strenuous*.

Water availability: None.

Elevation gain: 4,280 feet.

Maximum elevation: 7,670 feet.

Topo maps: Shingle Mill Mountain, Thatcher.

Jurisdiction: Safford Ranger District, Coronado National Forest.

Finding the trailhead: Take Main Street south from the town of Pima. This paved road turns west, then angles southeast past an airstrip. As it curves westward again, Forest Road 681 takes off to the left. Follow this primitive road for 5 miles to the spot where the trail (Forest Road 35) departs.

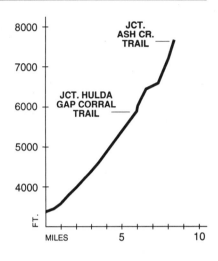

An old tramway tower in Upper Shingle Mill Canyon.

40 Ash Creek
41 Shingle Mill Trail

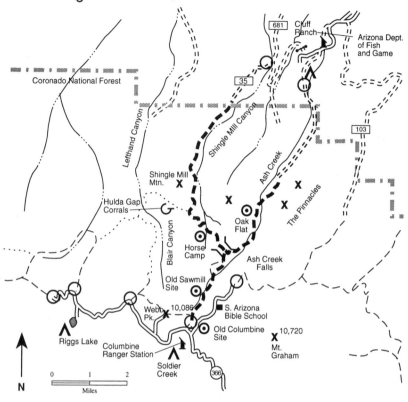

0.0	Jeep trail #35 leaves FR 681.
5.8	Junction with Hulda Gap Corrals trail. Bear left.
6.1	Horse Camp.
8.4	Junction with Ash Creek trail.

The trail: This route follows old jeep trails into the northern end of the Pinaleños. It begins on a primitive road that winds upward across rounded *bajadas* around the mountains. Creosote bush and mesquite gradually give way to prickly pear cactus as the track gains altitude. The massive inner peaks of the Pinaleños are reflected in the north by the distant Blue Mountains. At the national forest boundary, the road becomes a rocky jeep trail that makes its way to the edge of a steep dropoff overlooking Shingle Mill Canyon.

As the canyon penetrates the mountains, the rounded bulk of Shingle Mill Mountain guards its western entrance; a much craggier summit that bears no name stands sentinel to the east. The trail climbs into desert grasslands on the northern slopes of Shingle Mill Mountain, but these soon give way to a desert

upland community of scrubby oak, juniper, and manzanita as the trail continues upward. The track fades on several occasions as it crosses gulches choked
with enormous boulders. In general, each tricky spot marks a jog to the east,
and the track becomes apparent just beyond the boulders.

After rounding Shingle Mill Mountain, the trail descends to the floor of the
canyon. The first ponderosa and Chihuahua pines make their appearances
here, and a spur trail runs westward, climbing into the saddle that holds the
Hulda Gap Corrals. From this junction, the Shingle Mill trail continues along
the west side of the wash for a short time, then crosses it and climbs up the
ridge to the east. It reaches the crest just south of a cone-shaped point, then
turns upward to follow the ridgeline for a short distance. There are fine views
of the nameless ridge to the east, with its crags projecting high above Shingle
Mill Canyon.

The trail crosses a ridge shelf, then wanders onto its eastern slope. It passes
an old tram tower that once serviced a sawmill in Shingle Mill Canyon. The
roadbed runs level for a time, then climbs again around folds in the hillside.
At the top of the grade, the trail ends at a high saddle containing a junction with
the Ash Creek trail, Trail 40 in this book.

42   BLAIR CANYON

General description: A wilderness route down
a ridgeline above Blair Canyon, 2.8 miles.
Best season: May-October.
Difficulty: Moderate** south to north; strenu-
ous** north to south.
Water availability: None.
Elevation loss: 2,850 feet.
Maximum elevation: 9,270 feet.
Topo map: Webb Peak.
Jurisdiction: Safford Ranger District, Coronado
National Forest.

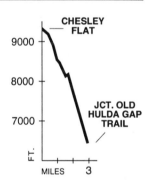

Finding the trailhead: South of Safford off U.S.
Highway 191, take Swift Trail (Arizona Highway 366) 33 miles into the
Pinaleños to reach Chesley Flat. The track runs north from the information
plaque along the edge of the meadow.

0.0   Chesley Flat trailhead.
0.2   Junction with Webb Peak trail. Bear left.
1.0   Trail peters out and becomes a map and compass route.
2.8   Junction with abandoned Hulda Gap Corrals trail.

The trail: This trail is maintained only for the distance that it covers in the
upper reaches of Lefthand Canyon. Once the trail makes it to the ridgeline,
it becomes extremely faint and difficult to follow. At its lower terminus, it

Webb Peak bares a rocky shoulder above Blair Canyon.

connects with two equally unmaintained and primitive routes at a series of 1950s-era trail signs that are easy to miss.

The trail begins in Chesley Flats, a grassy meadow where the Chesley family built their summer cabin in the 1890s. A roadside marker indicates the spot. The trail hugs the eastern edge of the clearing as it runs down a shallow grade. Just inside the forest, it reaches a marked junction with the Webb Peak trail. Bear left and descend into Lefthand Canyon, a shallow gulch wooded in Douglas-fir and quaking aspen. The path crosses the valley floor and begins to sidehill across the eastern wall of the valley. When it ultimately reaches the ridgetop, travelers can jockey for position to get a fine view of Blair Canyon, and the sheer cliff extending northward from Webb Peak that overlooks it.

From this point on, the trail exists only as faint vestiges that have escaped the wear of erosion and encroaching brush. The route follows the ridgetop down through a dense growth of aspens and locusts that sprang up following an extensive fire in 1973. After rounding a high knob, the pines return in force and the loose-knit forest allows excellent vistas of the surrounding country. To the north, the summits of the Santa Teresa Range rise to graceful points above the surrounding flats. The old trail sticks to the ridgeline for the remainder of the steep descent, and a couple of old trail signs mark its junction with the Lefthand Canyon and Hulda Gap Corral trails.

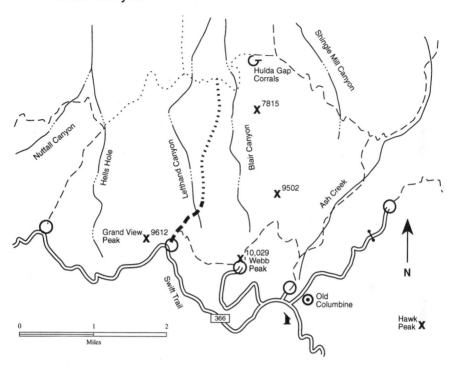

---

43 *JOHNS CANYON*

General description: A day hike along Johns Canyon Ridge, 6.8 miles.

Best season: March-November.

Difficulty: Moderate** southeast to northwest; moderately strenuous** northwest to southeast.

Water availability: None.

Elevation loss: 3,360 feet.

Maximum elevation: 8,600 feet.

Topo maps: Blue Jay Peak, Tripp Canyon.

Jurisdiction: Safford Ranger District, Coronado National Forest.

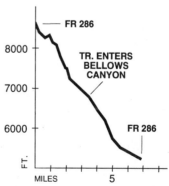

Finding the trailhead: Tripp Canyon Road leaves U.S. Highway 191 just north of Pima. Follow this improved, fair-weather road for 20 miles across the flats, following signs for Tripp Canyon. As Forest Road 286, this road climbs to the top of West Peak. (The last 2 miles require four-wheel-drive.) A jeep trail splits away to the right near the top of the peak; the hike starts here.

0.0	Trailhead.
0.2	Junction with old Colter Spring trail. Bear right.
0.6	Several unmarked junctions. Bear right.
3.4	Trail enters Bellows Canyon.
5.5	Trail adopts old jeep trail, #5540.
6.2	Track crosses Johns Canyon wash.
6.8	Trail reaches Tripp Canyon Road.

The trail: This little-used trail makes a nice day trip in the northern end of the Pinaleño Mountains. Parties that have two vehicles can leave one at the mouth of Johns Canyon and drive the other one to the top of the grade, thus avoiding uphill hiking entirely. The trail is often very hard to follow, and map and compass skills are a must for travelers who attempt this route. Once the trail makes its way onto Johns Canyon Ridge, the route-finding problems disappear. A tangle of jeep trails surrounds the camping area at the trail's lower terminus, making it difficult to approach the route from below.

Begin on the Blue Jay Ridge trail (#314), a two-rut jeep trail departing from Forest Road 286 near the summit of West Peak. This jeep track passes immediately through a cut in the hillside, whereupon a path marked by cairns drops downslope to the right. This is the Johns Canyon trail; it switchbacks down the slope, passing through country that was heavily burned in 1973.

In short order, the path reaches a trail sign that marks the departure point of the now-defunct Colter Spring trail. Turn right, following cairns and flagging as the trail heads southwest to a flattened saddle. A fallen signpost indicates the Durkee Ridge spur, while the Johns Canyon route drops onto the north side of the ridge to enter a stand of tall pines.

After a brief return to the ridgeline, the trail does something unexpected: it drops from the ridge crest down the southwestern slope of the hill, and finally runs out onto the much lower Johns Canyon Ridge. A bulky hilltop rises 400 feet above its crest, a distinctive feature that identifies the proper ridge for travelers who become confused at this point. The trail follows this lower ridge to the base of this hilltop, then skirts north to avoid the point, descending all the while. As the path negotiates this obstacle, it traverses steep terrain and is often cribbed with cunning stonework above dropoffs. Chollas and clumps of bear grass are scattered amid the scrubby pines and oaks, and openings in the woods allow fine views of the steep country surrounding Johns Canyon.

Beyond the bulky hill, the trail returns to the sinuous crest of Johns Canyon Ridge at a low saddle, then follows a barbed-wire fence along the south slope of the ridge to reach a similar depression. Travelers can take in sweeping views down 2E Wash, featuring the lonely expanse of the Sulphur Springs Valley and the rugged eastern front of the Galiuros beyond it. The trail then swings northward into the formless foothills, and the woodland closes in around the trail. It passes between two round knobs to enter the Bellows Canyon drainage, then swings south to take in the folds and draws that form the head of this valley. The trail sticks to the western slope of the drainage as it descends toward the canyon floor through an oak-juniper woodland.

43   Johns Canyon

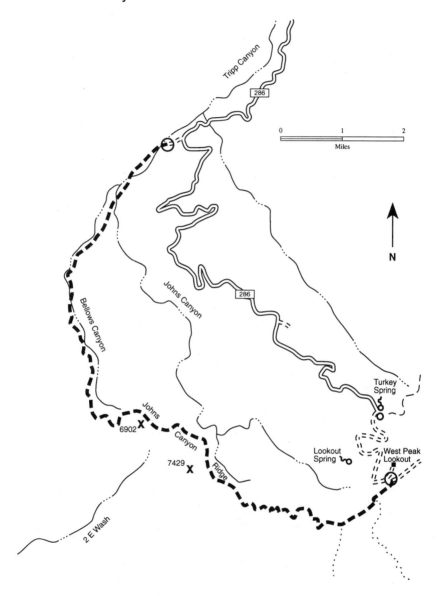

As the path nears the bottom of the grade, a rib of exposed bedrock rises from the hillside ahead to break the monotony of wooded slopes. As if sensing that this formation is an impassable obstacle, the trail drops to the canyon floor and begins to cross the wash repeatedly. The pathway ultimately becomes an extremely rough jeep track. It follows the floor of Bellows Canyon to its confluence with Johns Canyon, then continues along the bolstered streamcourse to reach a primitive camping area beside Tripp Canyon Road.

General description: A day hike that makes a circuit around Blue Jay Peak, 3.2 miles overall.

Best season: April-October.

Difficulty: Moderate*.

Water availability: None.

Elevation gain: 160 feet.

Elevation loss: 1,090 feet.

Maximum elevation: 8,660 feet.

Topo maps: Blue Jay Peak (inc.), Tripp Canyon (inc.).

Jurisdiction: Safford Ranger District, Coronado National Forest.

Finding the trailhead: Tripp Canyon Road leaves U.S. Highway 191 just north of Pima. Follow this improved, fair-weather road for 20 miles across the flats, following signs for Tripp Canyon. As Forest Road 286, this road climbs to the top of West Peak. (The last 2 miles require four-wheel-drive.) A jeep trail splits away to the right near the top of the peak; the hike starts here.

A granite outcrop on Blue Jay Peak.

44   Blue Jay Ridge

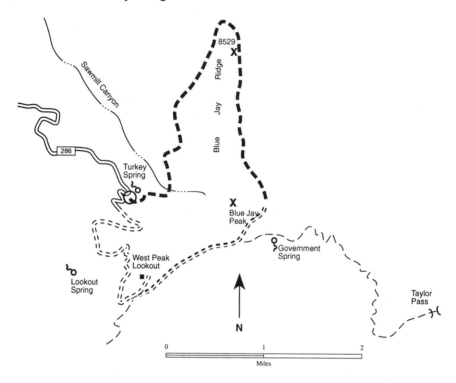

0.0	Jeep trail leaves FR 286.
0.1	Junction with Johns Canyon trail. Stay on jeep road.
0.7	Junction with Taylor Pass route. Bear left.
1.1	Jeep road ends, trail becomes a footpath.
2.0	Trail drops from Blue Jay Ridge.
3.2	Trail meets FR 286 at Turkey Spring.

The trail: This little-known trail forms a nice day loop around Blue Jay Peak, in the remote northern end of the Pinaleño Range. The trek begins near the top of West Peak as a two-rut jeep trail. It descends on a southerly bearing through open country. The summit of Blue Jay Peak burned in an intense forest fire in 1973, and the resulting destruction of forest now allows fine views of the Galiuro Mountains. A few larger pines were able to survive the blaze, but at the time of this writing the vegetation was mainly bracken fern and woolly mullein. These plants put on a fiery display of yellows and oranges as they prepare to shed their leaves in late October.

After a mile, the faint Clark Peak trail descends along an overgrown road grade, and the Blue Jay Ridge trail rounds the mountainside high above Taylor Pass. From this point, the jagged ridges of the central Pinaleños hover across a deep gulf of air. As the trail draws even with Blue Jay Peak, the jeep trail

141

changes to an overgrown footpath lined with boulders. This path continues north across an open slope sprinkled with outcrops of granite. It then switchbacks down the spur ridge to the north, and infrequent trail maintenance has resulted in Gambel oak and New Mexico locust saplings rising from the trailbed. The trail passes an enormous face of solid granite, then drops past a succession of pine-clad saddles before running onto the eastern slope of the ridge. Here, low-growing scrub offers a final view of the central Pinaleños.

Upon reaching the next ridgetop saddle, a trail sign marks the spot where the trail heads sharply south as it descends onto the western face of the ridge. The path crosses the steep and rocky west face of Blue Jay Peak, bearing for Turkey Spring. A mixed forest of Gambel oaks and enormous ponderosa pines closes around the trail, although a handful of openings in the canopy provide glimpses of surrounding country. These vistas are of nearby pine ridges dotted with granite outcrops, and the distant peaks of the Santa Teresa Mountains rise to the northwest. The trail maintains a steady descent all the way to Turkey Spring, where it meets FR 286 at the point where it becomes impassable to two-wheel-drive vehicles.

SAGUARO NATIONAL PARK
AND SURROUNDINGS

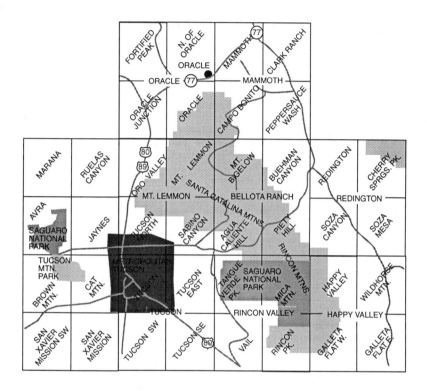

Saguaro National Park encompasses two extensive tracts of land on the outskirts of Tucson, protecting these outstanding examples of the Sonoran Desert cactus community from the ravages of land developers. Here, the mighty saguaro reigns above a rich assemblage of desert plants and animals. Wildflowers put on spectacular displays of color in early April, covering the desert *bajadas* and mountain slopes with bright blossoms. Wildlife within the park has lost its fear of humans; the area provides a unique opportunity for viewing desert animals in their natural habitat. Both units of the national park have visitor centers, nature trails, and extensive day-hiking opportunities.

The Rincon Mountain unit lies on the eastern outskirts of Tucson, and encompasses the lofty Rincon Range. The *bajadas* at its feet provide a network of hiking trails for day trips into the cactus lowlands, while an extensive system of backpacking trails provides access to the crest of the range. The popular Manning Camp area, on the crown of Mica Mountain, provides a piney oasis from the summer heat of the valley floor. Deep snow may be encountered in the high country from December through February. Backpackers must carry a free permit and camp only in designated campsites. There is an entrance fee for the Cactus Forest Scenic Drive, and the park's only campground is located here. Private land developers have closed off public access to the Madrona Canyon Ranger Station. The Forest Service administers the eastern trailheads into the Rincons, as well as the neighboring Little Rincon Mountains. They are accessed via an improved gravel road that may be impassable following rainstorms.

The Tucson Mountain unit is west of town, shielded from the city by the rugged Tucson Mountains. The geology here is so confused that scientists have named the formation the "Tucson Mountain Chaos." This volcanic range is too low to create rainfall, and as a result it is clothed entirely in sun-baked desert. Backcountry camping is not permitted in this part of the national park, although there several fine day-hiking trails.

To the south of this second unit is Tucson Mountain Park, an extensive municipal preserve set aside by visionary Tucsonians to protect the biological and recreational resources of the southern Tucson Mountains. It is administered by Pima County, and is crisscrossed with old mining roads that now serve as hiking and mountain biking trails. A crude map of the trail system is available at the Red Hills Visitor Center in Saguaro National Park. Other features of Tucson Mountain Park include an automobile campground as well as the Arizona–Sonora Desert Museum. This excellent museum offers a comprehensive look at the natural history of the Sonoran Desert, and includes zoo where desert inhabitants roam enclosures that are built to mimic their natural surroundings.

45   CACTUS FOREST COMPLEX

General description: A network of day-hiking trails in the low desert of Saguaro National Park.
Best season: October-April.
Difficulty: Easy to moderate.
Water availability: A tank at the junction of the Carrillo and Three Tanks trails has water year-round.
Maximum elevation: 3,800 feet (Three Tanks trail).
Map: A complete map of these trails (including mileages) is available free of charge from the visitor center.
Jurisdiction: Saguaro National Park, Rincon Mountain Unit.
Finding the trailheads: On the eastern edge of Tucson, there are trailheads at the ends of Speedway Boulevard, Wentworth Road, and Broadway Boulevard, as well as along Cactus Forest Scenic Drive within the park itself.

The trails: This intricate network of well-maintained trails crisscrosses the lowlands and foothills of Saguaro National Park's northwestern corner. There is a large number of trailheads to choose from. Hikers who start from Cactus Forest Scenic Drive will have to pay an entrance fee; this is not

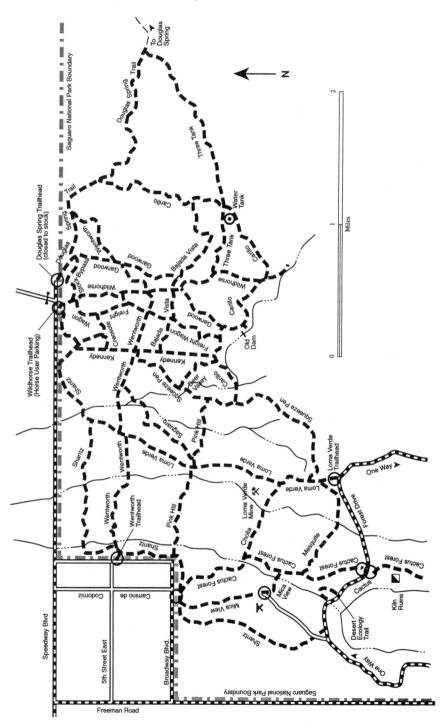

Saguaros along the Shantz Trail.

required for the other trailheads. The Douglas Spring trailhead (at the end of Speedway Boulevard) is notorious for break-ins; hikers should always lock their cars with the windows shut and all valuables safely stowed out of sight. The Cactus Forest is open for day hiking and horse use only; overnight camping is not permitted here.

This area offers a pristine example of Sonoran Desert vegetation, highlighted by an astonishing variety of cacti. The star of the show is the enormous saguaro, which grows to the height of a small tree and may live more than 200 years. This amazing plant is perfectly adapted to its desert environment. Its leaves, the major source of water loss in most plants, have been modified into spines. Photosynthesis occurs in the spongy trunk, which is deeply pleated so that it can expand like an accordion to hold more water. The whole structure is held aloft by a ring of woody rods, which lends rigidity while still allowing the flesh around it to expand or contract. The area is also home to several species of cholla and prickly pear; barrel, Christmas, hedgehog, and pincushion cacti are also spotted here. The green-barked palo verde and the spiny ocotillo also do much of their photosynthesis in their trunks and only bear leaves for a brief part of the year.

This rich desert environment provides sanctuary for a diverse and abundant assemblage of wildlife. Rodents and reptiles of all sorts sally forth from their burrows to forage on the desert floor. Herds of javelina and packs of coyotes scavenge along dry washes during morning and evening. During daytime, the desert belongs to the birds. Coveys of Gambel's quail scurry among the shrubs of the desert floor. Cactus wrens, flickers, Gila woodpeckers, and phainopeplas are often spotted among the shrubs and cacti, while raptors soar on thermals overhead. Move slowly and quietly and stay alert; under the protection afforded by national park status, the original inhabitants may show themselves with uncommon boldness.

The landscape covered by the Cactus Forest complex can be divided into three plant communities. The lowlands of the northwestern corner hold mostly low shrubs; a riparian scrub community grows along the washes there. This community is dominated by thorny shrubs such as mesquite and palo verde. Creosote bush is also fairly common, while cacti are relatively sparse. A broad band of well-drained *bajadas* leads to the foothills. These aprons of alluvial debris are covered in cactus thorn scrub of amazing diversity. The far-eastern trails of the Cactus Forest complex climb into the foothills plant community. Here, outcrops of bedrock rise from the thin desert soil to provide platforms for cacti and other desert shrubs. Jojoba makes its appearance here, and such wildflowers as brittlebrush and California poppy provide explosions of color in early spring.

There are several features of historical note scattered throughout the area. The Loma Verde Mine, located on the Loma Verde trail just north of the Cholla trail, was worked for copper in the early 1900s. It produced quantities of high-grade ore, but was abandoned when the copper market collapsed. The remains of an old lime kiln stand along the section of the Cactus Forest trail that bisects the scenic drive. Limestone caliche, the hardpan that underlies the desert soil here, was dug up and superheated to form lime, used in the making of concrete. The firing of the kiln demanded a great deal of firewood, which accounts for the current sparseness of mesquite and palo verde near the old kiln foundations. An old concrete dam beside the Carrillo trail, just east of its junction with the Garwood trail, was used to impound runoff so that ranchers could water their cattle. Finally, a deep, metal stock tank stands at the junction of the Carrillo and Three Tanks trails. This tank collects water from a spring and supported a thriving population of goldfish (of all things) when this book was written.

46   DOUGLAS SPRING

General description: A backpack from the national park boundary to the Chiminea Canyon trail, 10.2 miles.
Best season: September–May.
Difficulty: Moderately strenuous*.
Water availability: Douglas Spring and Grass Shack Spring run seasonally.
Elevation gain: 3,521 feet.
Elevation loss: 975 feet.
Maximum elevation: 6,100 feet.

Topo maps: Tanque Verde Peak, Mica Mountain, *Rincon Mountains*.
Jurisdiction: Saguaro National Park, Rincon Mountain Unit.
Finding the trailhead: In Tucson, take Speedway Boulevard east all the way to its end to find the trailhead.

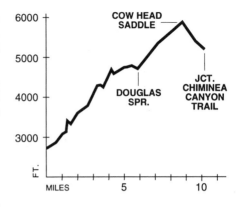

0.0   Trailhead.
0.2   Junction with Wentworth trail. Stay left.
2.3   Junction with Three Tanks trail. Bear left.
2.5   Junction with spur path to Bridal Wreath Falls. Stay left.
5.8   Douglas Spring camping area.
8.8   Cow Head Saddle. Junction with Tanque Verde Ridge trail. Keep going straight.
10.2   Junction with Chiminea Canyon trail.

The trail: This trail follows the northern border of Saguaro National Park, climbing steadily through the foothills of the Rincon Mountains. It begins in a typical Sonoran desert community of mixed cactus and desert scrub, climbs through high desert grasslands, and winds up in oak-pine woodlands at Cow Head Saddle. Here it links up with the Tanque Verde Ridge trail, which backpackers can follow all the way to Manning Camp on the Mica Mountain massif. Alternately, travelers might choose to drop down into Chiminea Canyon to camp at Grass Shack Spring.

The trail begins on the desert flats at the end of Speedway Boulevard, and travels through a diverse community of desert plants highlighted by saguaro, palo verde, cholla, and prickly pear. It runs east to the mouth of an arid draw. The Douglas Spring trail meets the Wentworth trail here, then climbs into the draw. The cactus-clad hills are interrupted here and there by low cliffs and outcrops of banded gneiss, and ocotillos and jojoba bushes soon become commonplace along the path. After the initial grade, the trail passes through a series of tiny basins, and a diverse assortment of desert birds give voice to territorial songs and warning calls. At the top of the escarpment is a rolling plateau, and the cacti give way to desert grasslands punctuated by an occasional sotol.

Soon after meeting the Three Tanks trail, the Douglas Spring route reaches an unmarked junction on the bluffs above a dry wash. The main trail seems to veer to the right and follow the wash, but this track is merely a dead-end spur that covers the short distance to Bridal Wreath Falls. Following wet weather, a thin trickle of water drops 20 feet from an overhanging sill to form the waterfall. Meanwhile, the main trail runs straight ahead from the unmarked junction, crossing the wash and following the crest of a low finger ridge that runs eastward. The path soon begins another bout of climbing across grassy *bajadas* overlooking Redington Pass and the Santa Catalina Mountains.

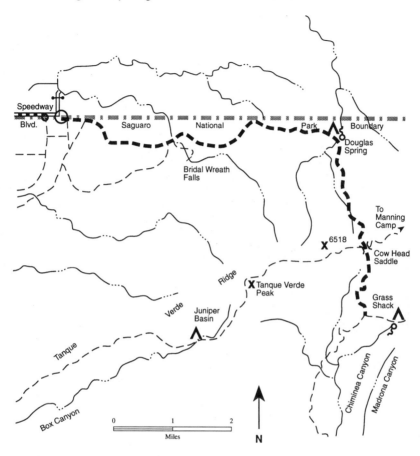

About 2 miles short of Douglas Spring, the ascent eases as the trail wanders among rolling hills. Junipers and clumps of bear grass frequently interrupt the grasslands, and there are fine views of Mica Mountain. Helens Dome is the rocky outcrop that rises from its crest. The trail then drops into a shallow drainage to reach Douglas Spring, with its campsites scattered along the western bank of a stony streamcourse. The spring is unreliable, and often dries up by midsummer and stays dry through autumn.

From the Douglas Spring camping area, the trail crosses the wash and follows a grassy hilltop southward. The Chiva Fire burned here in 1989, killing the shrubs and renewing the dominance of the grasses. The trail soon enters a maze of tight ravines as it makes its final ascent to Cow Head Saddle. A few piñon and ponderosa pines lend shade to the trail as it approaches the divide, where it meets the Tanque Verde Ridge trail.

The Douglas Spring Trail offers fine vistas of the Santa Catalinas.

GRASS SHACK OPTION

The Douglas Spring trail continues south from Cow Head Saddle, descending gently into a broad basin filled with oak scrub and spiny lechuguilla. After 1.4 miles, the trail terminates at a junction with the Chiminea Canyon route (officially called the Manning Camp trail). Follow this trail eastward for 0.6 mile, crossing a low and rocky ridgetop to reach Grass Shack Spring. This spring rises from the course of Chiminea Canyon where a band of gneiss forces underground water to the surface. The spring is unreliable and, like Douglas Spring, it is likely to be dry during midsummer and autumn. A designated camping area is located beneath the spreading canopies of evergreen oaks and ponderosa pines beside the spring.

General description: A backpack from the Javelina picnic area to Manning Camp, 14 miles.

Best season: March-November.

Difficulty: Moderately strenuous*.

Water availability: Manning Camp (at the end of the trail) has a permanent spring.

Elevation gain: 6,197 feet.

Elevation loss: 1,397 feet.

Maximum elevation: 8,100 feet.

Topo maps: Tanque Verde Peak, Mica Mountain, *Rincon Mountains.*

Jurisdiction: Saguaro National Park, Rincon Mountain Unit.

Finding the trailhead: From the visitor center, take Cactus Forest Scenic Drive to the Javelina Picnic Area. The trail departs from its southeastern edge.

0.0	Trail leaves Javelina Picnic Area.
0.7	Trail climbs onto the toe of Tanque Verde Ridge.
5.9	Juniper Basin Camping Area.
7.8	Short spur trail runs to summit of Tanque Verde Peak. Through traffic bear left.
10.2	Cow Head Saddle. Junction with Douglas Spring trail. Keep going straight ahead.
13.2	Junction with North Slope Trail. Bear right.
13.3	Junction with Fire Loop trail. Bear right.
14.0	Manning Camp.

The trail: This trail offers a long, arid journey along the spine of Tanque Verde Ridge, which projects westward from the main mass of the Rincon Mountains. Views are sweeping along the entire route, and wildlife may be encountered at any time. Camping is allowed in designated sites in Juniper Basin and at Manning Camp at trail's end. Backpack-

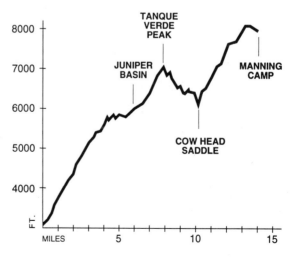

ers who wish to stay overnight between these two areas can drop from Cow Head Saddle to either Douglas Spring, to the north, or Grass Shack Spring,

Rugged walls of gneiss gird the flanks of Tanque Verde Peak.

to the south. There is no water along the route, although side trips to Douglas or Grass Shack springs might yield water on a seasonal basis, and there is a permanent spring at Manning Camp. The Chiva Fire of 1989 damaged the section of trail between Tanque Verde Peak and Cow Head Saddle, and as of this writing it was a bit tricky to stay on the route in this area.

The trail begins at Javelina Picnic Area and runs southward through broken country of rock and cactus. Saguaros rise everywhere around the trail, and teddy bear chollas, Englemann prickly pears, and ocotillos are all well-represented here. The path soon climbs onto the toe of Tanque Verde Ridge, revealing views of Rincon Peak and Box Canyon to the south, as well as of the massive Santa Catalinas to the north. The trail then works onto the northern slope of the ridge, where it climbs in fits and starts through an arid landscape. The cacti are fast disappearing by the time the trail returns to the ridgeline, but impressive views stretch away on all sides to compensate for the reduction in plant diversity.

The saguaros disappear as the trail climbs above 5,000 feet, to be replaced by a high desert grassland dotted with clumps of bear grass, sotol, and lechuguilla. Far below, vehicles crawl like sparkling insects across the sprawling grid of metropolitan Tucson. Live oaks and junipers crowd in clumps as the ridge resolves itself into a collection of rounded hillocks. Upon approaching one of the larger hilltops, the trail turns southeast and drops into Juniper Basin.

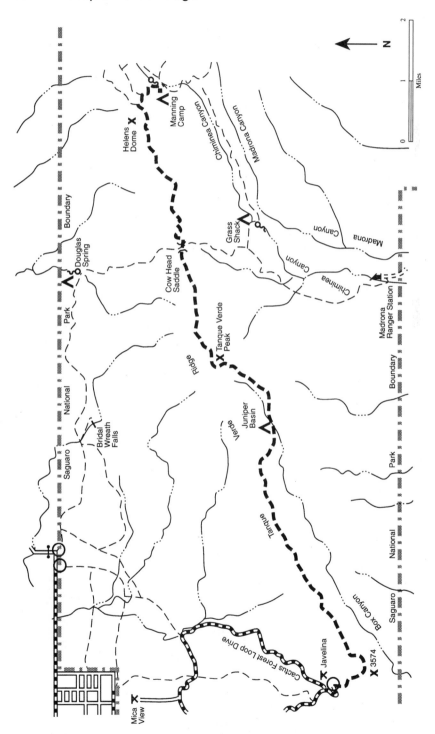

It soon crosses a bedrock streamcourse that may hold water following rains, then resumes its climb across the hummocky valley. Unexpectedly, the path breaks out of the scrub at the Juniper Basin camping area, set amid the piñon pines and alligator junipers that crowd a sandy wash.

The trail follows this wash uphill, becoming faint and hard to follow in some spots. The basin is a favorite haunt of javelinas, which run in herds through the scrubby trees, foraging on pine nuts and insects. At the upper end of the basin, the trail seeks the southern rim, which it follows toward Tanque Verde Peak. Near the summit, picturesque rock formations interrupt the wooded slopes of the mountain. A spur path about 100 yards long leads to the top of Tanque Verde Peak, where a register allows visitors to sign in and record their impressions. A little bouldering is required to gain the actual summit. From this lofty perch, fantastic views stretch in all directions. Rincon Peak rises regally to the southeast, with the Dragoon and Whetstone ranges visible in the distance. The Santa Rita Mountains soar skyward in solitary majesty to the south, while the Tucson and Santa Catalina mountains complete the encirclement of the Tucson basin.

The main trail follows the descending ridgeline eastward, and enters the Chiva burn. A fire raged here in 1989, and the trail is now hard to follow as it runs through a riot of regrowth. It never wanders far from the ridgetop, however, and old stone check dams mark the path's course to Cow Head Saddle. The trail meets the Douglas Spring trail as it crosses this low pass. Reaching Douglas Spring itself requires a 3-mile descent to the north, while a 1.4-mile drop to the south accesses the Chiminea Canyon trail near Grass Shack Spring.

The path officially becomes the Cow Head Saddle trail as it continues its eastward journey by climbing the next ridgeline. It makes a workmanlike ascent, passing several knobs of sculpted bedrock as it climbs. The oak-juniper scrubland found here also burned during the Chiva Fire, and the clearing of the trees created fine views of Tanque Verde Peak. As Chihuahua pines begin to creep into the surviving scrub, the trail levels off and passes into a shallow, south-facing basin filled with a mixed woodland of pines, junipers, and oaks. The route requires several bursts of vigorous climbing in between its longer, gentler stretches.

The path ultimately returns to the ridgetop, passing a beehive-shaped outcrop above an intermittent waterfall. It then climbs a last, steep grade to reach a rocky knob that allows views of Helens Dome rising from the ridgetop. The trail then drops into a wooded draw, which it follows toward the base of this striking rock formation. After passing the foot of Helens Dome, the path meets the North Slope trail (see Trail 48 in this book) and veers southward. After passing the Fire Loop trail, it descends gently through pines to reach its end at Manning Camp. Here, a former summer home dating to the turn of the century has become a National Park Service storehouse, and a nearby camping area and spring offer respite for the weary.

General description: A network of trails atop Mica Mountain, accessible after a full day of backpacking.

Best season: March-December.

Difficulty: Easy to moderate.

Water availability: Manning Camp has a perennial spring; Deer Head, Italian, and Spud Rock springs and Devil's Bathtub may be dry.

Maximum elevation: 8,666 feet (Mica Mountain).

Topo maps: Mica Mountain, *Rincon Mountains*.

Jurisdiction: Saguaro National Park, Rincon Mountain Unit.

Finding the trails: These remote trails can be accessed via the Tanque Verde Ridge, Douglas Spring, Turkey Creek, Heartbreak Ridge, or Italian Spring trails.

The trails: This network of well-maintained trails provides a spectrum of loop hikes atop the highest peak in the Rincon Mountains. The shortest access route is via the Turkey Canyon trail, while the Douglas Spring, Tanque Verde Ridge, and Heartbreak Ridge trails provide longer but more scenic routes. All of these trails are sufficiently long to ensure that travelers who visit the Mica Mountain complex will have to plan an overnight trip.

Mica Secondary.

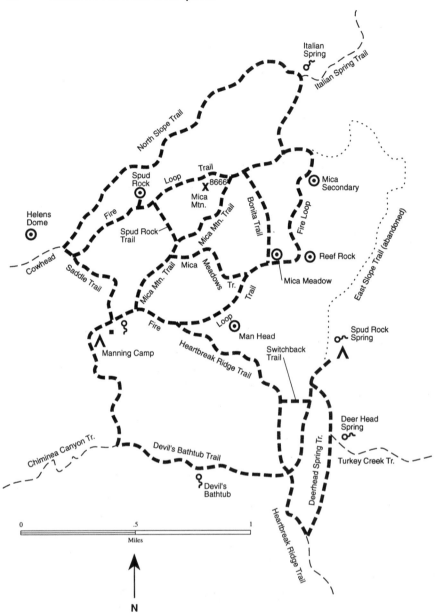

Manning Camp is an attractive base for explorations because of its central location and permanent water supply. There is a smaller camping area at Spud Rock Spring, on the eastern side of the massif. Mica Mountain was largely spared from the Rincon Mountain Fire of 1994 (except for the East Slope trail, which was completely obliterated). Here, cool mountain breezes course through the lofty pines. High overlooks and interesting rock formations are sprinkled liberally around the mountaintop, providing constant and varied scenery for travelers who make it into this remote corner of Saguaro National Park.

FIRE LOOP TRAIL

This 5-mile loop was once the daily stroll for fire crews stationed at Manning Camp. To start the loop, follow the Cow Head Saddle trail up and northward through the pines from Manning Camp. After 0.4 mile, The Fire Loop trail splits away to the right, ascending along a ridgetop studded with exposed sheaves of bedrock. The trail reaches its high point at Spud Rock (mile 1.2), and a spur path follows the east side of this formation before climbing to the top of it. Here, hedgehog cacti grow from fissures in the gneiss, and views encompass Man Head, Helens Dome, and the distant point of Rincon Peak rising far to the south. The path then drops into a low saddle, where it meets the Spud Rock trail (mile 1.4).

From this saddle, the Fire Loop climbs eastward along the ridgetop to the penultimate summit of Mica Mountain (mile 1.7). This rounded dome is loosely forested, and concrete blocks mark the spot where a lookout tower once stood. A few Douglas-firs are scattered among pines near the summit, which is the highest point in the Rincon Mountains. The trail then dips to the east, meeting the Mica Mountain trail (mile 1.8) and running onto a grassy ridgetop. From here, the Santa Catalinas can be glimpsed to the north. The Bonita trail drops to the south at a marked intersection (mile 1.9). The Fire Loop descends the ridgeline, passing a junction with the North Slope trail (mile 2.1) and turning south at the marked intersection with the old East Slope trail (mile 2.4).

The trail soon reaches a rocky promontory known as Mica Secondary, which commands a sweeping vista of the basins and ranges to the east. It then dips and rises through a forest cleared by ground fire during 1994. Many pines were saved from death by their thick bark, and grasses and bracken ferns flourish in the understory. A spur path runs onto the top of Reef Rock (mile 3.2), a cliff allowing outstanding views of Rincon Peak to the south as well as the more arid ranges to the east. The Fire Loop trail turns west here, climbing onto a flat hilltop where grassy Mica Meadow lies cupped in a forest of pines. The Fire Loop passes junctions with the Bonita (mile 3.7) and Mica Meadow (mile 3.9) trails, then heads to higher ground crowned by Man Head. This massive, solitary boulder is perched on the ridgetop like some plaything forgotten by an irresponsible giant. The path then drops into a gully to meet the Heartbreak Ridge trail (mile 4.4), which it joins for the westward descent to Manning Camp.

MICA MOUNTAIN TRAIL

From Manning Camp, this trail follows a wash bottom northeast through tall pines. After 0.5 mile, the gradient steepens and the trail intersects the Mica Meadow and Spud Rock trails in rapid succession. Spud Rock can be glimpsed through the trees to the north until the path jogs east around a hillside. The track then climbs into a grassy savannah dotted with ponderosa and Chihuahua pines. Hikers who travel silently might surprise a herd of Coues whitetailed deer here. The lone rock that rises above the forest to the south is Man Head. The Mica Mountain trail bends northward, climbing through a forested swale to reach a junction with the Fire Loop trail (mile 1.3). The summit of Mica Mountain rises 0.1 mile to the west along this latter trail.

SPUD ROCK TRAIL

From the Mica Mountain trail, this path offers a stiff climb of 0.5 mile to meet the Fire Loop at a junction that is 0.2 mile west of Spud Rock. The trail travels among a few smallish outcrops along the way and offers good views of Man Head to the south as well as Spud Rock itself.

MICA MEADOW TRAIL

This 0.6-mile trail connects the Mica Mountain and Fire Loop trails. It climbs over a small hill, then drops through a wooded draw before rising steadily to the western edge of Mica Meadow. The forest along the trail was scorched by a low-intensity ground fire in 1993. The blaze killed a number of seedlings and saplings, but the older pines were insulated from the fire by their thick bark.

BONITA TRAIL

This trail cuts off the eastern lobe of the Fire Loop trail. From its north end, the little-used path descends gradually across rolling uplands. The loose-knit pine forest found here is interrupted frequently by glades that project a sense of tranquillity. The trail ends by slanting across Mica Meadow to rejoin the Fire Loop after an overall distance of 0.8 mile.

NORTH SLOPE TRAIL

This trail departs from the Cow Head Saddle trail at Helens Dome, 0.6 mile north of Manning Camp. It is a bit harder to follow than most trails on Mica Mountain; hikers will have to pay attention in places to stay on the trail. The trek begins by passing Helens Dome, which presents its broadside through openings in the pines. Gambel oaks soon grow amid the conifers, splashing color in late October as they shed their leaves. The path takes to a steep, open slope allowing excellent views of the Santa Catalinas to the north, as well as another view of Helens Dome.

After rounding a spur ridge, the trail passes Douglas-firs and white firs rising prominently from the canopy, creating a forest community unique to this trail. The path crosses a series of finger ridges on its way east, each one crowned by a sculpted formation of gneiss that invites further exploration. As the trail winds onto the eastern slope of Mica Mountain, evidence of the 1994 Rincon fire becomes apparent in the form of blackened snags and fire-scarred pines. The trail dips to reach Italian Spring (mile 2.4), where it meets a little-used trail from the lowlands to the north. Italian Spring is an algae-choked pool that occupies a shallow depression, but it is more reliable than most other springs on Mica Mountain. The trail then climbs steadily to reach the Fire Loop trail (mile 3.0) on a grassy ridge.

COW HEAD SADDLE TRAIL

This trail is discussed in detail in the description for Trail 47, covering Tanque Verde Ridge.

DEVIL'S BATHTUB TRAIL

From Manning Camp, follow the Chiminea Canyon route (officially called the Manning Camp trail) as it descends past the camping area on a southwesterly bearing. This trail crosses the headwaters of Chiminea Canyon and follows this rather impressive little defile for a time past sheer walls and undercut grottos. It then finds a way onto the finger ridge to the east, passing through mixed forest of evergreen oak and pine. After 1 mile, the Devil's Bathtub trail takes off to the east. It crosses increasingly arid terrain, dotted with yuccas and bare gneiss. After crossing a low rise, the trail descends to the Devil's Bathtub, which marks the head of Madrona Canyon. Here, a spring trickles from the earth, then dribbles down a 50-foot face of bedrock into a broad and deep pool surrounded on three sides by naked stone. Beyond this point, the trail climbs across the bedrock and up a shallow ravine to meet the Heartbreak Ridge trail at Four Corners after 1.2 miles of travel from Manning Camp.

HEARTBREAK RIDGE TRAIL

See Trail 51.

EAST SLOPE TRAIL

This trail was heavily damaged by the 1994 Rincon fire. It can be followed with some difficulty between Four Corners and Spud Rock Spring, but has been completely obliterated beyond that point.

SWITCHBACK TRAIL

This 0.3-mile route descends from the Heartbreak Ridge trail to meet the East Slope trail, speeding access to Spud Rock Spring. The open nature of the pine forest allows sweeping vistas of the Little Rincon and Galiuro mountains.

DEER HEAD SPRING TRAIL

This trail sidehills from a low saddle to Spud Rock Spring. Along the way, its passes a junction with the Turkey Creek trail (mile 0.8), and Deer Head

Spring lies 0.1 mile down this side trail. The Deer Head Spring trail can be quite brushy as it continues northward for the remaining 0.6 mile to Spud Rock Spring. This spring emerges in an aspen grove beside an old cabin site. A camping area lies in the grassy meadow below it, with fine views of Reef Rock.

49   CHIMINEA CANYON

General description: An extended trip from Madrona Ranger Station to Manning Camp, 8.7 miles.
Best season: March-November.
Difficulty: Moderate northeast to southwest; moderately strenuous southwest to northeast.
Water availability: The pools at Madrona Ranger Station usually hold water. Grass Shack Spring may be dry; Manning Camp has a permanent spring.
Elevation gain: 4,760 feet.
Elevation loss: 190 feet.
Maximum elevation: 7,930 feet.
Topo maps: Mica Mountain, *Rincon Mountains*.
Jurisdiction: Saguaro National Park, Rincon Mountain Unit.
Finding the trail: This remote trail can be accessed from Manning Camp or from the end of the Douglas Spring trail.

Gneiss formation in Chiminea Canyon.

0.0	Trail leaves Madrona Ranger Station.
4.2	Junction with Douglas Spring trail. Turn right.
4.4	Grass Shack Spring camping area.
8.7	Manning Camp.

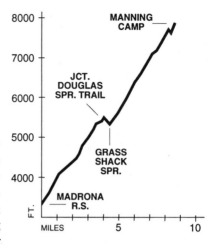

The trail: This route, known officially as the Manning Camp trail, was once the most direct and popular way for hikers to get to the top of Mica Mountain. It follows Chiminea Canyon from the Rincon Creek basin to Manning Camp, a popular jumping-off point for the Mica Mountain complex. An exclusive land development company, citing problems with vandalism, has long since closed off public road access to the Madrona Ranger Station. The lower segment of the trail is now used chiefly for backcountry patrols, but the upper section of the trail can be

49   Chiminea Canyon

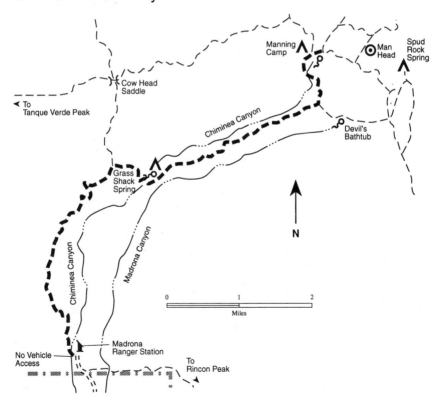

combined with the Tanque Verde Ridge and Douglas Spring trails for an extended loop trip. The *tinajas*, or natural pools, near the Madrona Ranger Station make a worthy destination themselves, although access by trail is a bit lengthy for most travelers' tastes. The pools are reached via a short trail that drops to the creek bottom from a hilltop water storage shed located just north of the ranger station.

From the Madrona Ranger Station corrals, the trail crosses Chiminea wash and begins its ascent across slopes studded with gigantic saguaros. The path arcs westward as it climbs, distancing itself from Chiminea Canyon. Watch for barrel cacti, ocotillos, and chollas in the midst of this diverse desert scrub community. The cactus-clad slopes ultimately turn to elevated, sandy flats populated by dense thickets of mesquite. After crossing these broad shelves, the trail climbs again, and the cacti grade into oak-studded grasslands. A waterfall graces a rocky cleft during the wet season; it is visible from a distance as the trail swings back toward Chiminea Canyon. The path turns west again before reaching the edge of the main canyon, and continues its climb on steep slopes.

At the top of the grade, the trail crosses a rocky feeder wash where hikers have to follow cairns across shelves of bare bedrock. The trail becomes evident again as it resumes a northward course to meet the Douglas Spring trail. Turn right at the junction as the trail climbs over a low finger ridge before descending to reach Grass Shack Spring. There is a designated campsite here, positioned in a grove of tall live oaks and pines beside the wash of Chiminea Canyon. Grass Shack Spring occupies the wash at a spot where bedrock forces groundwater to the surface. It provides water for most of the year, but may run dry during summer and autumn.

The trail picks up again on the far side of the streamcourse and ascends a low finger ridge to the east. The path follows the ridge crest through live oak scrubland punctuated by such succulents as lechuguilla and sotol. These desert plants disappear as the trail gains altitude. Piñon pine becomes commonplace among the oaks and junipers. To the left, the north wall of Chiminea Canyon rises into a wooded slope studded with gneiss outcrops. The gentler valley of Madrona Canyon is occasionally visible to the south of the trail. Vigorous ascents interrupt the lazy ridge-running, and the gradient of the trail increases near the head of the canyon. Before the forest closes off all views, the rounded formations guarding the upper reaches of the valley can be seen to the north.

As ponderosa and Chihuahua pines close in around the trail, the Devil's Bathtub trail joins the Chiminea Canyon route from the east. The main trail swings northward here, climbing through the woodlands, then sidehilling across steep slopes to meet the canyon floor. Sheer rock faces rise on both sides of the canyon here. These walls are pockmarked with grottos and depressions worn into the stone by wind and water. As the path crosses the streamcourse, travelers may find water that has flowed down from the spring at Manning Camp. The trail makes a brief but strenuous climb through the pines to reach Manning Camp itself, where it joins a suite of other trails that form the Mica Mountain complex.

General description: A backpack from Happy Valley to the Deer Head Spring trail, 6.2 miles. See map on page 166.

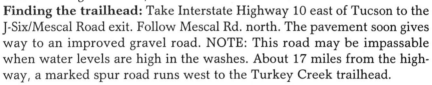

Best seasons: March-May; September-December.
Difficulty: Moderately strenuous*.
Water availability: Deer Head Spring is reliable; Mud Hole Spring dries up frequently.
Elevation gain: 3,030 feet.
Elevation loss: 80 feet.
Maximum Elevation: 7,200 feet.
Topo map: *Rincon Mountains Hiker's Map*
Jurisdiction: Saguaro National Park, Rincon Mountain Unit; Santa Catalina Ranger District, Coronado National Forest.
Finding the trailhead: Take Interstate Highway 10 east of Tucson to the J-Six/Mescal Road exit. Follow Mescal Rd. north. The pavement soon gives way to an improved gravel road. NOTE: This road may be impassable when water levels are high in the washes. About 17 miles from the highway, a marked spur road runs west to the Turkey Creek trailhead.

0.0   Turkey Creek trailhead.
1.6   Jeep track ends and trail begins.
6.1   Deer Head Spring.
6.2   Junction with Deer Head Spring trail.

The trail: This trail climbs the eastern side of the Rincon Mountains, providing the shortest route to Manning Camp and the Mica Mountain complex. It is the only trail open to horses that provides access from the eastern side of the range. The entire length of the trail was burned during the Rincon Mountain fire of 1994, so the scenery will have a charred and desolate aspect until grasses and shrubs can recolonize the burned area. The trail is easy to follow for most of its length but is tricky to locate near the top as it passes through lightly burned country.

The trek begins on a two-rut jeep trail that climbs straight up a finger ridge from the Turkey Creek parking area. This low country was touched only lightly by the fire, and a sea of new grass is interrupted occasionally by clumps of evergreen oak, mesquite, and manzanita. The Rincons can be seen from end to end, rising like a fortress wall from a maze of grassy foothills. The jeep trail ends after 1.6 miles, and the trail becomes a narrow but well-defined path that continues to follow the exposed spine of the ridge.

After rounding the north side of a substantial hill and crossing the Saguaro National Park boundary, the trail enters a devastated area where the blaze burned with its greatest intensity. Charred stumps rise from a mineral soil scoured bare of its organic layer. The trail is deeply gullied in places, but it is always easy to follow as it climbs through the moonscape. The trees return as the path nears Mud Hole Spring, although most were girdled by the blaze and now stand lifeless. Mud Hole Spring is little more than a trickle under the best of circumstances and is known to have an unreliable flow.

Follow the orange course markers as the trail snakes upward through a featureless maze of hillocks and draws. Travelers will pass Deer Head Spring near the top of the grade. This spring is known for its sweet water and is a fairly reliable water source— but be sure to treat the water before drinking. It is indeed a likely place to spot Coues white-tailed deer, especially in early morning and around dusk. The trail ends at a junction with the Deer Head Spring trail (covered under Trail 48), only a stone's throw from the Spud Rock Spring camping area.

51 HEARTBREAK RIDGE

General description: A backpack from Happy Valley to Manning Camp, 10.3 miles.
Best seasons: March-May; September-December.
Difficulty: Moderately strenuous*.
Water availability: Devil's Bathtub and Deer Head Spring are a short distance off the trail; Manning Camp has a permanent water supply. Miller Creek has no water in the dry months.
Elevation gain: 4,608 feet.
Elevation loss: 913 feet.
Maximum elevation: 8,270 feet.
Topo map: *Rincon Mountains.*

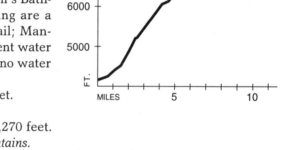

Jurisdiction: Saguaro National Park, Rincon Mountain Unit; Santa Catalina Ranger District, Coronado National Forest.
Finding the trailhead: Take Interstate Highway 10 east of Tucson to the J-Six/Mescal Road exit. Follow the Mescal Rd. north. The pavement soon gives way an improved gravel road. NOTE: This road may be impassable when water levels are high in the washes. Some 16.6 miles from the highway, a marked spur road runs west to the Turkey Creek trailhead.

0.0   Miller Canyon trailhead.
4.4   Junction with trail to Rincon Peak. Turn right.
5.6   Junction with spur to Happy Valley Lookout. Bear left for Manning Camp.

A view of Reef Rock from Heartbreak Ridge.

7.9   Junction with Deer Head Saddle trail. Bear left.

8.4   Four Corners junction (with East Slope and Devil's Bathtub trails). Keep going straight ahead.

8.9   Junction with Switchback trail. Keep going straight.

9.6   Junction with Fire Loop trail. Bear left.

10.2   Junction with Mica Mountain trail. Bear left.

10.3   Manning Camp.

The trail: This trek combines the Miller Creek trail with a well-worn path running along Heartbreak Ridge. The route passes Happy Valley Lookout along the way and ends by connecting with the Mica Mountain complex of trails. It provides a rather long but scenic route for travelers who are destined for Manning Camp. There is no water along the route, but there are several fairly dependable springs a short distance away from the trail as it enters the Mica Mountain complex; Manning Camp, at the trail's end, has a permanent supply of water. The first part of the hike (from Happy Valley to the crest of the Rincon Mountains) is discussed under Trail 52, the Rincon Peak trail description. This section of trail is closed to horses, but the Heartbreak Ridge section is not and can be accessed at its northern end via the Turkey Creek trail.

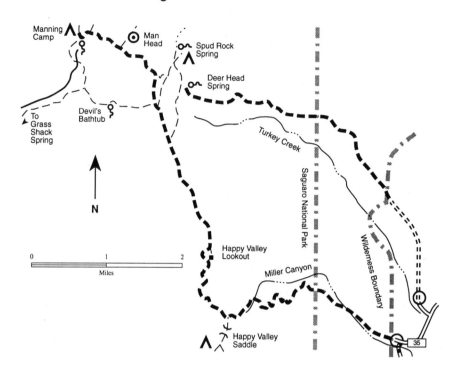

The trek begins by following the Miller Creek trail up the eastern slope of the Rincon Mountains to reach a junction at its crest (see Trail 52 for details). Turn north at this junction as the Heartbreak Ridge trail climbs onto boulder-strewn slopes covered with a loose growth of evergreen oak and piñon pine. As the path ascends a major summit to the north, it passes through country scorched by the fire of 1994. Flowering herbs were the first plants to take advantage of the flush of nutrients that was liberated by the blaze. These delicate plants grew and bloomed among the blackened stumps later in the same year. Evergreen oaks are bouncing back from the fire by sending out stump sprouts from their still-living roots.

The top of the peak was spared from the flames, as if the lookout on its summit had exerted some sort of magical protection. The trail climbs into the living trees as it rounds the western slope and runs level to a saddle on its northern flank. Here, an 0.2-mile spur trail climbs gradually to the Happy Valley fire lookout. Amid grassy meadows on the rounded summit, one of the ugliest lookouts in the Park Service boasts one of the finest views in the Rincons. Rincon Peak rises dramatically to the south, while the forested massif of Mica Mountain blocks out views to the north. Looking eastward, travelers see the Little Rincons as the nearest of a numberless series of arid ranges stretching away to the horizon.

The main trail follows the ridgetop northward, with occasional views of Reef Rock on the eastern face of the Mica massif. It surmounts two lesser points on its way to a pine-clad saddle, where it meets the Deer Head Spring trail. The Heartbreak Ridge route bears northwest here, climbing a substantial ridge. Near the top, it reaches an intersection known locally as "Four Corners." The Devil's Bathtub trail runs westward from this point, and the East Slope trail drops away to the northeast. The Heartbreak Ridge trail continues straight up the hill. Near the top, the trail swings onto an eastern slope for a fine view of the Little Rincons. It then crosses a saddle and meets the Switchback trail, which drops to the right on its way to join the old East Slope trail.

The Heartbreak Ridge route continues to climb gradually through the pines, rounding into a gulch that offers a good glimpse of Man Head atop the ridgeline to the north. The path passes a huge slab of bare stone that is set atop a broad pedestal. It then drops down into a wooded draw to meet the Fire Loop trail. Continue straight ahead, over another stony prominence and across a finger ridge of naked rock. The path then drops steadily into the forested basin beyond and crosses a dry wash to meet the Mica Mountain trail. Bear left, following the wash downhill for a short distance, to reach the trail's terminus at Manning Camp.

52   RINCON PEAK

General description: A long day hike or backpack from Happy Valley to the summit of Rincon Peak, 8.1 miles.
Best season: Year-round.
Difficulty: Moderately strenuous*.
Water availability: Miller Creek has no water during the dry months.
Elevation gain: 4,375 feet.
Elevation loss: 110 feet.
Maximum elevation: 8,450 feet.
Topo map: *Rincon Mountains.*
Jurisdiction: Saguaro National Park, Rincon Mountain Unit; Santa Catalina Ranger District, Coronado National Forest.

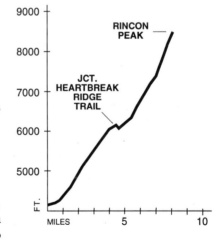

Finding the trailhead: Take Interstate Highway 10 east of Tucson to the J-Six/Mescal Road exit. Follow the Mescal Rd. north. The pavement soon gives way an improved gravel road. NOTE: This road may be impassable when water levels are high in the washes. Some 16.6 miles from the highway, a marked spur road runs west to the Turkey Creek trailhead.

Looking down on the Little Rincons from Rincon Peak.

0.0   Miller Canyon Trailhead.
4.4   Junction with Heartbreak Ridge trail. Turn left for Rincon Peak.
4.7   Junction with trail to Madrona Ranger Station. Turn left.
8.1   Summit of Rincon Peak.

The trail: This popular hike climbs from Happy Valley on the east side of the Rincon Mountains to the summit of Rincon Peak. The Miller Creek portion of the trail is closed to horses. Horse parties bound for Rincon Peak can follow the Turkey Creek trail to the crest of the range, then follow the Heartbreak Ridge trail westward to link up with the Rincon Peak trail at Happy Valley Saddle. Horse users must tether their horses about 0.5 mile short of the summit because the final pitch is extremely steep and vulnerable to erosion. There is no water along the trail, so travelers should bring plenty of their own for the long and arduous ascent. The reward for all of this climbing is an outstanding panorama of the surrounding ranges unmarred by the city of Tucson, which can barely be seen.

The trail begins on national forest land and follows the wash of Miller Creek northwest through the grassy live oak savannahs of Happy Valley. The path crosses the streamcourse numerous times, but never stays in the stream bed for long—watch for the track to pick up again on the far bank. At a muddy seep, the path veers west and leaves the main wash in favor of a narrow gulch. It then

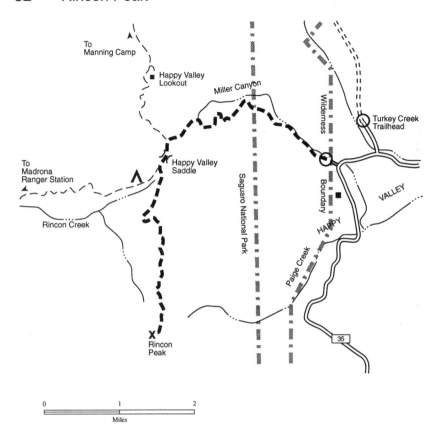

works its way cross-country to reach the stony foothills of the Rincon Mountains. A gate at the Saguaro National Park boundary marks the beginning of the climb, which proceeds upward through a maze of rounded boulders. The trail follows the southern boundary of the Rincon fire of 1994, where patches of oak and manzanita were scorched. Grasses sprang up in the wake of the blaze and now grow vigorously with the help of minerals put into the soil by the fire.

As the trail moves upward, outstanding views unfold to the east. The arid foothills dwindle like ripples in a grassy sea, finally ending in the pastoral basin of Happy Valley. Beyond this grassy bowl, the Little Rincons rise to low, tortured summits that stretch toward the northern horizon. The path may be tricky to spot in places; watch for cairns and a return of well-trodden trail tread (it never disappears for long). The trail tops a rise of weathered rocks and piñon pines, then drops into the head of Miller Creek Canyon. The path passes through a relatively lush growth of evergreen oaks during its gradual, final assault on the crest of the Rincon Mountains.

Atop the range, turn left at the trail junction. The trail will drop gradually through groves of tall ponderosa pines on its way to Happy Valley Saddle. Here, a second junction marks a trail that descends westward to Madrona Ranger Station via a camping area that lies only a few yards away. Turn left at the junction as the Rincon Peak trail runs southward along the crest of the range. This trail appears quite faint at first, but soon widens into a distinct track that is easy to follow. It crosses a rolling upland covered in pine-oak woodland, then ascends the northwest face of a rocky knob. Views to the north open up along the way, featuring the long finger of Tanque Verde Ridge rising toward dome-shaped Mica Mountain, the tallest peak in the range. Rising from the crest of this peak is the rocky cockscomb of Helens Dome. The trail levels somewhat as it traverses the western slope of the knob, then climbs steadily into a pine-clad saddle. The route meanders through rolling forest here, bearing south toward the palisades of Rincon Peak. Travelers may occasionally catch a glimpse of its summit through gaps in the forest canopy.

A signpost marks the beginning of the final pitch. All horses must be tethered at or below this point. The path zigzags aggressively up the eastern flank of the peak. This slope is wooded in Douglas-firs, pines, and even an occasional grove of aspens. Near the summit, the trees give way to arid chaparral and outcrops of a gneiss. An enormous cairn marks the summit, and an old ammunition box contains a register for visitors that reach the top. This windswept aerie commands a sweeping vista of desert basins and lonely ranges that seem to rise at the edge of the earth. The workings of humans appear insignificant when viewed from this height, surrounded as they are by the vast and unconquerable desert.

53 HIDDEN PASTURE

General description: A wilderness route into the Little Rincon Mountains, 3 miles.
Best season: September-May.
Difficulty: Moderately strenuous.
Water availability: Hikers may find pools in the wet months.
Elevation gain: 900 feet.

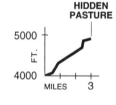

Maximum elevation: 4,900 feet.
Topo maps: Galleta Flat West, *Rincon Mountains.*
Jurisdiction: Santa Catalina Ranger District, Coronado National Forest.
Finding the trailhead: Take Interstate Highway 10 east of Tucson to the J-Six/Mescal Road exit. Follow the Mescal Rd. north. The pavement soon gives way an improved gravel road. NOTE: This road may be impassable when water levels are high in the washes. The road enters Coronado National Forest, then passes through the private lands of the Mackenzie Ranch. The extensive pullout from which the route begins lies 0.2 mile beyond the end of the ranch property on the right side of the road.

Rugged country in the Little Rincons.

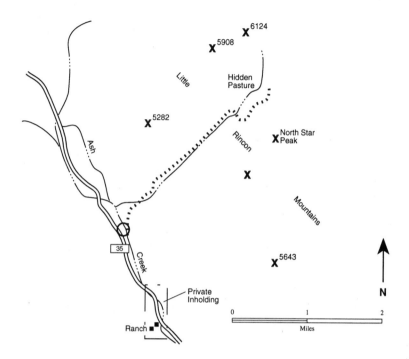

0.0   Parking area.
0.3   Trail enters nameless canyon.
2.3   Ravine joins canyon from slopes of North Star Peak.
3.0   Hidden Pasture.

The trail: This wilderness route has no defined path and requires travelers to use map and compass skills to navigate a rocky valley floor. It penetrates the Little Rincon Mountains, an arid and remote range composed of granite that has weathered into rock formations of all sizes and descriptions. The entire route lies on national forest lands, but its starting point is not marked in any way.

From the small parking area-pullout, cross Ash Creek and follow the base of the hills northward. After 0.3 mile of dodging cat's claws and chollas, travelers will see a broad opening in the hills. This marks the entrance to the canyon. Follow the wash eastward as rugged slopes rise on either side, encrusted with fanciful outcrops of weathered stone. A steep-walled chasm looms ahead, and the preferred route runs up a spur ridge to the north of the wash in order to avoid the impasse. The route then returns to the streamcourse, which makes several large S-curves before ascending into a flattened basin. Here, the water has worn a circuitous course through resistant bedrock, twisting and doubling back to take advantage of weaknesses in the stone. The wash is guarded by a few gnarled oaks, and no thorn scrub grows within the confines of the streambed. One has only to wander a few yards onto the surrounding slopes, however, to find a diverse array of spiny vegetation: lechuguilla, ocotillo, and cat's claw are all well-represented. Grasses grow here as well, providing forage for the Coues white-tailed deer that can sometimes be spotted here.

Near the head of this narrow basin is an interesting formation in the streambed where water has drilled round holes deep into the rock. Hillocks of boulders crowd the wash as fantastic pinnacles and balanced rocks tower above the streamcourse. A 30-foot wall of sheer stone soon blocks the canyon, and the tiny cleft worn through it is much too narrow to accommodate a hiker; climb the slopes to the north in order to get around it. A steep ravine tumbles down from a cleft in North Star Peak, heralding the next chokepoint in the canyon. Here, a jumble of house-sized boulders blocks further progress. Scramble up the draw to the south to get around this obstacle. Beyond this point, travelers can follow the wash as it climbs through a few more twists through the stone. As the last outcrop is overcome, the narrow canyon abruptly widens into a broad, grass-filled bowl known as Hidden Pasture. This natural amphitheater is guarded to the south by North Star Peak, the tallest summit in the Little Rincons.

54 HUGH NORRIS TRAIL

General description: A day hike to the summit of Wasson Peak, 4.9 miles.
Best season: September-May.
Difficulty: Moderately strenuous.
Water availability: None.
Elevation gain: 2,347 feet.
Elevation loss: 220 feet.
Maximum elevation: 4,687 feet.
Topo map: Avra.
Jurisdiction: Saguaro National Park, Tucson Mountain Unit.

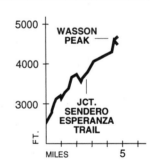

Finding the trailhead: From the Red Hills Visitor Center, drive northwest on Kinney Drive for 1 mile, then turn right on the Bajada Loop Drive. The trailhead is on the right after 0.7 mile.

0.0   Trailhead
2.7   Junction with Sendero Esperanza trail. Keep going straight.
4.1   Amole Peak.
4.6   Junction with King Canyon trail. Bear left for Wasson Peak.
4.9   Summit of Wasson Peak.

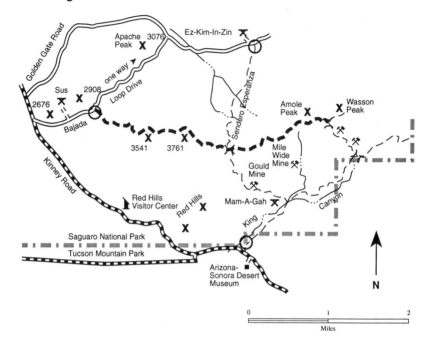

The trail: This trail is the premier hiking route in the Tucson Mountain Unit of Saguaro National Park. The trail begins by climbing up a small canyon studded with outcrops of granite and tall saguaros. Early views across the broad basin of the Avra Valley highlight the Roskruge, Waterman, and Silver Bell ranges as well as the loftier Santa Rosa Mountains beyond them. Upon cresting the ridgetop, the trail encounters a craggy summit. The trail climbs gradually as it skirts to the north of this high point. The footpath meets the ridgeline beyond the aforementioned peak and follows its crest eastward with occasional dips onto north-facing slopes. A magnificent reef of red rhyolite graces the flats to the north, and is topped by Panther Peak at its west end and Safford Peak in the center. The trail ultimately drops into a low saddle, where the Sendero Esperanza trail drops away on either side of the ridge.

From this saddle, the trail climbs steadily up the ridgetop toward Amole Peak. The saguaros thin out with increasing altitude, and finally disappear altogether as the trail makes its way across the slopes of this peak. A low gap in the hills provides a breather before the trail climbs the final pitch to reach a high notch in a twin-topped mountain. There is a trail junction just beyond this notch; a short spur runs east to the summit of Wasson Peak for unobstructed view of the Tucson basin. The Santa Catalinas present a solid wall on the far side of the basin, while the volcanic spires of the Tucson Mountains rise beyond the Red Hills to the south.

An ocotillo guards an overlook of Golden Gate Mountain.

55   SENDERO ESPERANZA TRAIL

General description: A day hike to Mam-a-Gah Picnic Area, 3.2 miles.
Best season: September-May.
Difficulty: Moderate.
Water availability: None.
Elevation gain: 560 feet.
Elevation loss: 510 feet.
Maximum elevation: 3,620 feet.
Topo map: Avra.

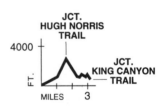

Jurisdiction: Saguaro National Park, Tucson Mountain Unit.
Finding the trailhead: From the Red Hills Visitor Center, drive northwest on Kinney Drive for 1.3 miles, then turn right on Golden Gate Road. The trailhead is on the right after about 5 miles.

0.0	Trailhead.
1.8	Junction with Hugh Norris trail. Keep going straight ahead.
2.5	Gould Mine site.
3.1	Mam-a-Gah Picnic Area.
3.2	Junction with King Canyon trail.

The trail: This trail crosses over a minor ridge and passes several old mines on its way to link Golden Gate Road with the Hugh Norris and King Canyon trails. The trail begins by following an old roadbed up a series of gently sloping *bajadas* that skirt the ridges to the south. Look for ironwood and barrel cacti early on; these plants soon disappear with increasing altitude. Phainopeplas are commonly spotted in the shrubs that border the dry washes. The male of this species has distinctive black plumage accented by white flight feathers; both sexes have a pointed crest. A substantial ridge of granite looms ahead, and the path snakes its way up a sinuous finger ridge to reach its crest. At the top of the grade is a ridgetop saddle; the Hugh Norris trail departs, following the ridgeline, while the Sendero Esperanza trail drops over the far side of the ridge.

As the path descends, old saguaros rise amid a diverse array of desert shrubs. The trail soon picks up an old mining road; turn left here (to the right, the road dead-ends at some abandoned diggings). Follow the road down into the site of the old Gould Mine. After passing a sealed shaft, the road runs past the shell of a stonework building. It then drops into a gully. A watchful eye will spot more tailings heaps a short distance up this gulch. The road then bears east to cross a low saddle and descends past the Mam-a-Gah Picnic Area. It ends at the wash of King Canyon, where it links up with the King Canyon trail.

Hiking through the saguaros of the Sendero Esperanza Trail.

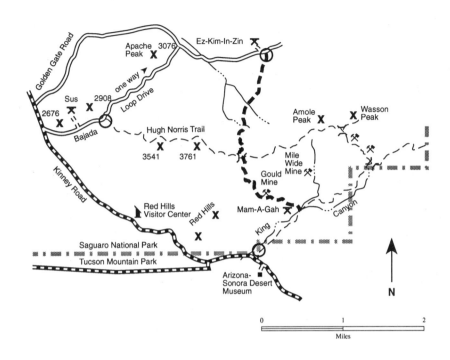

56 *KING CANYON*

General description: A day hike to the top of Wasson Peak, 3.5 miles.
Best season: September-May.
Difficulty: Moderately strenuous.
Water availability: None.
Elevation gain: 1,687 feet.
Elevation loss: 50 feet.
Maximum elevation: 4,687 feet.
Topo maps: Avra, Brown Mountain.
Jurisdiction: Saguaro National Park, Tucson Mountain Unit; Tucson Mountain Regional Park (Pima County).

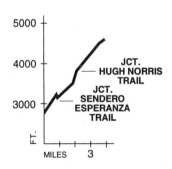

Finding the trailhead: From the Red Hills Visitor Center, drive southeast on Kinney drive for about 1.5 miles. The King Canyon parking area is to the east of the road, right across from the Arizona-Sonora Desert Museum.

56 King Canyon

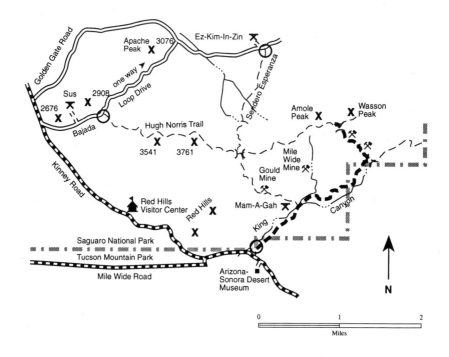

0.0 Trailhead.

0.9 Roadbed and streamcourse routes converge. Junction with Sendero Esperanza trail below Mam-a-Gah Picnic Area. Keep going straight.

2.3 Saddle at head of King Canyon. Junction with Sweetwater trail. Turn left.

3.2 Junction with Hugh Norris trail.

3.5 Summit of Wasson Peak.

The trail: This route begins in Tucson Mountain Park, but quickly enters Saguaro National Park and climbs through the cactus to link up with the Sendero Esperanza and Hugh Norris trails. The trek begins with a choice: one can follow an old road across the slopes to the south of the wash, or follow the streamcourse itself. The streamcourse of King Canyon provides easy walking across a level gravel surface occasionally interrupted by low stairsteps of emergent bedrock. Low cliffs of the same jointed stone line the outsides of curves where runoff water has carved into the hillsides. The slopes surrounding the gulch are dominated by stately saguaros, while barrel cacti, palos verdes, ocotillos, and chollas are also well-represented in this classic Sonoran Desert plant community. The streamcourse and the old road converge below the Mam-a-Gah Picnic Area, which was named after a Tohono O'odham Indian chief. It offers a shaded ramada and well-camouflaged rest rooms.

The Sendero Esperanza trail descends to this picnic area, while the King Canyon trail threads its way up a series of finger ridges to the north of the wash. Look back, since the valley walls frame an excellent vista of Kitt Peak, the northernmost summit of the Baboquivari Mountains. A look southward reveals the Red Hills, a series of low mounds that derive their color from lakebed deposits of iron oxide. The saguaros thin out as the trail gains altitude. The giant cacti are replaced by jojoba, prickly pear, and hedgehog cacti. The trail ends at a saddle looking over the Oro Valley, with Pusch Ridge and the rest of the Santa Catalinas rising regally beyond it. The Sweetwater trail descends eastward from this point on its way to the outskirts of Tucson, and the Hugh Norris trail climbs away to the north. From the junction, the main trail ascends vigorously northward, following the ridgeline past a number of abandoned mineshafts. Views of the Red Hills and Tucson Mountains expand until the trail reaches its terminus at a mountaintop junction. A short spur trail climbs eastward to the summit of Wasson Peak, while the Hugh Norris trail runs westward and descends a sinuous ridgeline.

57 YETMAN TRAIL

General description: A day loop through Tucson Mountain Regional Park, 6.7 miles.
Best season: October-April.
Difficulty: Moderate*.
Water availability: None.
Elevation gain: 592 feet.
Elevation loss: 822 feet.
Maximum elevation: 3,182 feet.
Topo map: *Tucson Mountain Regional Park*

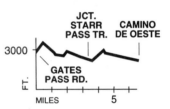

(available at Saguaro National Monument's Red Hills Visitor Center).
Jurisdiction: Tucson Mountain Regional Park (Pima County).
Finding the trailhead: From Tucson, take Speedway Boulevard west of town. This road becomes the paved Gates Pass Road and enters Tucson Mountain Regional Park. The Yetman trailhead is 0.2 mile beyond Gates Pass, on the left. The lower trailhead is at the end of the Camino del Oeste.

0.0	Gates Pass trailhead.
0.5	Junction with Golden Gate trail. Keep going straight ahead.
1.0	Junction with trail to Tucson Estates Road. Turn left.
3.9	Junction with Starr Pass cutoff trail. Bear left.
4.2	Junction with Starr Pass trail. Turn left.
4.6	22nd Street trailhead. Keep going straight ahead.
5.5	Ruins of Bowen Ranch.
6.7	Camino del Oeste trailhead.

The trail: This trail makes a long semi-loop into the heart of Tucson Moun-

57   Yetman Trail

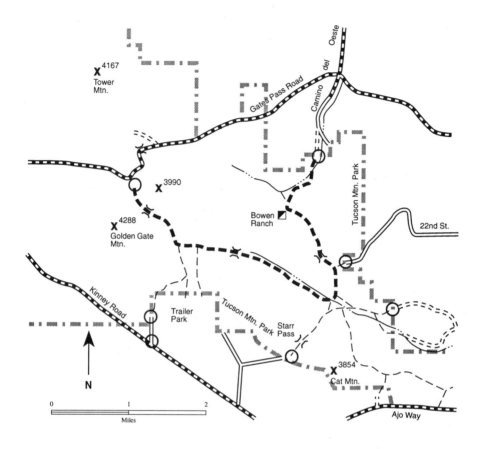

tain Park. From the Gates Pass trailhead, the track climbs gently southeast toward the low saddle behind Golden Gate Mountain. Jagged peaks rise all around, their reddish beds of volcanic rhyolite reaching to craggy heights above older and more crumbly beds of metamorphic stone. The low country is vegetated in a rich *bajada* community that features saguaro and cholla cacti, ocotillo, and palo verde. The Yetman trail meets the Golden Gate trail at the top of the pass, and fine views extend southward along the Tucson Mountains. Cat Mountain dominates the southern reaches of the range, while a sprawling trailer park crowds the southern boundary of the park.

As the path descends into a wide basin, a spur trail breaks away to the south, bound for the Tucson Estates trailhead. The Yetman trail swings eastward, crossing numerous washes on its way to a gap in the mountains. All traces of the city fall away as the trail appropriates an arroyo bed on its downward course. This draw soon empties out into a circular basin that is tucked in the midst of the mountains. A vigilant eye can detect evidence of mining activity

A southward view of Cat Mountain.

in this shallow depression. In the center of the basin, several trails break away to the right. Bear left; the Yetman trail swings north past the 22nd Street trailhead on its way back into the heart of the mountains. The path soon finds itself descending along a northwest-running wash. Bushmaster Peak rises regally in the distance. The path runs past the ruins of the old Bowen Ranch, a well-built structure of native stone that has survived intact excepting its roof. This ranch was built in the 1930s by an eastern newspaper editor who moved to Tucson after his wife developed heart problems. The climate apparently worked its magic, since she recovered from her illness; the couple was able to return to the East Coast.

After passing a sealed well shaft, the trail enters a broad wash and follows it northeast to leave the mountains. Colorful outcrops of volcanic rock adorn the banks of the arroyo. The arid slopes above it support a relatively depauperate community of saguaros, jojobas, and chollas. As the wash leaves the mountains, a jeep trail rises from the wash to carry the hiker the remaining distance to a parking area at the end of the Camino del Oeste.

THE SANTA CATALINAS

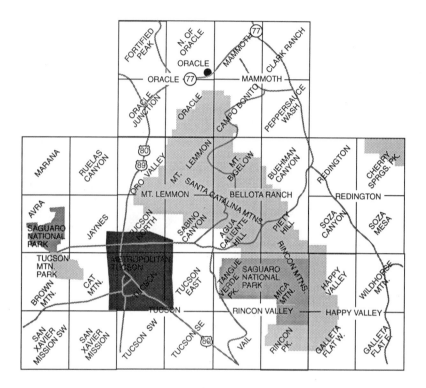

Rising to lofty heights just beyond the Tucson city limits, the Santa Catalina Range is regarded as a backyard playground by many Tucsonians: it has a small ski area, a town with summer cottages, numerous rock-climbing routes, campgrounds, and a diverse network of well-maintained trails. On summer days and weekends, the population of Tucson swarms into these accessible mountains to escape into the cool breezes and shady forests of the high country. The Sabino Canyon and Mount Lemmon/Marshall Gulch areas are particularly prone to crowding, and the trails that run up into the foothills from the edge of Tucson are rapidly becoming popular with trail runners. Hikers who are seeking a wilderness experience would do well to look elsewhere, although some of the more remote trails in the range receive very little traffic.

The Catalina Highway runs right to the top of the range. From it, travelers can approach most of the trails from the top-down, which saves climbing. Many mountain access points on the edge of Tucson lie on private lands, and there has been some difficulty in creating adequate trailheads for them. To the west of the range, Catalina State Park occupies a chunk of the Oro Valley below the foot of the range and offers access to the Romero Canyon and Sutherland trails for a small fee. Other Oro Valley access points are open only to four-wheel-drive vehicles.

The Pusch Ridge Wilderness Area encompasses the western arm of the range. It was created in large part to protect critical habitats of rare desert bighorn sheep. These sheep have lambing grounds on Pusch Peak, and visitors are asked to stay away from this sensitive area. The wilderness runs from the heights of Mount Lemmon all the way down to cactus flats at the edge of Tucson, and encompasses the rocky outer cordillera of the Santa Catalina Mountains. Machines (including mountain bikes) are not allowed in the wilderness, although leashed pets are permitted on a few outlying trails.

58   SABINO CANYON

General description: A day hike along Sabino Canyon to Hutch's Pool, 4.1 miles.
Best season: Year-round.
Difficulty: Moderate.
Water availability: Sabino Canyon has pools of water year-round.
Elevation gain: 1,260 feet.

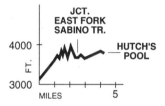

Hutch's pool.

Elevation loss: 710 feet.

Maximum elevation: 3,960 feet.

Topo maps: Sabino Canyon, *Santa Catalina Mountains.*

Jurisdiction: Pusch Ridge Wilderness, Santa Catalina Ranger District, Coronado National Forest.

Finding the trailhead: In Tucson, follow Tanque Verde Road to Sabino Canyon Road. Follow this second road to the visitor center at its end. The trailhead can be reached by walking or by shuttlebus.

0.0	End of Sabino Canyon shuttlebus road.
0.5	Junction with Phoneline trail. Turn left.
1.1	Overlook of Sabino Canyon.
2.5	Junction with East Fork Sabino trail. Turn left onto West Fork trail.
2.6	Trail crosses mouth of Box Camp Canyon.
3.8	Trail crosses Sabino Canyon streamcourse.
4.0	Junction with faint trail to Hutch's Pool.
4.1	Hutch's Pool.

58   Sabino Canyon

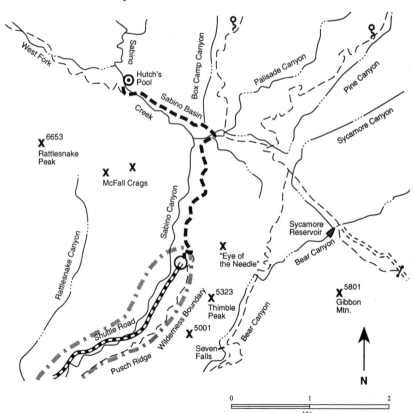

The trail: This hike is extremely popular, and the trail can be quite crowded during summer and on weekends. Its trailhead is at the end of the Sabino Canyon shuttlebus route; hikers can pay the rather exorbitant fee and ride the bus or hike to the trailhead along the road or via the Phoneline trail, which runs along the east wall of the canyon. The destination of the trek is Hutch's Pool, which carries water year-round. The pool receives heavy use during late spring and summer and has been a victim to heavy visitor impacts in the past. Be especially careful to leave no trace of your visit, and pick up any litter left by less-considerate visitors.

From the end of the shuttlebus road, the trail begins by zigzagging upward through spectacular canyon scenery to reach a junction with the Phoneline trail. On the way up, a rock formation known as The Eye of the Needle crowns the mountaintop above. After meeting the Phoneline trail, the Sabino Canyon trail swings north, traversing steep walls above a canyon floor littered with enormous boulders. It is believed that these chunks of stone were dislodged from the canyon walls by a strong earthquake in 1887. Across the valley, massive faces of striated gneiss form the summits of the McFall Crags. Other rocky points rise farther south.

After the path crosses a high spur, the landscape takes on a gentler aspect. Here, travelers will encounter a new assemblage of plants. Arid grasslands integrate the cactus scrub. The result is startling—giant saguaros can be found beside evergreen oaks. The path follows the canyon into the Sabino Basin, a wide east-west rift occupied by the several forks of Sabino Creek. The path bends eastward for a brief time, traversing a low gorge before descending to cross the East Fork of Sabino Canyon. On the far bank of a streamcourse is a marked junction; turn left on the West Fork trail to continue the trek.

The trail climbs onto grassy slopes as it passes the mouth of Box Camp Canyon. From these slopes the hiker can look back down the lower reaches of Sabino Canyon. The trail drops gradually to the valley floor, passing through sparse riparian forest interspersed with grassy flats. After 0.8 mile, the path crosses the streamcourse and continues a gradual ascent along its south bank. Watch for a faint track leading to the streambed as the main trail begins to switchback upward. This faint footpath drops to the watercourse, then picks its way among massive boulders to reach Hutch's Pool.

The pool is narrow, long, and deep. Low walls of metamorphic rock guard both sides. There is a natural dam of boulders at its lower end, and a sandy beach that is ideal for sunbathing. The main fork of Sabino Canyon bends north to enter the mountains just above Hutch's Pool, while the established trail runs along the West Fork on its way to Romero Pass.

General description: A day hike along Bear Canyon, 6.5 miles.

Best season: September-May.

Difficulty: Moderate to Seven Falls; moderately strenuous beyond.

Water availability: Bear Canyon has pools of water year-round.

Elevation gain: 2,000 feet.

Elevation loss: 540 feet.

Maximum elevation: 4,850 feet.

Topo maps: Sabino Canyon, *Santa Catalina Mountains.*

Jurisdiction: Pusch Ridge Wilderness, Santa Catalina Ranger District, Coronado National Forest.

Finding the trailhead: In Tucson, follow Tanque Verde Road to Sabino Canyon Road. Follow this second road to the visitor center at its end. The trailhead can be reached on foot or by shuttlebus.

59 Bear Canyon

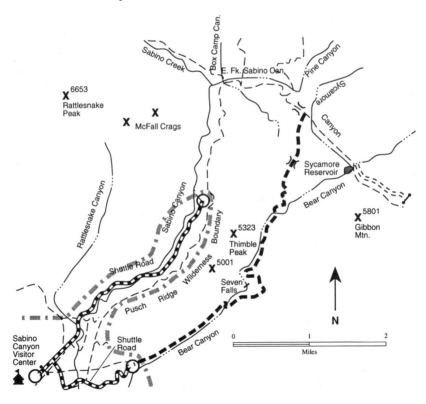

Seven Falls.

Sheer cliffs above Seven Falls.

0.0	End of Bear Canyon shuttlebus road.
2.1	Junction with spur trail to base of Seven Falls (0.2 mile, moderate). Bear right to continue the hike.
5.4	Overlook of Bear Canyon.
5.8	Trail crosses divide into Sycamore Canyon drainage.
6.5	Junction with East Fork Sabino and Sycamore Reservoir trails.

The trail: This trail offers another popular excursion from the Sabino Canyon visitor center. The trailhead can be reached by shuttlebus for a fee, or via a 1.7-mile footpath that parallels the road. This trail is quite popular on weekends, with hundreds of visitors strung out along the route on a busy day. The highlight of the trek is Seven Falls, a breathtaking chain of cascades, which drops more than 240 feet below soaring mountain peaks.

The hike begins at the mouth of Bear Canyon. Sloping walls covered in saguaro rise above a canyon floor choked with deep-rooted shrubs. There are several streamcourse crossings as the trail proceeds up the canyon; stepping stones provide dry passage when water levels are high. As the canyon penetrates the outer cordillera of the Santa Catalinas, soaring walls of gneiss rise high above the stream. This metamorphic rock is banded into distinctive black and white stripes. The cliffs reach a dramatic climax at Seven Falls. This fantastic cataract tumbles across stairstepped dropoffs, and magnificent saguaros rise on all sides. A spur trail drops to the edge of the lowermost plunge pool.

Beyond the falls junction, the main trail zigzags up at a steady pace. It ascends through the last dense stand of saguaro before shooting northward along the canyon. The path dips for a final stream crossing, then climbs the increasingly grassy slopes beyond the wash. This arduous pitch carries the traveler to a lofty overlook that boasts excellent views of Thimble Peak. The path then turns north into a hanging valley clad in oaks and meadows, and follows its bottoms to a narrow notch above the Sycamore Creek watershed. The trail bears northwest at this point, descending gradually along the rim of a wooded bowl. The trail ends at a pass above the East Fork of Sabino Canyon, where connecting trails lead both east and west.

60   ESPERERO CANYON

General description: A backpack from the Cactus Picnic Area to Window Rock, 8.5 miles.
Best season: Year-round.
Difficulty: Moderately strenuous to Bridalveil Falls; strenuous* beyond.
Water availability: Esperero Canyon has water seasonally.
Elevation gain: 4,520 feet.
Elevation loss: 1,595 feet.
Maximum elevation: 7,300 feet.

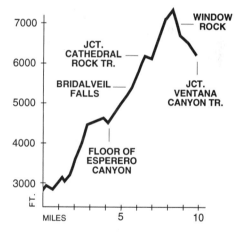

Topo maps: Sabino Canyon, Mount Lemmon, *Santa Catalina Mountains.*
Jurisdiction: Pusch Ridge Wilderness, Santa Catalina Ranger District, Coronado National Forest.
Finding the trailhead: In Tucson, follow Tanque Verde Road to Sabino Canyon Road. Follow this second road to the visitor center at its end. The trailhead can be reached on foot or by shuttlebus.

0.0	Trail leaves Cactus Picnic Area.
0.6	Junction with Rattlesnake Canyon cutoff trail. Turn left.
1.4	Trail crosses mouth of Bird Canyon.
3.0	Esperero Canyon overlook spot.
4.2	Trail reaches floor of Esperero Canyon.
5.6	Bridalveil Falls. Trail starts climbing.
6.5	Junction with Cathedral Rock trail. Turn left.
7.6	Saddle at head of Esperero Canyon.

60 Esperero Canyon
61 Ventana Canyon

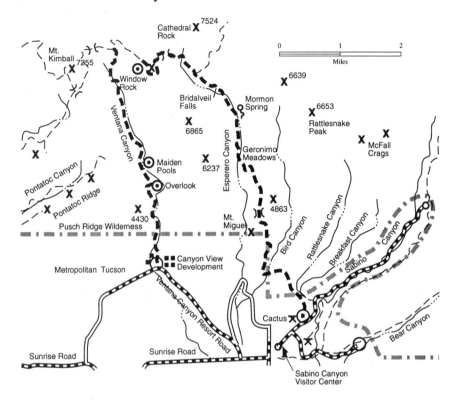

8.5 Window Rock.

9.7 Junction with Finger Rock and Ventana Canyon trails.

The trail: This trail climbs into the outer cordillera of the Santa Catalina Mountains, passing scenic landmarks that include Bridalveil Falls and Window Rock. From the Cactus Picnic Area, this trail runs northwest into the low foothills of the Santa Catalinas. After a short distance, the path drops into the broad mouth of Rattlesnake Canyon. This basin is home to some of the most vigorous stands of saguaro in the range. The trail crosses the basin, mounts low hills to the west, then drops into Bird Canyon. Look for hummingbirds here when the ocotillos and desert honeysuckles are in bloom. The trail heads straight across the streamcourse and climbs the south-facing slopes beyond it, bearing west as it seeks a nameless ravine. This draw bears the traveler into the mountains, climbing at a steady pace as grasses and upland shrubs appear among the cacti.

At the head of the draw, the trail climbs steeply to a high saddle that looks out over Esperero Canyon. A waterfall roars far below during the winter rainy season, and Cathedral Rock rises regally above the drainage. The trail crosses the sidehills to the east of the canyon, cutting through a grassland dotted with sotol, lechuguilla, and prickly pear. After crossing these open slopes, the trail enters a second saddle. This one is broad and sheltered by evergreen oaks, affording a fine (though waterless) camping spot. The path then descends to the canyon floor, where it enters a riparian forest that teems with bird life.

As the trail wanders upward through the bottomlands, towering palisades rise from the eastern slopes of the canyon. The western bank of the watercourse is overlooked by a dome of metamorphic rock, which is exfoliating, or shedding thin layers of rock, like an onion. Beyond the cliffs, a major draw enters from the east bearing Mormon Spring. The main canyon jogs northwest, and the trail follows it into the shade of a grove of Arizona cypresses. These stately trees have neatly ribbed bark and resemble firs in shape. However, they are not conifers at all; they are related to cypress and juniper. The trail follows the bottoms to Bridalveil Falls, a 15-foot cascade that pours over a sheer ledge of stone into an idyllic, shady pool.

The trail leaves the canyon floor at this point and climbs steeply to the top of a finger ridge. It follows this ridgetop to the base of Cathedral Rock, then cuts across the mountainsides, traveling westward along the southern slope of this peak. The Cathedral Rock trail departs from a marked junction, after which the Esperero trail sidehills toward the canyon floor. The path is overgrown and difficult to follow as it climbs along the floor of a draw, then zigzags upward aggressively to reach a saddle on the divide with Montrose Canyon.

A summit known locally as Window Peak looms to the southwest. The trail attacks its northwest corner in a series of switchbacks through heavy scrub. There are excellent views of Cathedral Rock along the way, and plenty of hair-raising dropoffs that encourage hikers to stay on the trail. The path crests a rocky ledge boasting good views of the pinnacles rising from the north face of Window Peak. It then travels to a saddle south of the summit before traversing northwest to regain the ridgeline. A steep descent leads to Window Rock, a soaring natural arch created by frost action; the arch is 15 feet high and 25 feet wide. It looks out over the head of Ventana Canyon, and also has good views of the spires adorning the north face of Window Peak. From here, a steep descent into the next saddle reaches trail's end at a junction with the Ventana Canyon and Finger Rock trails.

61   VENTANA CANYON

General description: A day hike through Ventana Canyon, 5.1 miles.
Best season: Year-round.
Difficulty: Moderately strenuous (* beyond Maiden Pools).
Water availability: Ventana Canyon has pools of water from winter through early summer.
Elevation gain: 3,180 feet.
Elevation loss: 60 feet.
Maximum elevation: 6,200 feet.

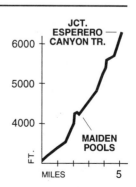

Topo maps: Sabino Canyon, Mount Lemmon, *Santa Catalina Mountains.*
Jurisdiction: Pusch Ridge Wilderness, Santa Catalina Ranger District, Coronado National Forest.
Finding the trailhead: In Tucson, take Sunrise Road to the northern arm of Kolb Road, which runs into the Ventana Canyon Resort. Park in the employee lot to the west of the resort headquarters and ask for a map to the trailhead, which is within the Canyon View Apartment complex.

0.0	Trail leaves Ventana Canyon Resort.
0.2	Trail enters Pusch Ridge Wilderness.
1.5	Trail leaves floor of Ventana Canyon and starts climbing.
1.9	Overlook spot.
2.3	Maiden Pools.
4.2	Trail leaves canyon floor.
5.1	Junction with Finger Rock and Esperero Canyon trails.

The trail: This trail begins on private lands at the edge of Tucson, and hikers should get permission by calling 299-4372 before using the trailhead. The trail is quite popular with locals, but it rarely sees traffic beyond Maiden Pools.

From the Canyon View complex, the trail runs northward, across the level uplands that lead to Ventana Canyon. Soon after entering the canyon, the path goes beyond the national forest boundary and enters the Pusch Ridge Wilderness. Massive cliffs of metamorphic stone slant skyward to sharp points above the floor of the canyon. Mesquite and other deep-rooted shrubs dominate the bottoms, while the slopes above them are sprinkled with saguaros and ocotillo. There are numerous crossings of the rocky streamcourse as the trail wanders northward, and the solid walls of the lower canyon rise into ragged pinnacles.

Upon reaching an impassable gorge, the trail jogs up a side draw that angles in from the west. The path follows this ravine upward for a short distance before turning east to continue the ascent on increasingly grassy slopes. The trail reaches its zenith atop a rounded spur ridge protruding into the heart of the canyon, offering spectacular views all around. Looking down the canyon, sharp spires frame a vista of the distant Santa Rita Mountains. To the north, a hanging valley ends at a dramatic pour-off, though the resulting falls cannot be seen from the trail. The path descends to the streamcourse at Maiden Pools. These shallow swimming holes are surrounded by flat shelves of rock that are ideal for basking in the sun. Low cliffs tower above the water, and evergreen oaks create pockets of shade. Just beyond the pools is a waterfall that carries a small stream into the canyon following rainy weather.

The trail follows the main streamcourse in Ventana Canyon, and the overhanging oaks and vigorous clumps of bear grass lend a tropical aspect to the otherwise arid landscape. The trail passes above a narrow cleft lined with inclined strata of gneiss. Oaks form a fairly solid woodland above this point, providing ample shade as the gradient steepens a bit. Hikers who stay alert may spot Hohokam mortar holes bored into flat boulders along the trail. These holes are perfectly round, about 3 inches in diameter, and were used by ancient Indians to grind seeds into a coarse flour.

The grade steepens as the path continues up the canyon. Near its head, the trail climbs into an eastern lobe of the valley to reach its end at a marked trail junction. The Finger Rock trail ascends to the west, while Window Rock is only a 1.2-mile climb along the Esperero trail to the east.

62   MOUNT KIMBALL

General description: A day hike along Finger Rock Canyon to the summit of Mount Kimball, 5.1 miles.
Best season: Year-round.
Difficulty: Moderately strenuous*.
Water availability: Finger Rock Spring may be dry.
Elevation gain: 4,135 feet.
Maximum elevation: 7,255 feet.
Topo map: *Santa Catalina Mountains*.
Jurisdiction: Pusch Ridge Wilderness, Santa Catalina Ranger District, Coronado National Forest.
Finding the trailhead: In Tucson, take Ina Road to Skyline, and follow this road to its junction with Alvernon Way. Turn left here and follow this road to the trailhead at its end.

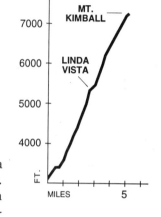

0.0	Trailhead. Follow the Finger Rock trail.
1.0	Finger Rock Spring.
2.7	Linda Vista overlook.
2.9	Junction with spur to a ridgetop saddle. Stay left.
4.5	Junction with Ventana Canyon and Pima Canyon trails. Turn left onto Pima Canyon trail for Mount Kimball.
5.0	Junction with spur trail to Mount Kimball. Turn right.
5.1	Summit of Mount Kimball.

The trail: This trail climbs to a high summit on Pusch Ridge, offering views of Finger Rock and a breathtaking overlook along the way. The trail begins by following the Finger Rock trail northward through tall saguaros and prickly pears. The broken foothills soon give way to the steep cleft of Finger Rock Canyon, with the sheer walls of Prominent Point towering above it. Finger Rock points skyward atop the wall, one of the most distinctive landmarks in the Santa Catalinas. The trail crosses the streamcourse at Finger Rock Spring, then begins a steep and rocky ascent of the eastern wall of the canyon. The climb eases at a grassy ledge known locally as

Linda Vista. This lofty perch commands a sweeping view down the canyon and out over the flats of Tucson.

As the trail continues upward, thorn scrub turns to grassy savannah dotted with evergreen oaks. Sheer outcrops of stone rise at odd intervals from the increasingly rolling landscape. The trail passes a spur that climbs into a ridgetop gap, then skirts the base of a cliff. Here, erosion along deep vertical joints in the rock has resulted in angular pillars. The path then drops into a wooded glen where ponderosa pines rise above a dense growth of oaks and junipers. After crossing the streamcourse, the path winds upward across an arid basin where stacked boulders rise like immense cairns above the scrub forest. The trail reaches the top of the grade at a saddle marking the divide between Finger Rock and Ventana canyons.

Straight ahead lies the trail to Ventana Canyon and beyond to Window Rock. To reach the top of Mount Kimball, turn left onto the Pima Canyon trail, which climbs its southern slope. This trail skirts the western side of the peak, then climbs to an overlook where an unmarked spur climbs to the right. The main path climbs across the summit of Kimball Peak to reach a ledge perched above a hair-raising dropoff. Mount Kimball is not an imposing peak, but by virtue of its strategic location it commands views in all directions around its summit. The most striking vista is to the east, where the rugged crests of Window and Cathedral rocks rise in front of forested Mount Lemmon.

Break time at Linda Vista.

62   Mount Kimball
63   Pontatoc Canyon

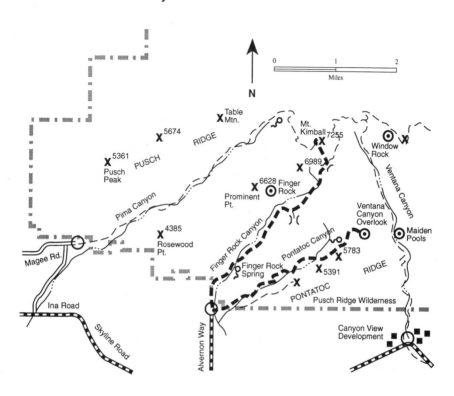

63   *PONTATOC CANYON*

General description: A day hike to an overlook above Ventana Canyon, 4 miles.
Best season: September-May.
Difficulty: Strenuous*.
Water availability: The spring at the head of the canyon is unreliable.
Elevation gain: 3,020 feet.
Elevation loss: 470 feet.
Maximum elevation: 5,740 feet.
Topo map: *Santa Catalina Mountains.*
Jurisdiction: Pusch Ridge Wilderness, Santa Catalina Ranger District, Coronado National Forest.
Finding the trailhead: In Tucson, take Ina Road to Skyline. Follow this

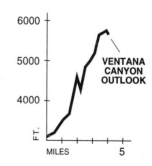

road to its junction with Alvernon Way. Turn left here and follow this road to the trailhead at its end.

0.0   Trailhead. Follow the Pontatoc Canyon trail.
0.8   Junction with Pontatoc Ridge trail. Bear right.
2.9   Junction with spur trail to ridgetop saddle. Stay left.
4.0   Overlook of Ventana Canyon.

The trail: This trail penetrates the arid foothills of the Santa Catalinas, carrying the hiker up a steady grade to an overlook of Ventana Canyon. The trail begins by gently climbing through rugged country populated by saguaros, prickly pears, and palos verdes. There are early views of the vertical rock faces of Prominent Point, including a distinctive formation known as Finger Rock. The hillsides steepen around Pontatoc Canyon, and the towering walls of Pontatoc Ridge rise to imposing heights straight ahead. The trail crosses the canyon floor and makes a brief climb onto the shoulders of Pontatoc Ridge. High on these slopes, the Pontatoc Ridge trail

The pinnacles of Pontatoc Ridge.

splits away to the right, while the Pontatoc Canyon trail drops back to the watercourse.

This is followed by a hard ascent up the far wall of the canyon, and the saguaros fall away to be replaced by lechuguilla and upland shrubs. From the heights, one can look out over the Tucson basin, rimmed by the volcanic Tucson Mountains. Beyond this range, the distant Sierritas and Baboquivaris rise on the horizon. The trail ultimately tires of the climb, and drops to the streamcourse. Tilted slabs of rock are exposed to the elements here, and waterfalls grace the canyon in winter. After a brief foray onto the south side of the canyon, the trail resumes a steep ascent on the north slopes. Grasses are abundant here, and sotol plants send up tall flowering stalks from basal rosettes of spiky leaves.

After passing the most rugged peaks of Pontatoc Ridge, the path crosses the draw and climbs to a saddle. Instead of passing through, it returns to the headwaters of Pontatoc Canyon. The upper reaches of the canyon are typified by rolling country sparsely wooded in evergreen oaks. The track becomes fainter as it rounds one last point on Pontatoc Ridge before climbing onto the saddle beyond. Follow the cairns northward up the ridgeline to pick up a well-worn path shooting eastward. Along the way, a small spring has been dug out of the mountainside; it may contain water in wintertime. Upon reaching the rim of Ventana Canyon, the trail drops onto a rounded knob that commands panoramic views of Tucson and the contrasting wild country of Ventana Canyon.

64   ROMERO CANYON

General description: A day hike to Romero Pools, 2.8 miles, or backpack to Romero Pass, 7.2 miles.
Best season: September-May.
Difficulty: Moderately strenuous*
(** beyond Romero Spring).
Water availability: Romero Pools and Romero Spring may be dry.
Elevation gain: 3,573 feet.
Elevation loss: 270 feet.
Maximum elevation: 6,020 feet.
Topo maps: Oro Valley, Mount Lemmon, *Santa Catalina Mountains.*

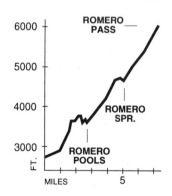

Jurisdiction: Catalina State Park; Pusch Ridge Wilderness, Santa Catalina Ranger District, Coronado National Forest.
Finding the trailhead: Drive 18 miles north of Tucson on U.S. Highway 89 to reach Catalina State Park. The trailhead is at the end of the main park road.

0.0   Trailhead.
0.6   Junction with Canyon Loop trail. Bear right.
1.1   Montrose Pools overlook. Trail enters Montrose Canyon.

2.6	Trail crosses divide into Romero Canyon.
2.8	Romero Pools.
5.1	Romero Spring.
6.4	Trail leaves Romero Canyon to ascend a side canyon.
7.2	Romero Pass.

The trail: This trek begins on the flats of Catalina State Park, ascends through the rugged foothills of the Santa Catalinas, then penetrates deep into the mountains. Most hikers travel only as far as Romero Pools, leaving the upper section of the trail fairly secluded. There is a good camping area near Romero Spring. From its terminus at Romero Pass, this trail links up with the Mount Lemmon and West Fork Sabino trails for extended trips.

The hike begins by crossing the prickly pear-mesquite flats that lead up to the foot of the Santa Catalinas. The rugged spires fronting the range are part of Pusch Ridge, a critical habitat for desert bighorn sheep. Hikers can pause at a perch that overlooks the mouth of Montrose Canyon, where pools of water often linger into the summer. The path then begins its ascent by climbing steadily up the hill to the north. Saguaros and ocotillos become increasingly prevalent as the trail traverses the high slopes above the north side of the canyon. These lofty slopes yield a bird's-eye view of the canyon as well a broad sweep of the Oro Valley to the west.

Outcrops of stone dominate the landscape as the trail approaches the Montrose-Romero divide. This is one of the most spectacular spots on the trail,

The rugged peaks of Pusch Ridge rise above Romero Canyon.

with craggy summits on all sides and a veritable rock garden of desert plants growing among the outcroppings. Lush clumps of sotol can be found in abundance here, and a substantial waterfall thunders through the depths of Romero Canyon during the wet season. The path turns southeast, becoming faint as it crosses bare stone on the flanks of a hillock. Watch for the cairns that mark the way. The trail follows the divide to a lower saddle separating the two canyons, then drops down the north side of the ridge to reach Romero Pools. These pools hold water most of the year, and groups of Tucsonians often bask on the rocks beside them.

The trail crosses the streamcourse and immediately turns up the valley, crossing a sandy bottomland clothed in grasses and yuccas. White-barked Arizona sycamores dominate the woody vegetation along the watercourse. There are numerous false trails here, and it will take some concentration to stay on the main path. As the flats come to an end, the trail crosses briefly onto the south bank of the watercourse. It returns to the north slope of the canyon for an arduous climb to avoid an impenetrable gorge. There is an overlook spot high atop a rocky spur; it commands fine views down the canyon and also offers a clear look at Cathedral Rock.

64   Romero Canyon

The trail continues to climb as it rounds a shallow draw, then descends to meet the wash again at Romero Spring. There is a good campsite here, although the water may dry up by midsummer and during autumn. Watch for clumps of cypress growing amid the increasingly vigorous oak woodland that fills the valley bottom. The path is much harder to follow beyond this point, since it is overgrown in many places and sometimes follows the beds of side channels as it ascends. Follow cairns whenever they can be found. The track makes seven crossings of the main wash as it ascends the valley, a fact that is poorly illustrated on most topographic maps. Pines soon make an appearance among the hardwoods, and the trail turns south to ascend a side drainage. A vigorous climb leads to Romero Pass, which is cloaked in forest. Drop over the divide a short distance to meet the Mount Lemmon and West Fork Sabino trails at a spot that looks out over the Sabino Basin.

65 ROMERO RUINS

General description: An interpretive loop through Hohokam and early Spanish ruins, 0.7 mile round-trip.
Best season: Year-round.
Difficulty: Easy.
Water availability: None.
Elevation gain: 35 feet.
Elevation loss: 35 feet.
Maximum elevation: 2,720 feet.
Topo map: Oro Valley (inc.).
Jurisdiction: Catalina State Park.
Finding the trailhead: Drive 18 miles north of Tucson on U.S. Highway 89 to reach Catalina State Park. The trailhead is 1 mile from the entrance, across from the day use area.

The trail: This short trail crosses Sutherland Wash to provide an interpretive loop through the ruins of a Hohokam Indian village. The Hohokam are thought to be the ancient forebears of the Tohono O'odham Indians, and contemporaries of the Anasazi. In contrast to their cliff-dwelling neighbors to the north, the Hohokam built villages on the flats. Highly advanced irrigation systems allowed them to grow crops with the minimal moisture provided by seasonal rains. Excavations have revealed the outlines of a stone wall that once surrounded the village here, as well as the foundations of pit dwellings. The centerpiece of the ruin is an oblong ball court, once the site of sports and games for the Indians who lived here centuries ago. A Spanish rancher by the name of Romero built his house on this site around 1850, and the rubble of this later structure stands amid the much older Hohokam ruins. The rugged cliffs of Pusch Ridge provides a striking backdrop for this fascinating archaeological tour.

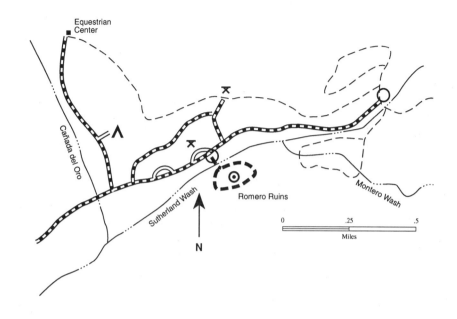

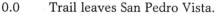

66   *GREEN MOUNTAIN*

General description: A day hike from San Pedro Vista to General Hitchcock Campground, 3.7 miles.

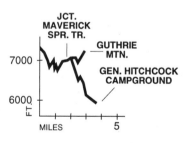

Best season: March-November.

Difficulty: Moderate north to south; moderately strenuous south to north.

Water availability: Maverick Spring generally has water; Horse Camp Spring is often dry.

Elevation gain: 440 feet.

Elevation loss: 2,000 feet.

Maximum elevation: 7,350 feet.

Topo map: *Santa Catalina Mountains.*

Jurisdiction: Santa Catalina Ranger District, Coronado National Forest.

Finding the trailhead: From Tucson, take Tanque Verde Road to the Catalina Highway. Follow this paved road into the mountains. San Pedro Vista is the upper trailhead, while General Hitchcock Campground is the lower one.

0.0   Trail leaves San Pedro Vista.

0.2   Junction with spur to summit of Green Mountain. Keep going straight.

0.3	Junction with Brush Corral trail. Keep going straight.
1.5	Junction with cutoff trail to Brush Corral route. Stay right.
1.7	Junction with spur trail to Maverick Spring (0.4 mile, moderate). Stay right.
1.9	Bear Saddle. Junction with Guthrie Mountain. spur (1.1 mile, moderate). Stay right.
3.7	Trail ends at General Hitchcock picnic area.

The trail: This trail offers a pleasant day hike that loops away from the Catalina Highway and then returns to it at a much lower point. It traverses secluded country with frequent views to the east. A large number of spur trails depart on an eastward heading, offering the possibility of side trips or longer loops incorporating a portion of the Brush Corrals trail. The habitat here is predominantly mixed pine-oak woodland, with conifers in the cooler sites and oaks prevailing on drier slopes. Coue's white-tailed deer are commonly sighted here, and birds congregate in the shady bottoms.

The trail begins by climbing over a pine-clad shoulder of Green Mountain. Heavy foot traffic has worn the forest floor bare in spots, and the trail is difficult to follow for the first hundred yards. It becomes obvious on the far side

A rocky spur of Green Mountain.

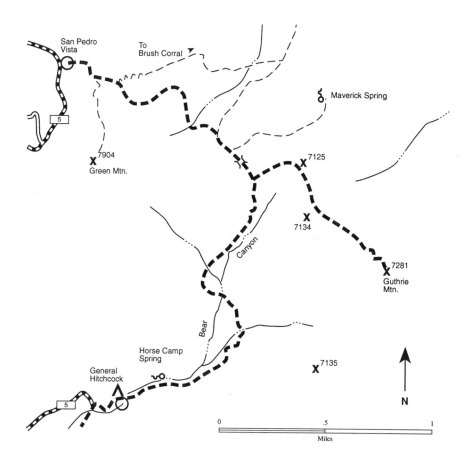

San Pedro Vista

To
Brush Corral

Maverick Spring

x 7904
Green Mtn.

x 7125

x
7134

x 7281
Guthrie
Mtn.

Canyon

Bear

Horse Camp
Spring

General
Hitchcock

x 7135

N

0　　　　　　　　　　　.5　　　　　　　　　　　1

Miles

of the rise as it descends the northeast slope of the mountain. A mixed forest of white firs, Douglas-firs, ponderosa pines, and evergreen oaks provides shady walking. Gaps in the canopy allow a sweeping vista of the Galiuro Mountains on the far side of a broad desert basin. As the trail passes a fingerlike projection of bedrock, an unmarked spur path climbs to the west on its way to the summit of Green Mountain. This steep track climbs steeply to rock outcrops that provide fine views of the surrounding country.

Meanwhile, the main trail levels off for a time, then makes several switchbacks down to meet the Brush Corrals trail. Bear southwest here as the Green Mountain trail sidehills across a steep slope, then wanders onto a low ridge to the east. This bare hilltop affords good views of Green Mountain's eastern face and the barren country of the San Pedro Valley. As the trail descends onto an east-facing slope, succulents grow amid the scattering of live oaks and manzanitas. These latter shrubs can be identified by the shiny red bark at the ends of their branches.

The trail passes a cutoff trail that links up with the Brush Corrals route; stay right as the main track climbs across rolling country. A spur path departs to the east for an 0.4-mile descent through ponderosa and limber pines to reach Maverick Spring. This clear trickle provides necessary moisture for water-loving plants such as mosses and ferns; wooden boxes have been embedded in the soil below it to catch the water. The main trail climbs from the junction with this spur path to a shallow saddle at the head of Bear Canyon. The Mount Guthrie spur trail runs southeast from the saddle and will be discussed in detail at the end of this section.

The Green Mountain trail drops into the shallow upper basin of Bear Canyon, rising and falling across the grain of the drainage pattern. It soon finds a finger ridge, which it follows for a rather abrupt descent. The path is deeply gullied here, and sometimes crosses exposed bedrock. It bottoms out amid tall pines and velvet ash trees beside a wash on the valley floor. The path crosses this wash several times as it wanders downward, passing the old site of Horse Camp Spring, which no longer offers any water. The forest diversifies as the trail approaches General Hitchcock Campground, and the understory supports such water-loving vegetation as bracken fern and canyon grape. Bird life is abundant here, and hikers are often serenaded by feathered songsters on the final leg of the hike.

MOUNT GUTHRIE OPTION

This 1.2-mile path follows a spur ridge southeastward from the Green Mountain trail to reach a scenic overlook. The trail dips and climbs on its way to the peak, and scrambles across naked bedrock just before the summit is reached. Look for prickly pear and hedgehog cactus growing from chinks in the stone. The summit of Mount Guthrie is clothed in dense live oaks and Douglas-firs that hide the distant views. However, an outcrop just beyond it along the ridgeline offers a fine panorama featuring Tanque Verde Ridge to the south and the rugged country of Bear Canyon to the southwest.

67 BRUSH CORRAL TRAIL

General description: A wilderness route to a long-abandoned ranger station site, 7.2 miles.
Best seasons: March-May; September-November.
Difficulty: Moderate** west to east; moderately strenuous** east to west.
Water availability: None
Elevation gain: 380 feet.
Elevation loss: 4,050 feet.
Maximum elevation: 7,350 feet.
Topo map: *Santa Catalina Mountains.*
Jurisdiction: Santa Catalina Ranger District, Coronado National Forest.

Finding the trailhead: From Tucson, take Tanque Verde Road to the Catalina Highway. Follow this paved road into the mountains. The trek departs from San Pedro Vista.

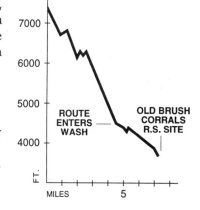

0.0 Trail leaves San Pedro Vista.
0.2 Junction with spur path to summit of Green Mountain. Stay left.
0.3 Junction with Brush Corral trail. Turn left.
2.2 Cutoff trail joins from the right. Keep going straight.
4.2 Trail ends. Descend southward into the wash.
5.1 Route leaves wash and ascends onto ridges to the south.
7.1 Route crosses Beuhman Wash.
7.2 Former site of Bush Corrals Ranger Station.

The trail: This trail descends the eastern slope of the Santa Catalinas, then runs onto the arid grasslands of the San Pedro Valley. The path is well-defined in its upper reaches, but upon leaving the mountains it becomes a wilderness route marked only by metal posts painted white at the tips, set apart at distances of up to half a mile. Its destination is the site of an old ranger station that was once a major administrative site before the building of the Catalina Highway. All traces of the old ranger station have long since been swallowed up by the desert. The upper portion of this trail can be combined with a cutoff path and the Green Mountain trail for a 4.6-mile day loop, or a 5.5-mile semi-loop that ends at General Hitchcock Campground.

The trek begins on the Green Mountain trail, which departs the Catalina Highway from San Pedro Vista. This trail runs across a bare dome of gravel, then cuts to the pine-clad flanks of Green Mountain. Several prominent pillars of stone allow views of the valley to the east, with the solid wall of the Galiuros rising like a wave beyond it. Bear left at two trail junctions. At the second intersection, the Brush Corrals trail splits away from the Green Mountain route and switchbacks relentlessly downward into the basin below. Pines and Douglas-firs are mixed with evergreen oaks here, but the conifers disappear as the trail bottoms out and ascends moderately onto a dry finger ridge. Look back at the Santa Catalinas for clear views of Green Mountain and Barnum Rock.

After following the ridgetop for a time, the trail drops into the valley to the east, which is thinly clad with pines and sprinkled with outcrops of weathered stone. The most prominent formation is a group of slabs exfoliating from the center like the petals of an opening bud. The trail passes close to this formation before traversing the basin floor to reach a wash, which it promptly crosses. The path then climbs vigorously for a short time. It levels off for a

Green Mountain and Barnum Rock.

straight stretch before its junction with the cutoff trail. This side trail climbs the hill to link up with the much higher Green Mountain trail.

Beyond this intersection is the last stand of the pine-fir forest. The trail then rounds a knob, passing through evergreen oaks and manzanitas that grow shorter and scruffier during the rapid descent. Alligator junipers raise contorted limbs to the sky from the dense mat of shrubbery, and a few sotols occupy the bare spots. The pathway is as wide as a boulevard here, but rolling rocks underfoot demand constant vigilance. Ahead, the ridge trails off like a crooked finger into the parched hills beyond. At one point, the trail disappears in a grassy saddle guarded to the east by a low knob that sports a copse of oaks. Stick to the ridgeline until several white-painted posts mark the spot where the route doglegs back into the arroyo to the south.

Travelers must now follow the wash (which may contain water in places) downstream for about half a mile. The streambed is littered with unstable boulders of white quartzite, and dark-gray bands of diabase bar the streamcourse in several places. The wash holds to a more-or-less constant eastward bearing, but the drainage ultimately jogs northeast as the ridge to the north sinks. On the north bank of the wash, a trail of sorts leads to a good

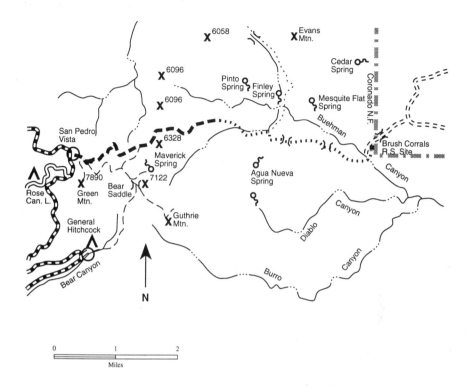

camping spot. (Cattle like this spot, too, and you may have to share it with them.)

Travelers bound for Evans Mountain should stick to the arroyo here, but the route to the Brush Corrals site leaves the wash at this bend and climbs southward through a low notch in the ridgetop. The terrain here is arid, with grass and thorn scrub of mesquite growing in sparse clumps, and ocotillo and cholla scattered across the parched south-facing slopes. The route skirts a draw, then strikes a course along the next eastward-running ridgetop—watch for cairns and white-painted posts that mark the route. The trail soon drops through a gap and onto a ridge to the southeast.

Watch the terrain on the far side of Beuhman Wash for clues to where the route descends to the Brush Corrals site. First, there will be a long, eastward-running ridge, then a convoluted hill, and finally a high, massive dome. The Brush Corrals site is on the north bank of Beuhman Wash just to the east of this dome. Travelers will encounter a section marker with one of the white posts. Keep going to the next white post, where the route follows a spur ridge down to cross the wash above a barbed-wire fence. A thicket of mesquite and a few towering saguaros occupy the flats where the ranger station once stood, and an abandoned jeep trail runs northeast into the desert through a gap in the low hills.

General description: A wilderness route from Palisade Ranger Station to Davis Spring, 9.4 miles.
Best seasons: March-May; September-November.
Difficulty: Moderately strenuous** west to east; strenuous** east to west.
Water availability: Pictograph, Araster, and Davis springs may be dry.
Elevation gain: 635 feet.
Elevation loss: 4,735 feet.
Maximum elevation: 8,275 feet.
Topo map: *Santa Catalina Mountains.*
Jurisdiction: Santa Catalina Ranger District, Coronado National Forest.
Finding the trailhead: From Tucson, take Tanque Verde Road to the Catalina Highway. Follow this paved road into the mountains. The trail departs the highway directly across from the Palisade Ranger Station.

0.0	Trail leaves Palisade Ranger Station.
0.5	Junction with Mount Bigelow Lookout trail. Keep going straight.
2.5	Junction with the Davis Spring trail. Turn right.
4.1	Petroglyphs.
4.2	Pictograph Spring.
5.9	Araster Spring.
6.4	Valley drains into Edgar Canyon. Junction with Knagge route. Turn left to follow the wash downward.
6.9	Trail climbs high onto hillsides to the north.
8.4	Route returns to floor of Edgar Canyon.
9.4	Davis Spring.

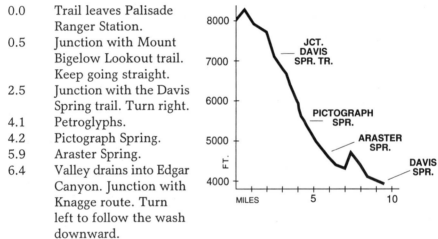

The trail: This very primitive trail runs from the crest of the Santa Catalinas into the cactus-filled canyons of the eastern foothills. Cairns and flagging mark the route from the Butterfly trail to Edgar Canyon; beyond this point, it is poorly marked and often quite faint. The trek begins at the Palisade Ranger Station and follows the Butterfly trail eastward to a high saddle on Mount Bigelow. The trail to Davis Spring runs over the far side of the hill, then turns north across slopes wooded in fir and pine. There is a fine vista spot along the way, and from here one can look out across the broad desert basin of the San Pedro Valley at the rugged Galiuro Mountains. The path then runs out onto a lofty spur ridge. An enormous block of bedrock crowns its top, and another scenic overlook waits at its eastern end. The path then zigzags down its steep eastern face to reach the saddle above Novio Spring. From a junction in the saddle, the Butterfly trail swings north as it descends to the spring, while the Davis Spring trail drops away to the east.

The navigation challenges begin here as the trail descends in fits and starts across the gentle slopes above Atchley Canyon. Plastic flagging may mark the trail as it descends through pines and firs to reach the oak woodlands of the middle elevations. The trail ultimately pops through a low saddle and drops across dry, south-facing slopes that allow good views of the basin below. At the bottom of the grade, the trail follows dry streamcourses to reach an overhanging boulder covered with Apache petroglyphs. Several tortoises adorn the surface of the stone, along with intricate birds and a dog-shaped figure. Just a short distance beyond this rock, Pictograph Spring offers a steady supply of clear water in the bottom of the gulch.

Beyond Pictograph Spring lies a long, shallow basin filled with evergreen oaks and manzanitas. The track is obscured by fallen leaves here, and travelers may have to rely on cairns and flagging to find the route. About halfway between Pictograph and Araster Springs, the track passes through a series of fenced paddocks. Just beyond them is a steep, sparsely wooded slope that offers fine views of rocky peaks that crown grassy foothills to the east. The trail crosses the streamcourse numerous times on its way down to Araster Spring,

A nameless peak in the foothills of the Santa Catalinas.

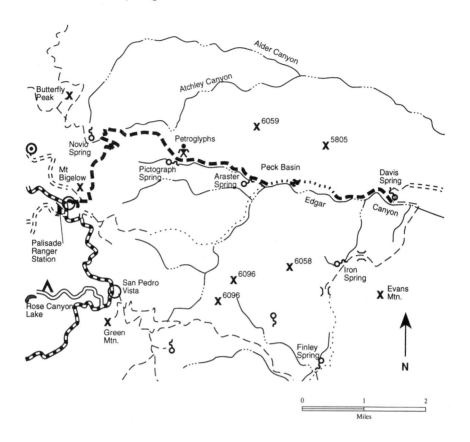

a natural (and muddy) seep located in a grove of mixed hardwoods. Beyond it, the path climbs quickly to the parched slopes above the east side of the wash, where it stays all the way down to Edgar Canyon.

At this confluence of valleys, a signpost marks the junction with the Knagge "trail"; this was the last overt trail marker along the route when this book was written. Turn east to follow the wash of Edgar Canyon for about half a mile. The watercourse soon makes a sharp bend to the south, and a steep track climbs up onto the slopes to the east. Follow this path onto the desert slopes that rise high above the north side of the canyon, where it peters out entirely. After crossing above the initial band of cliffs, stay high on the slopes to avoid a rocky impasse in the canyon below. The route traverses a steep vale dotted with ocotillo, mesquite, and evergreen oak. It then runs over the flat top of a finger ridge that extends out over the canyon. After crossing this ridgetop, the route descends steeply along the course of a dry gulch to reach the canyon floor.

After following the wash for a while, the trail runs onto a flat covered with evenly spaced mesquite trees of great age. A handful of cottonwoods and ivory-barked sycamores shade the wash here, and clumps of seep willow grow from the gravel bars. The seep willow is not actually a willow at all; this white-flowered bush is most closely related to rain forest shrubs of Central America. A major wash soon enters from the south, and Edgar Canyon jogs northward before bending sharply to resume its eastward course. The trail drops briefly into the arroyo at the second bend, then climbs onto a steep hillside covered with various species of mesquite, a few tall saguaros, and scattered clumps of prickly pear. Upon cresting a rise, the trail reveals a small flat dead ahead. Tall cottonwoods mark the stock tanks of Davis Spring. The trail runs through fenced paddocks as it passes them. The track then takes a sharp turn to the north, climbing steeply along the east wall of a small gulch. It tops out on the low tablelands of Davis Mesa, where it meets a primitive jeep track.

69   ASPEN LOOP

General description: A day loop through the high country near Mount Lemmon, 3 miles.
Best season: April-October.
Difficulty: Moderate.
Water availability: Marshall Gulch has water year-round.
Elevation gain: 755 feet.
Elevation loss: 755 feet.
Maximum elevation: 8,115 feet.
Topo maps: Mount Lemmon, *Santa Catalina Mountains.*
Jurisdiction: Pusch Ridge Wilderness, Santa Catalina Ranger District, Coronado National Forest.
Finding the trailhead: From Tucson, take Tanque Verde Road to the Catalina Highway. Follow this paved road into the mountains. Turn left into the town of Summerhaven; the trailhead is at the end of this road.

0.0	Marshall Gulch Picnic Area. Follow the Aspen trail.
1.8	Marshall Saddle trail junction. Turn right onto Marshall Gulch trail to complete the loop.
3.0	Trail returns to Marshall Gulch Picnic Area.

The trail: This trail offers a popular day loop through high montane country from the Marshall Gulch Picnic Area. It is often crowded during summer and early autumn, especially on weekends. The aspen stands for which the trail is named are among the largest in the state, and put on a brief fall color display that generally peaks in late October.

The trail begins on a southward bearing as it climbs the slopes above the west bank of Sabino Creek. After a short distance, a rocky overlook just below the trail offers views of the granite-walled canyon, sprinkled liberally with tall ponderosa pines. The path turns westward into a moist swale. This level glade is populated by groves of quaking aspen, their stately colonnades capped by clouds of bright-green leaves that tremble in the slightest breeze. The dark green spires of spruce and fir rise in the midst of the aspens, thrown into high relief by lighter foliage surrounding them.

The path begins to climb more vigorously, passing into a forest of Gambel oak that provides an annual banquet of acorns for fox squirrels and Coues white-tailed deer. Gambel oaks are the only oaks in Arizona that sheds its leaves in the autumn rather than remaining green through the winter. This grove of oaks accompanies the traveler to the top of the ridgeline, where an open savannah of ponderosa pine takes over.

The route follows the ridgetop westward, continuing to climb as it enters country that was swept by a low-intensity ground fire in the recent past. Look for charred stumps and "cat faces," or fire scars, at the bases of living trees; these offer reminders of the fire's passage. The trees close ranks as the trail climbs around a wooded summit. After reaching a high point, the path turns northward and drops into a rounded saddle before running northeastward onto the ridge at the head of Marshall Gulch. Here, a spur track leads to an outcrop of bedrock rising above the forest canopy. A brief scramble rewards the traveler with a fine view toward Cathedral Peak across the Wilderness of Rock.

69 Aspen Loop

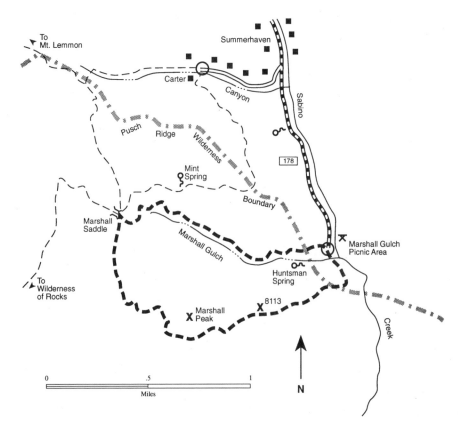

Some of the tallest aspens in the nation grow in the high country of the Santa Catalinas.

To the east, buff-colored fins of stone rise from the flanks of Mount Lemmon, the tallest peak in the Santa Catalinas.

The main trail passes a second outcrop on its way to Marshall Saddle, where it reaches a complicated intersection. To complete the loop, take a hard right onto the Marshall Gulch trail. This path winds eastward as it descends, crossing the wooded floor of a shallow basin. An intermittent stream joins the trail on its descent, providing necessary moisture for riparian plants such as columbine, box elder, and bigtooth maple. The pines soon give way to a bottomland forest of hardwoods that puts on a striking display of fall colors that begins in early October. Miniature walls of stone line the streamcourse, forming a foothold for mosses, ferns, and other trailing vegetation. The path splits, with the left fork descending drier slopes above the north bank of the watercourse, and the right fork following the bottoms along its south bank. These trails emerge in tandem beside the privy of the Marshall Gulch Picnic Area.

70 WILDERNESS OF ROCK

General description: A day hike or backpack into the Wilderness of Rock, 5 miles.
Best season: April-October.
Difficulty: Moderate*.
Water availability: Mint Spring may be dry; Lemmon Canyon has water year-round.
Elevation gain: 1,025 feet.
Elevation loss: 1,645 feet.
Maximum elevation: 8,065 feet.
Topo maps: Mount Lemmon, *Santa Catalina Mountains*.
Jurisdiction: Pusch Ridge Wilderness, Santa Catalina Ranger District, Coronado National Forest.
Finding the trailhead: From Tucson, take Tanque Verde Road to the Catalina Highway. Follow this paved road into the mountains. Turn left into the town of Summerhaven; turn right on Carter Canyon Road and follow it to the unmarked trailhead at its end.

0.0	End of Carter Canyon Road. Follow the Mint Spring trail.
0.8	Mint Spring.
1.3	Marshall Saddle trail junction. Turn west onto the Wilderness of Rock trail.
2.8	Junction with Lemmon Rock Lookout trail. Keep going straight.
3.2	Trail enters the Wilderness of Rock.
5.0	Junction with Mount Lemmon trail.

The trail: This route accesses a very popular area of pine forests and striking granite formations. The Wilderness of Rock receives particularly heavy visitor use from late spring through early fall, and travelers should go to

Granite formations in the Wilderness of Rock.

extra effort to ensure that they leave the area unscarred by their passage. The rugged nature of the country makes it hard to find a level campsite, and campers should be especially careful to conceal their tents from passersby. Water can generally be found in the wash of Lemmon Canyon. Route-finding skills will prove useful here, since the path often crosses broad stretches of bare stone.

The trek starts by passing between several private homes on the Mint Springs trail. After clearing these last remnants of civilization, the route swings southeast to round a low finger of Mount Lemmon. The trail then dips eastward into the pine-clad basin of Marshall Gulch, passing Mint Spring along the way. This tiny seep is bordered by aromatic mint plants during late spring, and makes a pleasant rest spot. A brief climb then carries the traveler to Marshall Saddle, where the trail reaches a complicated intersection.

The Wilderness of Rock trail lies straight ahead, descending through pines on a westward tack. This path skirts the base of Mount Lemmon, winding among weathered outcrops that form a fitting prelude to the geological wonders that lie ahead. The route then turns south, following the crest of a sandy hillock robed with pine trees. At the bottom of this shallow grade is the streamcourse that ultimately forms Lemmon Canyon. The presence of small

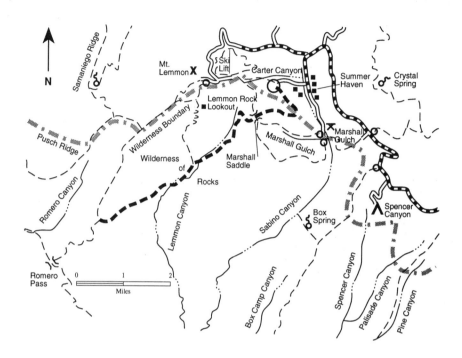

fishes in the sun-dappled waters indicates that this stream is one of the more dependable watercourses in the Santa Catalinas. The trail follows the waterway downward, and aspens and canyon grapes grow among the ever-present pines. After passing the Lemmon Rock Lookout trail, the landscape takes on a drier aspect. Live oaks and clumps of manzanita grow from the sandy soil found here.

The trail climbs over a low outcrop of stone that marks the eastern boundary of the Wilderness of Rock. The formations of weathered granite become increasingly spectacular as the pathway penetrates the heart of the rocks. Hoodoos, fingers, balanced rocks, and natural menhirs have been sculpted into the granite by the relentless forces of wind and water. To the north, enormous pillars of stone rise from the wooded slopes of Mount Lemmon. From the high points along Lemmon Canyon, the distant silhouette of Tanque Verde Ridge can be seen along the southern skyline. The trail may be a bit faint in places as the trail crosses stretches of naked bedrock; watch for cairns and look for the next spot where the well-worn path finds softer footing.

The rock formations reach a spectacular climax as the trail crosses a waterchiseled canyon. They recede a bit as the trail climbs into piney uplands bordering the western side of the basin. The granite here is shot through with veins of quartz, and huge chunks of this milky crystal have weathered out and lie scattered across the forest floor. After crossing a pocket-sized meadow occupying its own narrow vale, the pathway climbs a final moderate pitch to meet the Mount Lemmon trail. Just beyond it, uplands fall away dramatically into the depths of Romero Canyon.

71   *MOUNT LEMMON*

General description: A backpack from the top of Mount Lemmon to Romero Pass, 6.3 miles.
Best season: April-October.
Difficulty: Moderate* northeast to southwest; moderately strenuous* southwest to northeast.
Water availability: None.
Elevation gain: 230 feet.
Elevation loss: 3,450 feet.
Maximum elevation: 9,300 feet.
Topo maps: Mount Lemmon, *Santa Catalina Mountains.*

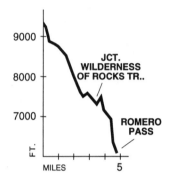

Jurisdiction: Pusch Ridge Wilderness, Santa Catalina Ranger District, Coronado National Forest.
Finding the trailhead: From Tucson, take Tanque Verde Road to the Catalina Highway. Follow this paved road into the mountains. Turn right at the Summerhaven junction and follow the Mount Lemmon Road to the trailhead at the summit of the peak.

0.0	Trail leaves Mount Lemmon Road.
0.1	Junction with Meadow trail. Keep going straight.
0.3	Junction with Lemmon Rock Lookout trail. Keep going straight.
0.5	Overlook spots.
0.7	Meadow trail rejoins Mount Lemmon trail. Keep going straight.
1.5	Junction with Sutherland trail. Bear left as the old road becomes a footpath.
3.3	Junction with Wilderness of Rock trail. Keep going straight.
3.5	Trail begins descent to Romero Pass.
6.3	Romero Pass. Junction with Romero Canyon and West Fork Sabino trails.

The trail: This trail drops from the heights of Mount Lemmon all the way down to the divide between Romero Canyon and the west fork of Sabino Canyon. It meets the Sutherland and Wilderness of Rock trails along the way, allowing short loop trips or extended hikes that end in Catalina State Park, below the western slope of the range. The trail's end allows access into Romero Canyon and the Sabino Basin, offering further possibilities for backpackers. Hikers will encounter a wide spectrum of life zones along the

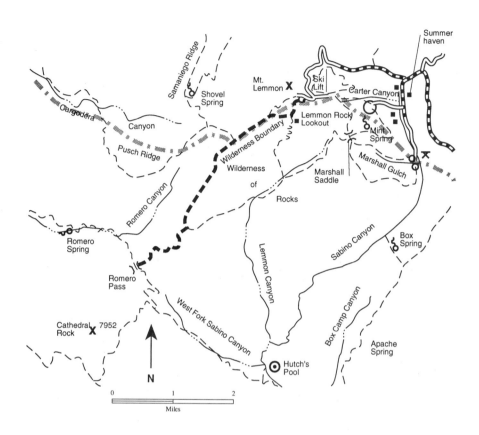

Summer haven

Samaniego Ridge

Shovel Spring

Mt. Lemmon **X**

Ski Lift

Carter Canyon

Oargodera

Canyon

Lemmon Rock Lookout

Mint Spring

Pusch Ridge

Wilderness Boundary

Wilderness

of

Rocks

Marshall Gulch

Marshall Saddle

Romero Canyon

Romero Spring

Sabino Canyon

Box Spring

Romero Pass

Lemmon Canyon

Box Camp Canyon

Cathedral Rock **X** 7952

West Fork Sabino Canyon

Apache Spring

Hutch's Pool

N

0   1   2

Miles

route, ranging from lush conifer forest to arid scrubland. The magnificent granite towers of Mount Lemmon are visible from the trail, and a short excursion into the Wilderness of Rock finds even more unusual formations of stone.

From the parking pullout that serves as a trailhead, the trek follows an old dirt road that runs southwest as it descends. The Meadow trail splits off to the right, offering a slightly longer alternate route through sun-dappled glades among the pines and aspens. The main trail makes a straight course downhill, and after 0.3 mile the Lemmon Rock Lookout trail splits away to the left. This trail runs a short distance to the lookout before dropping steeply into the Wilderness of Rock. Bear right to follow the Mount Lemmon trail along the rim of Mount Lemmon itself. A rocky overlook offers a panoramic view of the basin containing the Wilderness of Rock. Sheer towers of stone rise from the slopes nearby, and Rattlesnake Peak and Cathedral Rock guard the far edge of the Santa Catalinas. The grid of metropolitan Tucson sprawls across the basin beyond, and the Rincon and Santa Rita ranges rise in the hazy distance.

The Meadow trail soon rejoins the Mount Lemmon route, and the old roadway is soon swallowed by a forest of pines, firs, and a few aspen groves. The descent is gentle as far as the junction with the Sutherland trail, where the roadbed ends and the Mount Lemmon trail becomes a footpath. This narrow track drops down a pine-clad ridge with fine views of Cathedral Rock and the broken crags of Pusch Ridge. The descent eases as the ridge resolves itself into a series of rocky hillocks reminiscent of the *kopjes* found on the African veldt. Erosion has carved the granite bedrock into pillars and domes and pines and evergreen oaks are sprinkled at random amid the stone. At the bottom of a low saddle is a junction with the Wilderness of Rock trail, which descends gradually on an eastbound course.

The Mount Lemmon trail then climbs a rocky hillock; look backward for final views of the mountain. At the top of the hill, a level band of rimrock overlooks the broad vista of Romero Canyon. This is an outstanding perch for taking in the sunset. The trail then descends a steep face, weaving back and forth as it seeks an unobstructed path through the outcrops. Live oak and manzanita grow from every available fissure, and boulders of crystalline quartz lie scattered about. Before long, an outstanding view of Cathedral Rock presents itself. Beyond it, the tilted buttresses of Pusch Ridge rise skyward at crazy angles.

The trail makes for a ziggurat of cloven bedrock, which turns out to be the first point on a long spur ridge descending to Romero Pass. Look back for views of the sheer blocks of stone that line the rim of Romero Canyon. The spur ridge reaches a steep dropoff, and the trail weaves downhill. To the east, the West Fork of Sabino Canyon is guarded by Rattlesnake Peak and the McFall Crags, their faces deeply cleft with fissures and gullies. Piñon pine and manzanita are the dominant plants here, while yucca and agave occupy a sparse understory. The trail bottoms out in the low saddle of Romero Pass, where it meets the Romero Canyon and West Fork Sabino trails near some shady ponderosa pines.

72   THE BOX CAMP TRAIL

General description: A backpack from the Catalina Highway to the Sabino Basin, 7.1 miles.
Best seasons: March-May; September-November.
Difficulty: Moderate* north to south; moderately strenuous** south to north.
Water availability: Box Spring is reliable; Apache Spring is intermittent.
Elevation gain: 255 feet.
Elevation loss: 4,575 feet.
Maximum elevation: 8,130 feet.
Topo maps: Mount Bigelow, Mount

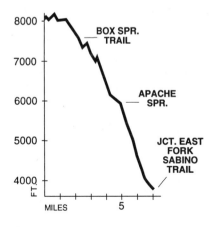

Lemmon, *Santa Catalina Mountains*.

Jurisdiction: Pusch Ridge Wilderness, Santa Catalina Ranger District, Coronado National Forest.

Finding the trailhead: From Tucson, take Tanque Verde Road to the Catalina Highway. Follow this paved road into the mountains. The trail leaves from a parking area 100 yards beyond the Spencer Canyon Campground road.

0.0	Trail leaves the Catalina Highway.
2.2	Junction with trail to Box Spring. Keep going straight.
5.0	Apache Spring. Trail becomes faint.
7.0	Trail crosses East Fork Sabino Canyon wash.
7.1	Trail joins East Fork Sabino trail.

The trail: This trail runs from the crest of the Santa Catalinas to the bottom of the Sabino Basin. It follows a ridgetop for most of its length, and offers good views as well as opportunities for wildlife viewing that improve as the trail penetrates the wilderness. The track is well-beaten and obvious at its upper end, but becomes overgrown below Apache Spring. Travelers are advised to hike this part of the route in the downhill direction, because the trail was almost impossible to pick up from the lower end at the time of this writing.

From its upper end, the trail begins as a lazy stroll among rounded hilltops covered in mature mountain pines. The path follows an undulating ridgetop for a short time, then drops into a shallow swale that bears southwest. The glens contain bracken ferns and grasses, lending a pastoral aspect to the landscape. The gradient is initially shallow, then steepens at a point where waterfalls splash through the rocks during spring runoff. The vale soon adopts a westward course, while the trail angles to the south across a steep hillside. The Box Spring trail drops westward onto the flats below, crossing a small ravine before descending the slopes of Sabino Canyon to reach the spring itself. Meanwhile, the main trail seeks the ridgeline, which has a more arid climate well suited to evergreen oaks and manzanitas.

The scrub shrinks as the ridge loses altitude, revealing excellent views of lower Sabino Canyon and the sprawling metropolis of Tucson. Directly to the east, a nameless canyon is lined with pillars of granite that have taken on fanciful forms in accordance with the whims of wind and water. The bedrock underfoot weathers into a fine gravel that rolls like ball bearings; tread carefully during the descent. The vegetation reflects increasing aridity as the trail gives up elevation, and sotol, agave, and yucca are common amid the chaparral. Lechuguillas (locally known as "shin daggers") creep in at the lower elevations, and a thorny shrub that is easily mistaken for an aspen seedling grows among the rocks.

The path fades as the descent steepens, and an outcrop of bedrock shaped like stacked pancakes looms directly ahead. The trail works its way to the foot of this formation, where it crosses the narrow gulch containing Apache Spring. This spring is rarely more than a thin film of water running across the rocks,

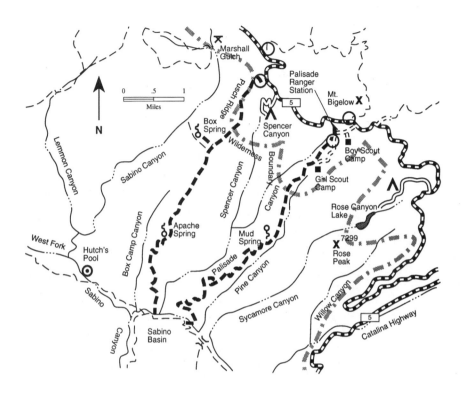

but in this dry environment, it is a powerful magnet for birds and small rodents. Red-fluted desert honeysuckle and yellow brittlebrush thrive on the ample supply of groundwater, and unleash an abundance of blossoms from time to time.

The path then skirts to the west of the outcrop and begins its descent into Box Camp Canyon. Thorny cat's-claw punishes the traveler who wanders from the trail here; it pays to stay on the old trailbed. Gnarled piñon pines are scattered across the slopes, growing from crevices in the stone. The trail dips onto the western side of the hill, then returns to the ridgeline for the remainder of its wandering descent. Speargrass seeds hitch rides in the socks of passing hikers, and chollas and lechuguillas provide a spiny incentive to stay on the faint track. Near the bottom of the grade, spindly ocotillos and grandiose saguaros dot the hillsides. Coue's white-tailed deer commonly are spotted in the draws during morning and evening, and golden eagles ride thermals overhead.

The trail finally drops into a forest of oaks that line the East Fork of Sabino Canyon. It promptly becomes lost in a maze of game trails; bear straight downhill to the course of the intermittent stream. Upstream of this point, the arroyo is often dry and is guarded by walls of rock on each bank. Below, water is often

Looking into Sabino Canyon.

found in pools, and the chalky white bark of Arizona sycamore stands out against a dark background formed by the more drought-tolerant oaks. The track picks up on the far bank of this border area, buried in a carpet of fallen leaves. The route runs a short distance across the flats to reach a signpost on the East Fork Sabino trail, which loops down into the bottomlands to meet it.

73 PALISADE TRAIL

General description: A backpack from Organization Ridge Road to the Sabino Basin, 6.2 miles.

Best seasons: March-May; September-November.

Difficulty: Moderate* north to south; moderately strenuous* south to north.

Water availability: Mud Spring is reliable.

Elevation gain: 40 feet.

Elevation loss: 3,880 feet.

Maximum elevation: 7,800 feet.

Topo maps: Mount Bigelow, Sabino Canyon, *Santa Catalina Mountains.*

Jurisdiction: Pusch Ridge Wilderness, Santa Catalina Ranger District, Coronado National Forest.

Finding the trailhead: From Tucson, take Tanque Verde Road to the Catalina Highway. Follow this paved road into the mountains. Turn left on the Organization Ridge Road, which departs to the left just before the Palisade Ranger Station. The trail leaves this primitive road across from the Showers Point group camp.

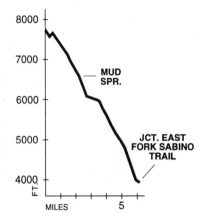

0.0	Trail leaves Organization Ridge Road.
0.5	Junction with spur to Girl Scout camp. Stay right.
2.3	Mud Spring.
3.6	Trail leaves Pine Canyon.
6.2	Junction with East Fork Sabino trail.

The trail: This trail starts near the Palisades Ranger Station and runs down the ridgetops to end in the East Fork of Sabino Canyon. It initially passes through pine forest, then descends through oak woodlands and ends up in arid grasslands sprinkled with ocotillos. The path is well-beaten for its entire length, and Mud Spring offers a fairly reliable water source along the way. The scenery features Pine Canyon along the middle part of the route, and near its end is a rocky bluff that commands a panoramic view of the Sabino Basin.

From the Showers Point group campground, the trail wanders through rolling country wooded in ponderosa pine. It soon runs out onto the slopes of a steep gully. This is the head of Palisade Canyon, and several spur paths drop to the floor of the gulch, where the Hidden Pools lie among boulders and slabs of bedrock. After 0.9 mile, a spur track from the Girl Scout camp joins the trail from the left. The main path then bears southwest down a sandy ridgetop clad sparsely in pines. The yellow cliffs of a nameless summit rise to the east, and after passing them the path drops into a wooded gully containing Mud Spring. A cement trough captures the water here, providing a reliable supply to travelers and local wildlife.

Evergreen oak replaces pine as the dominant tree as the trail continues down the gully, rounds a finger ridge, then continues its descent down a similar gulch. Here, Chihuahua and ponderosa pines are replaced by piñon pines and junipers, and the oaks take on a scrubby appearance. The draw opens dramatically onto a steep precipice above Pine Canyon. Rock towers loom into the canyon from its sides, and Thimble Peak rises beyond its mouth. The trail clings to the canyon wall, then climbs to the top. Here, it skirts westward across a shallow depression filled with wind-sculpted gneiss. The trail crosses windswept slabs of stone; it may be necessary to follow the cairns to stay on route.

Looking down Pine Canyon toward Thimble Peak.

After crossing the depression, the path drops over a hilltop and runs the rim of Palisade Canyon for a while. The trees are small and widely spaced here, and grasses become the prevalent ground cover. After wandering onto a lobe of stone that juts out over Palisade Canyon, the trail turns south into an arid fold in the hillside. It passes across level bands of rimrock before dropping onto steep slopes beyond, and these stony perches offer sweeping views of the Sabino Basin and the rugged peaks that surround it. The path passes a last cluster of stone pillars as it descends toward the featureless slopes below.

Sotol and lechuguilla interrupt the grasslands as the trail descends, and ocotillos and chollas are scattered across the lower skirts of the hillside. Saguaros are here in low numbers; only a few grace the parched slopes. The trail makes a long dogleg to the east on its final descent toward the valley floor. It meets the East Fork Sabino trail in the heavily wooded canyon bottoms, at the foot of the grade that climbs eastward into Sycamore Canyon.

General description: A day hike from the Mount Lemmon Road to the floor of the Cañada del Oro, 2.8 miles.

Best season: April-October.

Difficulty: Moderate south to north; strenuous north to south.

Water availability: No dependable sources.

Elevation gain: 70 feet.

Elevation loss: 2,520 feet.

Maximum elevation: 8,170 feet.

Topo maps: Mount Lemmon, *Santa Catalina Mountains.*

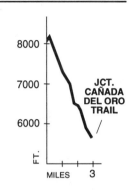

Jurisdiction: Santa Catalina Ranger District, Coronado National Forest.

Finding the trailhead: From Tucson, take Tanque Verde Road to the Catalina Highway. Follow this paved road into the mountains. Turn right at the Summerhaven junction, and follow the Mount Lemmon Road for 1.5 miles to reach a pulloff to the right. A rusting sign marks the trail.

74   Red Ridge

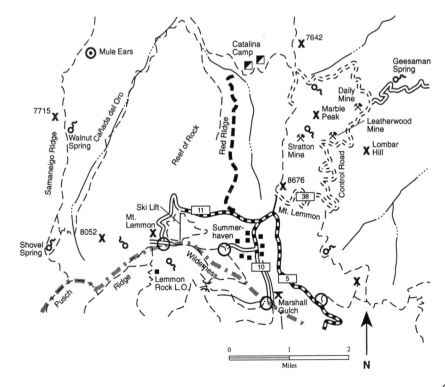

A spur of the Reef of Rock.

| 0.0 | Trail leaves Mount Lemmon Road. |
| 2.8 | Trail joins cutoff trails to Dan Saddle and Cañada del Oro. |

The trail: This trail descends steadily (and sometimes steeply) from the flanks of Mount Lemmon to the floor of the Cañada del Oro. It can be approached as a vigorous day hike, or can be combined with the upper portion of the Oracle Ridge trail for a short overnight loop. The trail provides excellent views of the Reef of Rock, one of the most striking geological formations in the Santa Catalinas. Carry plenty of water, because none will be found along the trail.

The trail begins by climbing over a low hill clad in a mixed forest that includes pines, aspens, spruces, and even subalpine firs. It then drops to a ridgeline and soon reaches a high overlook. The Reef of Rock drops away to the west. Straight ahead lies the broad basin of the Cañada del Oro and the distant Tortillita Range far beyond. A savannah of limber and ponderosa pines cloaks the ridge as it descends; look for fire scars at the base of the tree trunks. Low-intensity fires help to maintain this open forest of pines by weeding out thin-skinned trees and shrubs.

The climate gets hotter and drier with decreasing altitude, and the pines ultimately give way to a scrub forest of live oak, manzanita, and yucca. The Reef of Rock rises a few hundred yards to the west; its tilted sheaves of granite are an imposing natural presence. The rusty tint of the rocks underfoot derives from the oxidation of iron during natural weathering. This iron-bearing formation gives the ridge its name.

The trail drops to the valley floor, where it reaches a trail junction near Catalina Camp. Standing water can sometimes be found in the streambed here if it has rained recently. Travelers who explore the far bank of the watercourse may discover rusting machinery from the old copper-mining days. A path runs northward from the junction to connect with the primitive Cañada del Oro trail. Another track climbs eastward, passing Catalina Camp on its way to Dan Saddle and a meeting with the Oracle Ridge trail.

75   ORACLE RIDGE

General description: A backpack along the spine of Oracle Ridge, 13.2 miles.
Best season: March-October.
Difficulty: Moderately strenuous south to north; strenuous north to south.
Water availability: There is no water on the ridgeline.
Elevation gain: 1,700 feet.
Elevation loss: 5,100 feet.
Maximum elevation: 7,990 feet.
Topo map: *Santa Catalina Mountains.*
Jurisdiction: Santa Catalina Ranger District, Coronado National Forest.
Finding the trailhead: From Tucson, take Tanque Verde Road to the Catalina Highway. Follow this paved road into the mountains. Just before Summerhaven, turn right onto the Oracle Control Road and follow it downhill for 100 yards to reach the trailhead.

0.0	Trail leaves Oracle Control Road.
1.2	Stratton Saddle.
2.4	Dan Saddle. Junction with jeep trails to Catalina Camp and Geesaman Mine. Keep going straight ahead.
4.6	Trail meets jeep trail to Rice Peak. Follow it downward.
5.9	Junction with jeep road #4475. Keep going straight.
8.5	Trail passes Apache Peak.
9.8	Jeep track descends to the right. Keep going straight.
10.5	Jeep track descends to the right. Keep going straight.
10.7	Junction with American Flag trail. Turn right.
11.9	Junction with Highjinks Mine road. Bear left.
13.2	American Flag Ranch trailhead.

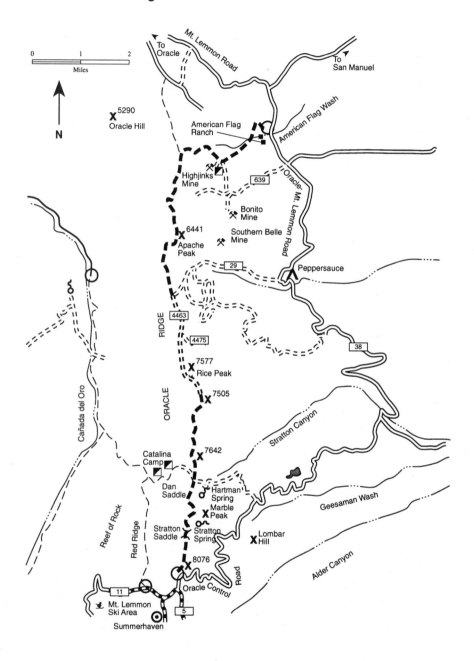

0   1   2
Miles

N

X 5290
Oracle Hill

Mt. Lemmon Road

To Oracle

To San Manuel

American Flag Wash

American Flag Ranch

Highjinks Mine

639

Oracle - Mt. Lemmon Road

Bonito Mine

Southern Belle Mine

X 6441
Apache Peak

29

Peppersauce

RIDGE

4463

4475

38

X 7577
Rice Peak

X 7505

Cañada del Oro

ORACLE

Stratton Canyon

X 7642

Catalina Camp

Dan Saddle

Hartman Spring

Marble **X** Peak

Geesaman Wash

Reef of Rock

Red Ridge

Stratton Saddle

Stratton Spring

X Lombar Hill

X 8076

Road

Oracle Control

Alder Canyon

11

Mt. Lemmon Ski Area

5

Summerhaven

trails. The Oracle Ridge trail curls around a rusting cattleguard and climbs straight up the ridgeline to the north. As it rounds the western side of the next point, distant ranges become visible to the west, beyond Samaniego Ridge. Agave, yucca, and sotol appear commonly among the gnarled oaks and junipers. The trail descends to the next saddle, then works its way onto the eastern slope of the ridge. The plant community found here is a chaparral of hardy upland shrubs, although a few conifers can be seen in a north-facing draw across the ravine. Hikers can look out across the flats of the San Pedro Valley to see the alkaline bed of a playa, or dry lake bed, near the copper smelter at San Manuel.

The ridgetop is fairly level as the trail makes its way north, and the footpath soon finds its way to a jeep trail that will bring the traveler into the next saddle. A steep road climbs from here to the summit of Rice Peak and dead-ends there; through-hikers will turn left at the road junction and descend steadily across the western face of the mountain. At its base, another jeep road marked 4463 takes off to the east. Stick to the ridgeline road, which maintains a level course for another mile or so before dropping down slopes to the east. The footpath picks up again at this point, following a barbed-wire fence along the ridgeline as it descends toward Apache Peak. This minor peak appears prominent when

The Reef of Rock as seen from Oracle Ridge.

viewed from the basins to the north; its rocky crest presides over slopes of grassy savannah. Its cooler north slope is heavily wooded in oak and manzanita.

The path jogs west to miss the peak, then embarks upon a long descent into the saddle beyond it. To the northwest, the cluster of white buildings out on the flats is Biosphere II. This research station is an attempt to determine whether a completely enclosed, self-sufficient system can be created as a long-term habitat for human beings. If successful, it could serve as a model for space stations or even colonies on other planets. After crossing the saddle, the trail embarks on a vigorous piece of climbing, and two old jeep trails rise from the east to join it. Just beyond the second road, the trail to the American Flag Ranch trailhead breaks away to the right. Since the old Oracle Ridge route ends up on private land, the American Flag trail will be described as the final portion of the hike.

This path wanders downward across hilly country, rising and falling frequently. Outcrops of bedrock dot the landscape here, and barrel cacti may be spotted amid the scrub. The path dodges north to avoid the Highjinks Mine, which is still in private hands. It then continues its winding descent into the sandy draw of American Flag Wash. The trail follows the streamcourse downward through a wooded basin, then jogs northward to avoid the outbuildings of the American Flag Ranch. The route makes its way over one final hilltop before descending to a well-marked parking area along the road to Mount Lemmon.

ORGAN PIPE CACTUS
NATIONAL MONUMENT

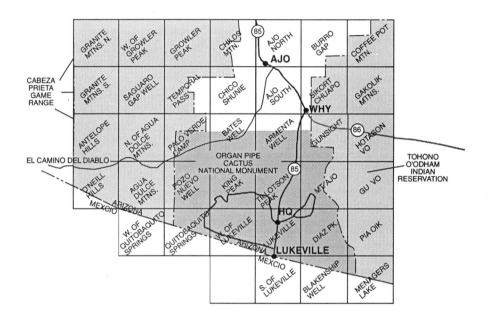

Organ Pipe Cactus National Monument encompasses some of the most pristine and diverse low desert flora in the United States. Organ pipe and senita cacti compete with the taller saguaros for primacy in this cactus-dominated ecosystem, and a rich abundance of smaller spiny plants grow among their giant cousins. Beginning in late March, the desert bursts into a profusion of wildflowers, highlighted by yellow brittlebrush and Mexican gold poppies. Colonies of Mexican leafcutter ants are perhaps the most exotic animals that call the monument home. The cactus scrub provides a habitats for a vast array of desert wildlife, from kangaroo rats to pronghorn antelope, from cactus wrens to golden eagles, and from rare Quitobaquito pupfish to Gila monsters. The landscape holds young mountain ranges of volcanic origin, raising their ragged peaks among expanses of low desert. These low basins are filled to a depth of thousands of feet with alluvial fill washed from the mountains: it could be said that these Arizona mountains are drowning in a sea of their own alluvial wastes.

In this vast desert, there are few trails that were established for hiking. Instead, most of the popular routes follow wagon trails left from the heydays of mining and cattle. Some of the routes visit old ruins that hark back to these hardscrabble times.

This is a land of wide open spaces. The monument has been divided into a series of backcountry zones, and the permits required for backpacking are allotted so that no one part of the backcountry ever gets crowded. Backpackers can get permits at the visitor center for no charge beyond the entrance fee, and must turn in their permits when the trip is over.

The emphasis in these parts is on map and compass skills, and visitors can test their self-reliance on extended trips into the trackless desert. Water sources are few and far between out here; the National Park Service requests that visitors tote their own water and leave natural sources for wildlife. Fires are not allowed in the monument for two reasons: wood is scarce and grows slowly, and fire sites left by visitors might confuse the ongoing archaeological search for ancient peoples who once roamed the area.

The Organ Pipe Visitor Center is located along U.S. Highway 85, 22 miles south of the community of Why. There is a developed campground near the visitor center, and there are a few primitive campsites at the end of Alamo Canyon Road, which can be reserved free of charge. Puerto Blanco and Ajo Mountain drives provide improved gravel roads into the monument, and Bates Well on its northern edge can also be reached by passenger vehicles via a road originating in Ajo, Arizona. This road goes on to become El Camino del Diablo, the Devil's Highway, a hardscrabble jeep track that runs west through the Cabeza Prieta Game Range all the way to Yuma. Permits are required for driving the road, and can be obtained from the game range headquarters in Ajo. The game range may be closed at any time, and is only open to four-wheel-drive vehicles. Its sand traps and unmarked junctions offer limitless possibilities to drivers who want to challenge their ability to survive.

76   *VICTORIA AND LOST CABIN MINES*

General description: A day hike to two historic mine sites, 3.8 miles in all.
Best season: October-April.
Difficulty: Moderate to Victoria Mine; moderate** beyond.
Water availability: None.
Elevation gain: 220 feet (to Lost Cabin Mine).
Elevation loss: 230 feet (to Lost Cabin Mine).
Maximum elevation: 1,680 feet.

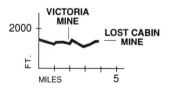

Topo maps: *Trails Illustrated.*
Jurisdiction: Organ Pipe Cactus National Monument (NPS).
Finding the trailhead: From the Organ Pipe Visitor Center, follow signs for 1.5 miles to the auto campground. The trail departs from its south end.

0.0	Trail leaves Campground Loop path.
1.7	Junction with old Sonoyta-Ajo Road. Turn left.
1.9	Victoria Mine.
2.1	Route crosses through pass in Sonoyta Mountains.
3.7	Stone Cabin ruins.
3.8	Lost Cabin Mine shafts.

The trail: This short trail runs from the auto campground to several historic mining ruins along the Sonoyta Mountains. From the southern end of the Campground Loop trail, the well-marked Victoria Mine route angles to the west. It wanders across well-drained hillocks where creosote bush and greasewood live sparsely amid a desert pavement of gravel and sun-baked sand. The path occasionally drops into small ravines as it crosses south-

76 Victoria and Lost Cabin Mines

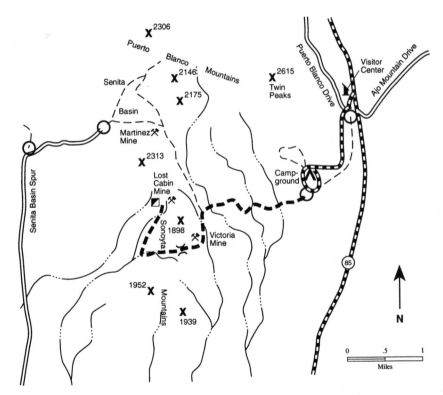

The shell of an old general store is one of the notable features of the Victoria Mine site.

ward-running washes. In these swales, greater moisture allows the growth of mesquite and palo verde, and permits cacti to grow abundantly. Looking northward up the washes, travelers can see a gap in the hills revealing the distant crest of Pinkley Peak. From the hilltops, the Sonoyta Valley seems bounded by the rocky wall of the Sierra Cubabi, across the Mexican border.

The trail approaches a low range of granite hills, whimsically named the Sonoyta Mountains. This range appears to be little more than a rumpled collection of bluffs, but in fact it is the oldest mountain range in Organ Pipe National Monument. A well-worn wagon track follows the base of the range, and the trail joins it just to the east of some prospect tailings. (These are visible on the hillside to the west.) The wagon track is actually the old Sonoyta-Ajo Road, which dates from times when the surrounding country was a part of Mexico. Turn south on this old track, which crosses a substantial wash before reaching the site of the Victoria Mine.

The Victoria Mine is the best-preserved historical ruin in the monument. It produced about $120,000 worth of gold, silver, and copper during its forty years of operation. The shell of the old mine store, built of native stone, stands amid mineshafts and glory holes harking back to the turn of the century, when a substantial quantity of silver and copper was removed from this site. Ajo and

Sonoyta were too distant to economically transport the raw ore there, so it was put through a crude smelting process right here. Rusted pieces of smelting machinery still lie amidst the diggings. The mineshafts have been sealed to prevent accidents, but shallow glory holes are still open to the sky. These were prospect holes, not actual mineshafts, and were dug along veins of quartz in the hopes of striking a paying lode.

LOST CABIN MINE OPTION

Travelers who are confident in their sense of direction can proceed to the site of the more remote Lost Cabin Mine. Hike due south from the ruins of the Victoria Mine store to strike a wagon track running westward to the Lost Cabin Mine. There is a low pass visible from the Victoria Mine; the wagon track runs through it, then descends into the basin beyond. Vigorous organ pipe and saguaro cacti abound on the eastern side of the divide, but the terrain strikes a markedly bleaker note beyond the pass. The wagon track descends onto the flats, then crosses a wash. It follows this dry arroyo westward along the base of the hills for 0.7 mile. The track then enters a comparatively lush oasis of desert plants. Saguaros, chollas, and organ pipe cacti all grow to large sizes here. Tall ironwoods and mesquites line the folds in the plain.

The track enters this diverse assemblage of plants, then crosses the wash as it doglegs sharply to the northeast. Several prospect holes can be seen near the banks of the wash to the west of the trail. The old wagon track makes a beeline for the Lost Cabin Mine; keep going straight as another track veers left. Upon reaching the base of a rocky hillock, the track encounters the remains of a stone cabin. It then turns sharply eastward, fading as it wanders the remaining distance to the mine site. There are several substantial shafts here, surrounded by fences to prevent the unwary from taking a fall.

77 SENITA BASIN LOOP

General description: A day hike through the Senita Basin, 2.8 miles round-trip.
Best season: October-April.
Difficulty: Easy*.
Water availability: None.
Elevation gain: 100 feet.
Elevation loss: 100 feet.
Maximum elevation: 1,760 feet.
Topo map: *Trails Illustrated.*
Jurisdiction: Organ Pipe Cactus National Monument (NPS).
Finding the trailhead: Take U.S. Highway 85 south from the visitor center. Turn right on Puerto Blanco Scenic Drive and follow this improved gravel road for 5.2 miles. Then turn right onto the Senita Basin spur road. The trail leaves from the picnic area at its end.

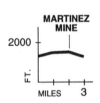

0.0	Trail leaves Senita Basin Picnic Area.
0.1	Trail splits. Bear left to begin the loop.
1.0	Trail joins old Sonoyta-Ajo wagon road. Turn right.
1.9	Martinez Mine site. Turn right to complete the loop.
2.8	Trail returns to Senita Basin Picnic Area.

The trail: The Senita Basin is a low depression surrounded by spurs of the Puerto Blanco Mountains. It is a good place to spot desert wildlife, especially javelinas and coyotes. It also features the abandoned shafts of the old Martinez Mine. The basin is famed for the occurrence of the rare senita cactus, which grows wild at only a handful of sites in the United States. This cactus has the same growth form as the organ pipe cactus, but has fewer, broader ribs and sparser needles. Its most distinguishing characteristic is a shaggy, beardlike growth of long, grayish needles at the tips of its stalks. Look for senita cactus near the picnic area where the trail starts, and keep an eye out for the stout, gray-barked elephant tree, also present in the basin.

77 Senita Basin Loop

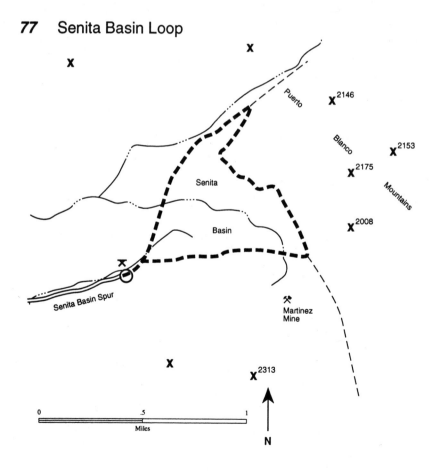

The pinched spots on this organ pipe cactus indicate frost damage in the recent past.

The trail leaves the northeast corner of the picnic area and bears east-northeast along a wash studded with overgrown mesquite, ironwood, and palo verde. Look for clumps of desert mistletoe among the branches of the larger shrubs. This parasitic plant is distributed almost exclusively by the phainopepla, a species of bird wherein the male looks like a black-and-white replica of the cedar waxwing. This tiny bird looks to desert mistletoe berries as a primary food source, and deposits the seeds of the parasite on the branches of unwitting shrubs. There are also plenty of cacti along the wash, dominated by mature organ pipes.

After a few hundred yards, the trail forks into two well-marked tracks. This description arbitrarily covers the hike in a clockwise direction, but its is equally easy to go either way. Take the left fork, which climbs onto arid flats that are covered richly in saguaro, cholla, and organ pipe cacti. After 1 mile, the track intersects the old Sonoyta-Ajo wagon road, which once serviced silver mines in this area. Turn south here, following the twin ruts across bleak uplands that contrast with the profuse growth along the arroyos. Nearing the southeastern corner of the basin, the old Sonoyta-Ajo road reaches a marked junction with track that forms the final leg of the loop.

Adventurous souls can hike cross-country from this junction to reach the Martinez Mine site, which occupies several low hilltops to the southwest. The site is honeycombed with glory holes and mineshafts, and its huge piles of tailings can be seen from the trail. The final leg of the loop bears northwest from the junction, skirting the foot of the low hills bordering the basin. It passes an old glory hole and crosses flats studded with organ pipe cacti. The trail completes the loop by rejoining its northern leg just east of the parking area.

78   MILTON MINE

General description: A day hike to the Milton Mine, 1.7 miles.
Best season: October-April.
Difficulty: Easy.
Water availability: None.
Elevation gain: 60 feet.
Maximum elevation: 1,620 feet.
Topo map: *Trails Illustrated.*
Jurisdiction: Organ Pipe Cactus National Monument (NPS).

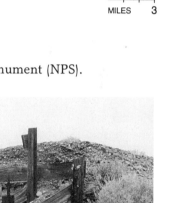

The remains of an old ore loading platform.

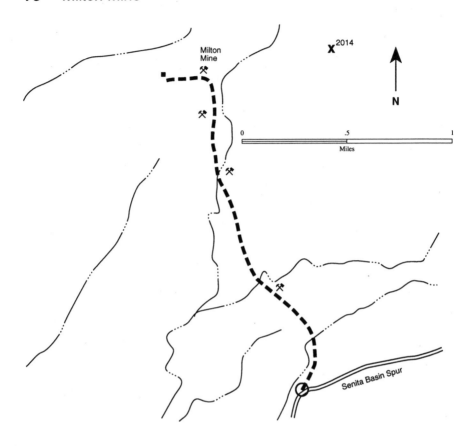

Finding the trailhead: Take U.S. Highway 85 south from the visitor center. Turn right on Puerto Blanco Scenic Drive and follow this improved gravel road for 5.2 miles, then turn right onto the Senita Basin spur road. After 3.6 miles, it curves to the east. The Milton Mine trail departs from this curve, but the nearest parking is 1 mile farther at the end of the road.

0.0   Trail leaves Senita Basin spur of Puerto Blanco Scenic Drive.
1.7   Milton Mine site.

The trail: This well-defined mining road runs north from the Senita Basin spur road to a mining site on the eastern edge of La Abra Plain. It first traverses a rolling desert of arid hills. After crossing the first major arroyo, the track wanders amid a complicated maze of hillocks and draws, richly populated with saguaro, cholla, and organ pipe cacti. The second major wash marks the beginning of mining activity, although the first two shafts are difficult to spot when approached from the south. The trail then follows a third arroyo toward the western tail of the Puerto Blanco Mountains, crossing the bleak fringes of La Abra Plain along the way. Creosote and bursage rule the flats, while a sparse collection of cacti grows along the wash.

A glory hole to the left of the trail marks the approach to the Milton Mine site. The old road hooks west and soon arrives at the remains of an old ore-loading platform. Behind it lies an extensive open-pit mine, surrounded by heaps of rubble. The bright aquamarine patina encrusting the rock is caused by the weathering of copper ore contained in the stone. A concrete foundation across the trail is really an old leaching vat. Watchful explorers may also discover an old explosives locker, dug into the rock so that the force of any blast would be directed harmlessly upward. Travel with care in this area to avoid causing damage to this historic site.

79 RED TANKS TINAJA

General description: A short day hike to a natural water pocket in the northern Puerto Blanco Mountains, 0.8 mile.

2000 ┤ RED TANKS
  ── TINAJA
FT.
  └─┼──┼──┤
  MILES   3

Best season: October-April.
Difficulty: Easy*.
Water availability: None. (The National Park Service requests that any water found in Red Tanks Tinaja be left for the wildlife.)
Elevation gain: 35 feet.
Elevation loss: 40 feet.
Maximum elevation: 1,875 feet.
Topo map: Trails Illustrated.
Jurisdiction: Organ Pipe Cactus National Monument (NPS).
Finding the trailhead: From the Organ Pipe Visitor Center, take Puerto Blanco Scenic Drive northwest for 4 miles to reach pullout #3. Park here and walk back 0.2 mile to pick up the trail on the south side of the road.

0.0   Track leaves Puerto Blanco Scenic Drive.
0.2   Red Tanks Well.
0.8   Red Tanks Tinaja.

The trail: This trail makes a nice day hike from the Puerto Blanco Road to a natural catch-basin that may contain water during the rainy season. This source of surface water is critical to desert wildlife, and hikers should tote their own water with them so that the tinaja does not become depleted. The trail begins as a narrow footpath, but soon merges with an old two-rut wagon trail. The wagon road runs southwest across desert flats studded with tall saguaros. Far to the east, the Ajo Range towers beyond the lesser crags of the Diablo Mountains. The cloud-rending spire of Pinkley Peak

A view of Pinkley Peak from Red Tanks Tinaja.

crowns conical hills to the north, while the crest of Twin Peaks rises above foothills to the south.

Just beyond the crossing of a shallow and brushy draw, the shaft and watering trough of Red Tanks Well stand abandoned to the north of the trail. This well was an important watering hole for cattle that once grazed throughout the monument. As the track descends into a shallow basin, the distant vistas fall and the old road fades. The road bears westward to the edge of a major wash, then bends south. After crossing the arroyo, the track climbs over the shoulder of a bluff, then returns to the streamcourse. Hike up the streambed for 200 feet to reach Red Tanks Tinaja. This interesting water pocket was sculpted into a band of rhyolite by centuries of seasonal floods. The majestic crown of Pinkley Peak can be seen from the *tinaja*, and provides a striking backdrop for the algae-tinted pools.

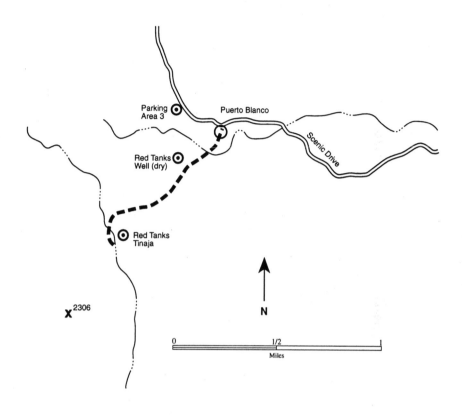

80 DRIPPING SPRINGS MINE

General description: A short day hike to a mine
site in the northern Puerto Blancos, 1.3 miles.
Best season: October-April.
Difficulty: Moderate**.
Water availability: None.
Elevation gain: 130 feet.
Elevation loss: 110 feet.
Maximum elevation: 1,930 feet.
Topo map: *Trails Illustrated.*
Jurisdiction: Organ Pipe Cactus National Monument (NPS).
Finding the trailhead: From the Organ Pipe Visitor Center, take the Puerto
Blanco Scenic Drive northwest for 12 miles. Park at pullout #9 and walk

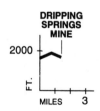

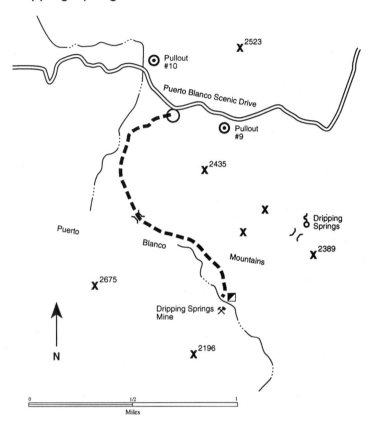

ahead or at #10 and walk back to find the trail, which departs from the
south side of the road.

0.0   Track leaves Puerto Blanco Scenic Drive.
0.7   Trail crosses pass in Puerto Blanco Mountains.
1.3   Dripping Springs Mine.

The trail: This route follows a faint wagon track deep into the most rugged corner of the Puerto Blanco Mountains. It begins by curving around a
sheer promontory of volcanic rock that is resplendent in red and ochre. The
path then ascends a dry valley, where cacti grow only sparsely. A dusky
peak of grayish andesite sits at the head of this basin. The roadbed climbs
steadily to reach a broad pass, then drops into the valley beyond. Cacti are
more diverse and abundant here. Look for hedgehog and barrel cacti among
the taller chollas, saguaros, and organ pipe cacti. The track descends along
the eastern side of the valley. Watch for desert mule deer as the track

crosses behind a solitary hillock. An astounding panorama of Pinkley Peak unfolds to the south as the path descends to the mine site.

Dripping Springs Mine occupies both sides of the main wash, with glory holes, tailings heaps, mineshafts, and collapsed sheds scattered across the landscape. Some of the shafts still have original plank cribbing in place; this can be seen clearly from outside barbed-wire fences surrounding the shafts. Dripping Springs is located beyond the tall divide of mountains to the east, and there is no trail to it. This is just as well, because the spring is a favorite gathering spot for the so-called "killer bees," which swarm at water sources throughout the monument.

81 GRASS CANYON LOOP

General description: A long day hike or backpack in the northern Ajo Mountains, 6.2 miles round-trip.
Best season: October-April.
Difficulty: Moderately strenuous**.

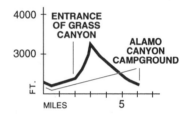

Vertical spires dominate Grass Canyon.

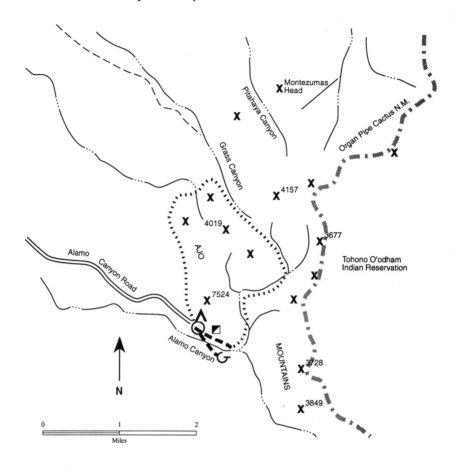

Water availability: None.
Elevation gain: 1,255 feet.
Elevation loss: 1,255 feet.
Maximum elevation: 3,455 feet.
Topo maps: Mount Ajo, *Trails Illustrated.*
Jurisdiction: Organ Pipe Cactus National Monument (NPS).
Finding the trailhead: Drive north from the Visitor Center on U.S. Highway 85 to mile 65.4. Turn east on the Alamo Canyon Road. Follow this improved gravel road for 3.3 miles to reach the parking area at its end.

0.0	Follow the foothills north from Alamo Canyon Campground.
2.2	Route enters the mouth of Grass Canyon.
3.1	Route crosses the pass above the head of Grass Canyon.
3.7	Route reaches the wash of North Alamo Canyon.
5.3	South Alamo Canyon joins at a major confluence.
5.4	Alamo Canyon corrals. Climb the south bank to pick up the trail.
6.2	Route returns to Alamo Canyon Campground.

The trail: This wilderness route offers a long loop trip from Alamo Canyon Campground. It crosses cactus-rich *bajada* slopes that offer sweeping views of the valley, then penetrates the northern end of the Ajo Range to take in some of the most striking mountain scenery in the monument. There is no trail, and the route is easiest to follow when approached from a clockwise direction. Remember that permits are required for backcountry camping and can be obtained at the Organ Pipe Visitor Center.

The journey begins with a northward trek across open *bajadas* at the base of the Ajo Range. A towering palisade of rhyolite rises sheer to the west, and saguaro and organ pipe cacti dot the flats. The alluvial fans at the base of the range are dissected by small arroyos and ravines, making for lots of small-scale ups and downs. The mountains bordering the far side of the Valley of the Ajo are dwarfed by the sheer vastness of the cactus-studded basin. A stout pillar of stone looms ahead, marking the entrance to Grass Canyon. As the route travels around the base of the pillar, the formation resolves itself into a thin blade of stone that rises from a conical mound of debris. Travelers should angle northeast as they round the promontory, passing the entrance to a box canyon to reach a second fin of volcanic stone.

The entrance to Grass Canyon lies beyond this second formation, and teddy-bear cholla and brittlebrush dominate the arid mounds of alluvium that occupy the mouth of the canyon. An enormous castle of stone rises above the south wall of the canyon, and it has been eroded into a striking collection of pillars and spires. Follow the canyon upward as it narrows into a steep v-shaped cleft studded with saguaros. The safest approach to the pass is to stay high on the middle slopes of the valley's south side, maintaining an altitude sufficient to avoid the steep and eroded ravines of the canyon bottom. These cooler slopes are home to high-desert plants such as jojoba and goldeneye. The climbing ends atop a narrow, cholla-strewn saddle overlooking a tributary that feeds into the North Fork of Alamo Canyon.

Once again, stay high on the south slope for the descent to Alamo Canyon's North Fork. Near the mouth of the side canyon, cliffs force travelers down into the wash, which is choked with hackberry and other thorny shrubs. The side canyon soon merges with the North Fork of Alamo Canyon. Turn right for easy traveling down the wash; rugged spires adorn the slopes above. After half a mile, several ancient junipers preside over a series of *tinajas* that fill with water during the rainy season. Shortly thereafter, the canyon reaches a bottleneck and numerous sills in the streambed; a painstaking scramble is required to negotiate these. The wash drops through a staircase of such sills, but the cliffs that surround the streamcourse offer few alternatives for travel. Organ pipe cactus thrives in great abundance here, growing from every conceivable chink in the stoneworks.

An even narrower defile soon enters from the west, and the wash bends due south as the canyon widens. Two impressive side canyons join it from the east, rimmed by towering pinnacles and massive cliffs of volcanic rock. The wash soon meets the South Fork of Alamo Canyon, and an old well sits abandoned on the south bank of the streamcourse, downstream from the confluence. Climb up the bank and into the corrals to strike a footpath that follows the arroyo westward. This path soon crosses the streambed and becomes a two-rut track. Sharp pinnacles rise to either side as the track leaves the canyon, passing the brick ruins of an old ranch house as it does. This house was once inhabited by one of the scions of the Gray family, who began ranching in the present-day Organ Pipe National Monument in 1920. The track then crosses the flats to return the traveler to the Alamo Canyon camping area.

82   ARCH CANYON–BOULDER OVERLOOK

General description: A day hike/wilderness route to a high overlook in the Ajo Mountains, 1.1 miles.
Best season: October-April.
Difficulty: Moderate* in Arch Canyon; strenuous** to overlook.
Water availability: None.
Elevation gain: 1,110 feet.

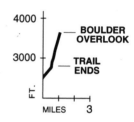

82   Arch Canyon—Boulder Overlook

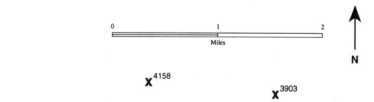

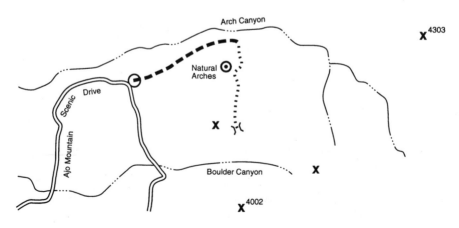

Maximum elevation: 3,670 feet.

Topo map: *Trails Illustrated.*

Jurisdiction: Organ Pipe Cactus National Monument (NPS).

Finding the trailhead: From the Organ Pipe Visitor Center, cross U.S. Highway 85 to get on Ajo Mountain Scenic Drive. Follow this improved gravel road for 9.5 miles to reach pullout #13, from which the trail originates.

0.0	Trailhead.
0.5	End of trails. Route commences climb out of Arch Canyon.
1.1	Boulder Canyon overlook.

The trail: Arch Canyon is named for a pair of natural arches that decorate a cliff wall high above its entrance. The larger arch is 90 feet wide, and a tiny, gracile arch is perched atop it. These arches are best viewed from the entrance of the canyon; as the path penetrates the cleft, they are hidden from view. The track is well-defined for the first half-mile as it follows the main canyon. Beyond this point, the route becomes a steep scramble marked by cairns as it climbs to an overlook of Boulder Canyon.

From the parking lot, the footpath winds eastward through a dense growth of low shrubs. It enters Arch Canyon and rises and falls as it progresses between towering walls of rhyolite. The track stays high on the southern edge of the canyon floor, climbing moderately as it approaches a broad gulch that enters from the south. Here, the path splits. A faint track drops into the wash ahead and disappears, while cairns mark a route across bare stone, climbing toward the Boulder Canyon overlook.

This route skirts the base of the cliffs, often crossing friction pitches of gently inclined stone and scrambling up boulder-choked gullies. The bedrock is streaked in many places with a black substance known as "desert varnish." This substance is a layer of manganese oxide deposited on the stone by dripping water. It may be quite slippery when wet. The path climbs high into a desert grassland, where yuccas, agaves, and junipers rise beside shrubs and bunchgrasses. Behind, the sheer walls and pinnacles of Arch Canyon tower to the north; straight ahead lies the narrow saddle to Boulder Canyon. The saddle hardly does justice to the grandeur of Boulder Canyon's massive walls. However, travelers who are not prone to vertigo can walk out onto a small promontory jutting out over the canyon, yielding outstanding views of the chasm as well as a look at the distant ranges to the east.

---

83   BULL PASTURE–MOUNT AJO

General description: A day hike to Bull Pasture overlook, 4.1 miles round-trip, or wilderness route to Mount Ajo, 5 miles one-way.

Best season: October–April.

Difficulty: Moderately strenuous* to Bull Pasture; strenuous** to Mount Ajo.

Cliffs of rhyolite and tuff soar above Estes Canyon.

Water availability: None.
Elevation gain: 900 feet (to Bull Pasture);
2,568 feet (to Mount Ajo).
Elevation loss: 120 feet (to Mount Ajo).
Maximum elevation: 3,260 feet (Bull
Pasture); 4,808 feet (Mount Ajo).
Topo map: *Trails Illustrated.*
Jurisdiction: Organ Pipe Cactus
National Monument (NPS).
Finding the trailhead: From the visitor
center, cross U.S. Highway 85 to get on the

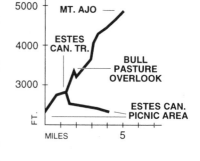

Ajo Mountain Scenic Drive. Follow this improved gravel road for 11.4 miles
to reach the Estes Canyon Picnic Area, from which the trail originates.

0.0   Trail leaves Estes Canyon Picnic Area.
0.1   Trail splits. Turn right onto Bull Pasture trail.
1.3   Estes Canyon trail joins Bull Pasture trail.
1.8   Bull Pasture overlook.
3.8   Mount Ajo route reaches the crest of the range.
5.0   Summit of Mount Ajo.

83 Bull Pasture—Mount Ajo

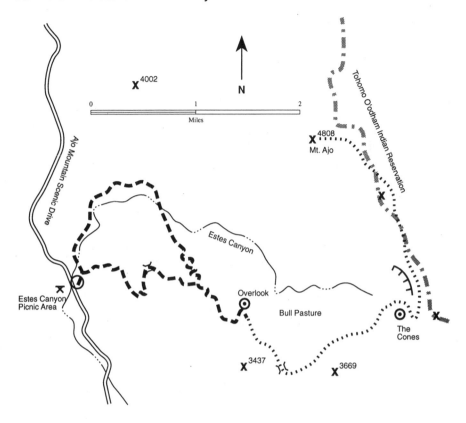

2.3   Jct. of Bull Pasture and Estes Canyon trails. Turn east to complete the loop.

2.7   Estes Canyon trail reaches floor of Estes Canyon.

4.0   Trails converge. Bear right for the trailhead.

4.1   Trail returns to Estes Canyon Picnic Area.

The trail: The trail to the Bull Pasture overlook is a fine day loop that features the rugged western wall of the Ajo Mountains. A well-defined and heavily traveled track, it is the closest thing to an established trail found in Organ Pipe Cactus National Monument. The route to the summit of Mount Ajo is also a defined path, but is very tricky to follow. It crosses steep and potentially unstable slopes and presents several false paths that could lead a hiker into trouble. Hikers who choose this route should be absolutely confident in their route-finding abilities. Overnight camping is not allowed anywhere in the Estes Canyon drainage, which encompasses both routes.

The trail begins by crossing the main wash of Estes Canyon, and soon splits into the Estes Canyon and Bull Pasture sections of the trail. The Bull Pasture trail will be covered first in this description. It begins with an immediate climb into the low, cactus-studded hills that border the wash to the southeast. As it climbs, watch for switchbacks as the path ascends to a crown of bedrock atop a sinuous ridge. The trail then follows the ridgeline around the head of a pocket in the hills, offering clear views of Mount Ajo as it does so. As it curves around to a southeasterly bearing, the track passes onto the back side of a hulking outcrop of beige stone. It makes its way toward a narrow chasm to the south, and the Estes Canyon trail rises to join it at a signpost.

Thus bolstered, the trail continues southeast. Black stripes of desert varnish adorn the cliffs facing the trail. The path soon zigzags to a saddle, then continues climbing to the top of a low spur ridge. Here, a trail register marks the Bull Pasture overlook. It offers an outstanding platform for viewing the Bull Pasture, once an important summer range for local ranchers. The Ajo Range rears impressive walls of rhyolite and tuff beyond this elevated grassland. The route to the top of Mount Ajo (discussed later in this section) departs from this point; the return trip to the trailhead via Estes Canyon will be discussed next.

To complete the loop, hikers can retrace their steps and follow the Estes Canyon trail down into the valley from its signpost junction. This path descends sharply to the flat basin of Estes Canyon, a natural amphitheater surrounded by towering cliff walls. The track wanders northeast through dense thorn scrub, then climbs onto drier ground, home to saguaro and organ pipe cacti. At the foot of the basin, the path crawls over several rolling hills that allow a last view of the forbidding Ajo Range. It then drops back to the wash, crossing the streamcourse before making a beeline through tall shrubs to the parking lot.

MOUNT AJO OPTION

From the Bull Pasture overlook, three distinct footpaths head southward. Follow the lowermost path, which descends gradually to the bottom of a shallow draw. The track follows this draw to a low divide that looks south toward Diaz Spire. It then turns east to pass beneath the northern face of a rugged finger of the Ajo Mountains. This track gains altitude at a gradual pace, finally reaching a broad gully in a crotch that is overlooked by rounded pillars of stone. These pillars are called The Cones, and are made up of compressed volcanic ash (tuff) that was never welded together by hot flows of magma that formed the range. The ash tuff weathers easily, resulting in the rounded shapes seen here.

Turn uphill at The Cones, ignoring paths that lead onward, and follow a track zigzagging upward immediately to the east of these rounded towers. The path reaches a high col behind them, then continues to switchback up, passing a small natural arch as it does so. The trail then climbs above a jagged outcrop of stone and sidehills northeast, skirting a sill of buff-colored stone. This stone is welded tuff, which was formed when an advancing flow of lava buried beds of volcanic ash, and the immense heat and pressure transformed the ash into solid and unyielding stone. The lava flow formed the reddish beds of rhyolite rising above the route at this point. After crossing the band of welded tuff, the trail angles uphill across scrub-covered slopes to reach the crest of the range.

The trail turns north here, following the ridgeline toward the summit of Mount Ajo. The first summit is a false one; the path begins to climb again, swinging onto its eastern slope. The wide-open view to the east encompasses the desert basins of the Tohono O'odham Indian Reservation. Once beyond this lower peak, the trail returns to the ridgetop and continues north toward the true summit of Mount Ajo. The capstone of this peak is made up of a volcanic conglomerate called "breccia." It was created when lava flows picked up chunks of older rock as it flowed, and these stones were incorporated into the cooling lava. A little scrambling is required to reach the top of the peak, which rewards the traveler with inspiring views of the Ajo Range and the sweep of desert surrounding it.

84 SWEETWATER PASS

General description: A wilderness route to a low pass through the Ajo Mountains, 3.5 miles.
Best season: October-April.
Difficulty: Moderate**.
Water availability: None.
Elevation gain: 500 feet.
Elevation loss: 78 feet.
Maximum elevation: 2,550 feet.
Topo maps: Diaz Peak, *Trails Illustrated.*
Jurisdiction: Organ Pipe Cactus National Monument (NPS).
Finding the trailhead: From the Organ Pipe Visitor Center, cross U.S. Highway 85 to get on Ajo Mountain Scenic Drive. Follow this improved gravel road for 13.4 miles to reach pullout #18, from which the route originates.

SWEETWATER PASS
3000
FT.
MILES   5

0.0   Route leaves Ajo Mountain Scenic Drive.
1.8   Route encounters major wash that drains the valley to the north. Turn north along this wash.
2.9   Tributary wash enters from the east. Turn right to follow it.
3.5   Sweetwater Pass.

The trail: This route crosses the broad basin that separates Diaz Spire from the northern marches of the Ajo Mountains. Sweetwater Pass was once an important route for Tohono O'odham Indians, who used it to travel west into the Valley of the Ajo to gather the fruits of the organ pipe cactus. Long before their time, bands of Archaic people hunted and gathered in the basin to the west of the pass. Keep an eye out for signs of ancient Indian culture. Round mortar holes in the bedrock aided the grinding of seeds, and circular

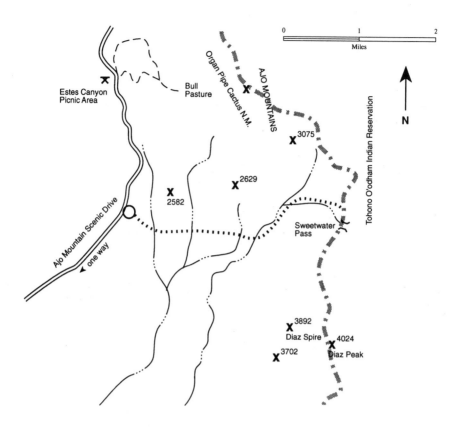

arrangements of boulders indicate sleeping areas. The route to Sweetwater Pass is strictly map-and-compass; there are no established paths.

From the pullout, chart a course that runs south of the smaller of two joined hillocks extending southwest from the Ajo Range. Turn due east after rounding this conical hill, and begin crossing broad alluvial flats that are dotted with saguaro and organ pipe cacti. The imposing summit to the southeast is Diaz Spire; Diaz Peak is hidden behind it. The colorful southern buttresses of Ajo Peak unfold to the north as the route runs eastward. Navigate for an isolated hill of brownish red stone, then chart a path that runs just south of the next series of chalky white hills. The second of these hills is conical, and upon rounding it the traveler will see a long valley extending northeast into the mountains.

Follow this valley upward, aiming to pass around the toe of a sinuous finger ridge to the east of the valley. A pillar of stone rises from the end of this finger ridge, and the valley splits into two branches at the terminus of the ridge. Turn east along a tributary wash to reach Sweetwater Pass. It is best to stick to the higher ground on the way to the pass, because the steep-sided arroyos that dissect the floor of the draw are choked with thorn scrub. The pass itself

Diaz Spire is the dominant landmark along the route to Sweetwater Pass.

is in the bottom of the ravine and offers no views. For a fine vista of the ranges to the east, climb to the hilltop immediately to the north of the pass.

85 BATES MOUNTAINS

General description: A wilderness route through a rift valley in the remote Bates Mountains, 4.6 miles.

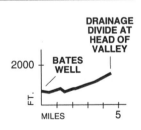

Best season: October-April.
Difficulty: Moderate**.
Water availability: None.
Elevation gain: 510 feet.
Elevation loss: 60 feet.
Maximum elevation: 1,810 feet.
Topo maps: Bates Well, Kino Peak, *Trails Illustrated*.
Jurisdiction: Organ Pipe Cactus National Monument (NPS).
Finding the trailhead: Take U.S. Highway 85 south from Ajo to the enormous copper tailings heap. Turn left onto the improved gravel road that runs along its southern edge. Bear left at all major forks (the road is always wide) and this road ultimately becomes the Bates Well Road. After 12 miles, the road enters Organ Pipe Cactus National Monument, and 4 miles

later it arrives at Bates Well. Park here and hike south from the ranch.

0.0	Bates Well. Bear south to reach Growler Wash.
0.2	Route reaches Growler Wash.
0.5	Route leaves Growler Wash and heads south at low hills.
1.5	Route encounters westward-running arroyo. Follow it upward.
4.6	Pass at head of rift valley.

The trail: This unmarked route follows an ancient migration corridor of the Hohokam Indians. These ancient people migrated hundreds of miles to reach the Sea of Cortez at the mouth of the Colorado River. They left fragments of seashells along their paths, leading archaeologists to identify the rift valley of the Bates Mountains as an important route for pre-Columbian trading. The route follows a natural trench that splits the Bates Mountains into two separate cordilleras. This wild and remote range looks much the same as it did when Europeans first laid eyes upon it, and showcases a classic Sonoran Desert ecosystem dominated by giant cacti.

85 Bates Mountains

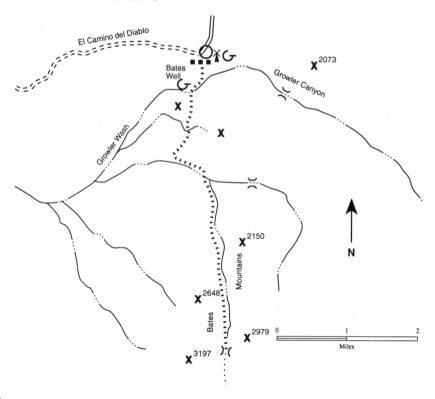

Pinnacles of rhyolite and tuff in the heart of the Bates Range.

The trek begins at Bates Well, headquarters of the Robert Gray family ranching operation, which began in 1920. Grazing has long since ceased, but the buildings, windmills, and corrals look largely the same as they did when the ranch was abandoned. Bear south from the ranch to intercept Growler Wash, and follow this broad highway of loose gravel downhill as it charts a southwesterly course. Some low hills rise on the south bank of the arroyo, and the route breaks away from the streamcourse to run along the western side of these hills. Follow the low swales southward along the base of a massive dome rising to the east. A gentle uphill grade through creosote bush and bursage leads to a shallow divide, and vigilant travelers might find an old horse trail running southwest down the next draw to reach a substantial arroyo.

The route now turns southeast to follow the arroyo upstream, as saguaros and chollas poke up from a sparse growth of desert shrubs. The flat benches above the wash make for easy traveling as the route swings south into a wide rift penetrating the heart of the Bates Mountains. The most impressive spires of this range rise to the west of the valley, in the form of great blocks and pinnacles of ancient lava and solidified volcanic ash. Look backward at this point for a panoramic view of the Growler Range, which rises to the north of the monument boundary. Near the head of the drainage, a network of tributary arroyos compels travelers to descend into the main wash and follow its course uphill. Great chocolate pinnacles of breccia now crown the range to the west, and organ pipe cacti scatter across the surrounding slopes.

The route tops out at a narrow saddle overlooked by the blocky summit of Kino Peak, the loftiest point in the Bates Mountains. A jagged ridge of volcanic rock trails away from its southern face, and the craggy cordillera that is formed by this ridge represents a southern extension of the Bates Mountains. Looking southward along the next trench, the rounded summits of the Cipriano Hills rise from the heart of Organ Pipe Cactus National Monument. Hikers with strong route-finding abilities can proceed southward from this point, following the next rift valley onto the flats, and from there can navigate southwest to intersect Puerto Blanco Scenic Drive.

APPENDIX A: A GLOSSARY OF SOUTHWESTERN TERMS

NOTE: In Spanish, the double L (ll) is pronounced like a "y," and "j" is pronounced like an "h." The tilde (ñ) is pronounced as "ny".

adit- a mine shaft sunk horizontally into the rock.

adobe - a building material consisting of bricks made of alluvial mud mixed with grasses and left to bake in the sun. Adobe dwellings are stout-walled and have a high thermal mass, which keeps them cool in the summer and warm in the winter.

agave - this large succulent is composed of a basal rosette of pointed leaves edged with dark-colored spines. An agave may live to an age of 30 years, then use all of its reserves to send up a flowering stalk. The plant dies soon after flowering.

altiplano - Spanish for "high plain," and generally applied to high-elevation grasslands.

Anasazi - cliff-dwelling people, contemporaries of the Hohokam, who inhabited Northern Arizona before the coming of the Europeans.

Apache - a confederation of hunting and gathering tribes that originally ranged throughout southeastern Arizona and New Mexico. There are several Apache Reservations, which are centered to the north of the Gila River.

arroyo - a well-established wash that has cut a shallow course into the alluvium of the desert floor.

bajadas - skirts of alluvial debris fanning out around the bases of mountains. *Bajada* soil is typically composed of unsorted material that is highly porous, and this quality typically leads to a diverse plant community of both shrubs and cacti.

butte - a solitary tower of stone, usually faced on all sides with cliffs.

caliche - a layer of limestone hardpan that forms a foot or two beneath the surface of the desert in some places. It holds rainwater near the surface of the soil, where shallow-rooted cacti can make maximum use of it.

cañoncito - Spanish for "little canyon."

chaparral - a fire-dependent shrub community that inhabits desert uplands and is typically dominated by manzanita.

cholla - a cactus that grows in a brachiated form like a tree. The cholla is renowned for the sharpness of its hooked spines.

cienega - a small desert wetland found on the valley floor, usually dependent on groundwater to maintain its water level. The root of the word is "cien aguas," Spanish for "100 springs."

coati - an omnivorous mammal related to the raccoon. Coatis are highly social and typically travel in troops. Males of the species are called coatimundis.

cordillera - a continuous arc of mountains.

desert varnish - a deposit of manganese and iron oxide that coats stones on the desert flats and streaks canyon walls. This film of minerals is leached out of the bedrock by runoff waters and is deposited as it drips or flows slowly across the surface of the stone.

draw - a narrow gully or ravine, usually dry.

glory hole - a shallow shaft dug to prospect for metal ores. Glory holes were never deepened into mineshafts because they failed to strike a lode, or paying deposit of ore.

Hohokam - a pre-Columbian group of Indians who shared a culture centered around the irrigation of southern Arizona's desert basins.

jacal - a crude hut or shed made from materials that can be gathered from the desert.

javelina - a small, pig-like mammal that inhabits the low deserts and travels about in small herds.

jojoba - a common shrub of the desert uplands. The jojoba turns its leaves parallel to the rays of the sun to slow water loss, and an extract from its edible nuts serves as a substitute for whale oil.

lechuguilla - locally known as "shin daggers," this low-growing succulent grows in dense mats and has sharp needles at the end of its leaves that can pierce the sole of a tennis shoe.

mesa - a small, flat-topped plateau surrounded by cliffs.

mesquite bosque - a plant community of the arid valley floors that is dominated by mesquite and other thorny shrubs of the acacia family. These plants enrich the soil by adding nitrogen to it through symbiotic bacteria in their root nodules.

ocotillo - a desert shrub with long, unbranched stalks that are covered with thorns and have no leaves for most of the year. The ocotillo leafs out and flowers following desert cloudbursts, but sheds its leaves after several weeks and is capable of a minor amount of photosynthesis through the bark of its stems.

palo verde - the Arizona state tree and a common dweller of Sonoran desert lowlands. Palo verde is Spanish for "green branch," and this shrub has bright green bark which it uses for photosynthesis; it rarely leafs out at all.

playa - the dried-up bed of a seasonal lake that fills only following rains. Playas typically have beds of whitish grit that is highly alkaline and this prevents the growth of most plants.

prickly pear - a low-growing cactus that is identified by its chains of linked pads that have a round or oblong shape. Its fruits, or *tunas*, are prized for jams and jellies.

ramada - a covered porch or veranda; commonly used for covered picnic tables emplaced to provide shade in desert recreation areas.

saguaro - the largest of the cacti, the saguaro grows in an erect column that grows side branches in old age. Saguaros may reach heights of 60 feet or more.

sierra - Spanish for "mountain range."

sotol - a large, upland succulent characterized by a basal rosette of spiky leaves that gives rise to a tall flowering stalk.

tank - a small reservoir (or sometimes merely a large metal tub) used for watering livestock.

Tohono O'odham - The modern native tribe of southwestern Arizona, originally sedentary and agricultural. This is the proper name for the tribal people who were once called the Pimas and Papagos.

tinaja - a natural water pocket that is formed in the bedrock and carries water through a substantial part of the year.

wash - an established streamcourse that only carries water during floods and is dry for most of the year.

yucca - also known as the "soap tree," this relative of the agave has long, dagger-shaped leaves atop a stout stalk.

APPENDIX B: USEFUL ADDRESSES

Coronado National Forest

Coronado National Forest Headquarters, 300 West Congress, Tucson, AZ 85701. Phone (520) 670-4552.

Douglas Ranger District, Rural Route 1, Box 228-R, Douglas, AZ 85607. Phone (520) 364-3468.

Nogales Ranger District, 2251 Grand Avenue, Nogales, AZ 85621. Phone (520) 281-2296.

Safford Ranger District, P.O. Box 709, Safford, AZ 85548-0709. Phone (520) 428-4150.

Santa Catalina Ranger District, 5700 North Sabino Canyon Road, Tucson, AZ 85715. Phone (520) 749-8700.

Sierra Vista Ranger District, 5990 South Highway 92, Hereford, AZ 85615. Phone (520) 378-0311.

Campground Reservations line: (800) 280-2267.

National Park Service

Chiricahua National Monument, Dos Cabezas Route, Box 6500, Willcox, AZ 85643. Phone (520) 824-3560.

Coronado National Monument, 4101 East Montezuma Canyon Rd., Hereford, AZ 85615. Phone (520) 366-5515.

Fort Bowie National Historic Site, P.O. Box 158, Bowie, AZ 85605. Phone (520) 847-2500.

Organ Pipe Cactus National Monument, Route 1, Box 100, Ajo, AZ 85321. Phone (520) 387-6849.

Saguaro National Park, 3693 Old Spanish Trail, Tucson, AZ 85730. Phone (520) 733-5100 (Rincon Mountain Unit); (520) 296-9576 (Tucson Mountain Unit).

Tumacacori National Historic Park, P.O. Box 67, Tumacacori, AZ 85640. Phone (520) 398-2341.

Bureau of Land Management

Safford District, 711 14th Avenue, Safford, AZ 85546. Phone (520) 428-4040 (district office); (520) 357-7111 (West Aravaipa Canyon Ranger Station); (520)828-3380 (East Aravaipa Ranger Station).

U.S. Fish and Wildlife Service

U.S. Fish and Wildlife Ecological Services Field Office,
3616 West Thomas Road, Phoenix, AZ 85019. Phone (520) 379-4720.

State of Arizona

Arizona Office of Tourism, 1100 West Washington, Phoenix, AZ 85007. Phone (800) 842-8257.

Arizona State Parks, 800 West Washington, Phoenix, AZ 85007. Phone (520) 542-4174.

Catalina State Park, P.O. Box 36986, Tucson, AZ 85740. Phone (520) 628-5798.

The Nature Conservancy

Arizona State Office, 300 East University Boulevard, Suite 230, Tucson, AZ 85705. Phone (520) 622-3861.

Aravaipa Canyon Preserve, Klondyke Station, Willcox, AZ 85643. Phone (520) 828-3443.

Muleshoe Ranch, Rural Route 1, Box 1542, Willcox, AZ 95643. Phone (520) 586-7072.

Patagonia-Sonoita Creek Preserve, P.O. Box 815, Patagonia, AZ 85624. Phone (520) 394-2400.

Ramsey Canyon Preserve, 27 Ramsey Canyon Road, Hereford, AZ 85615. Phone (520) 378-2785.

Other Private Associations

Arizona-Sonora Desert Museum, 2021, North Kinney Road, Tucson, AZ 85743.

The Amerind Foundation, P.O. Box 400, Dragoon, AZ 85609.

Friends of Madera Canyon, P.O. Box 1203, Green Valley, AZ 85622.

Southwest Parks and Monuments Association, P.O. Box 2173, Globe, AZ 85502. Phone (520) 425-8184.

Southwest Natural and Cultural Heritage Association,
P.O. Drawer E, Albuquerque, NM 87103. Phone (505) 345-9498.

ABOUT THE AUTHOR

Erik Molvar discovered backpacking while working on a volunteer trail crew in the North Cascades of Washington. A newfound taste for the wilderness experience inspired him to choose a career in the outdoors, and he soon found himself at the University of Montana pursuing a bachelor's degree in wildlife biology. Montana's craggy ranges were his playground for the next five years, and his experiences inspired his first book, *The Trail Guide to Glacier and Waterton National Parks*. He is also author of trail guides to the Bob Marshall Wilderness complex and Olympic National Park.

An adventurous spirit has led Erik to embark upon backpacking expeditions throughout the Rocky Mountains, the Great Basin, western Canada, and Alaska. Along the way, he earned a master's degree studying moose behavior in Denali National Park, Alaska. Erik has hiked hundreds of miles in Arizona's Cactus Country, including all of the trails featured in this book. It is his hope that this book will inspire a greater interest in and appreciation of our desert wilderness, which are fast disappearing in the face of economic development.

Author Erik Molvar takes a break in the Tucson Mountains.